Faces of Nationalism

D0746751

Faces of Nationalism

Janus Revisited

◆

TOM NAIRN

VERSO

London · New York

First published by Verso 1997
© Tom Nairn
All rights reserved

Verso
UK: 6 Meard Street, London W1V 3HR
USA: 180 Varick Street, New York NY 10014–4606

Verso is the imprint of New Left Books

ISBN 1–85984–823–0
ISBN 1–85984–194–5 (pbk)

British Library Cataloguing in Publication Data
A catalogue record for this book is available from the British Library

Library of Congress Cataloging-in-Publication Data
A catalog record for this book is available from the Library of Congress

Typeset by SetSystems Ltd, Saffron Walden, Essex
Printed by Biddles Ltd, Guildford and King's Lynn

Millicent:

Love, touch my heart with who you are
And sleep, history, sleep.

Contents

Preface

The essays in this volume were written over a period of nearly eighteen years, too long and too varied a time for all of the author's real acknowledgements and thanks to be expressed. He has to confine himself to relatively recent events and people. Chief among these must be David McCrone of Edinburgh University's Sociology Department, who encouraged a belated return to academic life in 1993–94 and helped set up a course for the study of nationalism at the Graduate School in Social Sciences. Others who helped in the initiative include Neil McCormick, the former Provost of the University's Faculty of Law and Social Science; his successor in this post, Professor Anthony Cohen; and Professor Malcolm Anderson of the International Social Science Institute. All four belong to a group of like-minded teachers at Edinburgh which has since the 1970s wholly changed the approach to this area of study. It includes Lindsay Paterson and Alice Brown, as well as a growing number of younger scholars and researchers grouped around them. The way for its formation was partly prepared in the 1970s and the early 1980s by Henry Drucker, a co-founder of the Unit for the Study of Government in Scotland (who has also assisted me more personally in recent times). Thanks to this broad community of thought something of the former spirit of Scottish Enlightenment returned before the Edinburgh Parliament did, and I have been fortunate enough to benefit from its influence.

Another community which played a part in the book's genesis was the shorter-lived one formed around Ernest Gellner, in the city of Prague. He returned there to set up his Centre for the Study of Nationalism, in the former Prague College of the Central European University. But that project endured for all too short a time. Together with the assorted political and financial problems afflicting the College, his sudden death in November 1995 ended what could have become the principal centre for research and publication in the subject. An abiding sadness at this loss is qualified (but not much) by gratitude for my luck in being there during the academic year 1993–94, and learning so much. Among the Prague friends it is a particular pleasure to mention were Ernest's assistants Robin Cassells and Gaye Woolven, and scholars like Sukumar Periwal, Peter Pithart and John A. Hall.

As anyone can see from various items in the book, acknowledgement is also due to a much more enduring thought community associated with the *New Left Review* and its publishing house Verso. So far it has survived everything history has thrown at it: the expiry of 1960s hopes, the end of both empire and the Cold War, and the collapse (or identity change) of both communism and Western social democracy. Robin Blackburn's personal help brought the volume to its present state, as did suggestions and encouragement from other Verso authors like Benedict and Perry Anderson. Since 1995, I have also been fortunate enough to receive very useful assistance from Geoff Mulgan and his colleagues at Demos. Anthony Barnett has encouraged and invigilated this production in his inimitable way, from both sides of the Atlantic. A similarly constant influence has been that of Jean-François Revel, the *miglior fabbro* of most of what I have written since the 1960s. And as I mentioned before, there have been simply too many other inputs to list or acknowledge properly for such a volume, notably from Neal Ascherson, Willie Storrar, John Osmond, Willie Thompson and Jean McNicol of the *London Review of Books*. A number of the essays first appeared there, and I am very grateful for the sustained support and interest of the *London Review*: editor Mary-Kay Wilmers' is another of those indispensable communities of thought to which I have belonged since 1994. Thanks to Jim Singh-Sandhu I became a Visiting Professor at the University of Northumbria in 1997. I am also grateful to Jim, Monica Shaw, Bill Lancaster and David Welsh for letting me learn something of the republic-to-be in the north-east of England. Work on the book was concluded in an older Republic, under the welcoming eaves of Henk Van Kerkwijk's home in Roscommon.

Kilmore, Ireland, 1997

On Studying Nationalism[1]

More than once, Ernest Gellner remarked that the true subject of all modern philosophy is industrialisation.[2] It was the kind of remark which he loved most, an acrid mixture of surprise, denigration and humour. Modern philosophers (i.e. since David Hume) may believe they have been ruminating upon universal standards, the Soul, God, Infinity and other capital-letter constructions. In truth, all they have been trying to do is cope with the after-effects of the steam-engine.

As usual with his jokes, the point becomes more obvious the longer one thinks about it. Yes, industrialisation and its prolonged after-shock, 'modernity', have actually altered or had inescapable results for everything metaphysicians could conceivably think about. Yes, this does include human values as well as science and technology: ethics, aesthetics, science, nature, souls and gods. The steam-engine changed human beings and set them on the route to the personal computer and the World Wide Web. Hence it changed everything: the 'whole universe', or at least their ideas about it, which (as Immanuel Kant went on to observe) is all we can ever discuss anyway.

Agreeable though it is, Gellner's astringent *aperçu* still seems to me incomplete. It does not go far enough. For reasons I will come back to, he drew back from another more radical conclusion, even though it was implicit in his general and constantly reiterated theory of the transition from traditional agrarian society to modern times. One key point in that transition is nationalism. Gellner made the decisive advance in understanding why this is so in 1964, when the famous essay 'Nationalism' appeared in his collection *Thought and Change* (1964). For those concerned with understanding nationality politics, that was the 'Eureka!' cry which founded the social-scientific theory of nationalism. So, he demonstrated how industrialisation produced modern political nationalities; yet did not go on to suggest that the true subject of modern philosophy might be, not industrialisation as such, but its immensely complex and variegated aftershock – nationalism.

'Modernisation Theory'

What was the gist of his theory about modernisation and nationalism? Well, what he showed was how the salience of nationality in modernisation was

1

neither an accident nor (as his colleague and friend at the LSE Elie Kedourie had argued just a few years before) the product of idealism and wilfulness.[3] However important ideology and conspiracy may have been in engendering nationality-based politics, Gellner objected, such importance is bestowed upon them by other factors. It is the impact of socio-economic change which gives them this new significance, turning them into levers of change rather than bookish preoccupations or weekend antics. It is the advent of capitalist industry and agriculture, and of the middle and working classes which alters all social conditions. In these conditions – or sometimes, in hope of them – politics also changes its character. It becomes a non-elite, then a majority, concern; 'representation' becomes, or pretends to be, more egalitarian, until modern democracy is the result. As schoolbook histories used to put it, Kings and Lordship had to give way to the Common Man, then the Common Woman too – even if the former did take their time about it and spent most of the nineteenth and early twentieth centuries in rearguard or defensive operations which slowed down, even if they could not reverse, 'the inevitable'.

Gellner's addition to this commonplace view was a recognition that the Common Person was really a nationalist. The statement was never literally true, as Gellner also loved pointing out, since in themselves people were just nationals, or 'natives', or ethno-persons – that is, the products of one non-elite culture or another, either illiterate or unversed in whatever high culture went on around them or 'above their heads'. The '-ism' was potency only. And yet, this potential was bound to be realised on a large scale (if not absolutely everywhere) because the rapidly undertaken business of industrialisation required a general culture and language to make it work, and the effective culture was usually the popular-national one – the demotic rather than the highbrow, the dialect rather than the refined tongue of court, academy or salon. One form or another of demotic is raised up and made a respectable tongue by modernisation. Hence natives acquired a vital and economically sustained interest in their cultures, in what distinguished and identified them as well as what might provide them with jobs and their children with accessible schooling. Growing numbers of natives became cultural specialists, teachers, journalists, writers, politicians and assorted symbol-operators. That was inevitable too, in spite of Kedourie's complaints. There was nothing generally 'wilful', egregiously 'idealist' or romantic about the process at all: Gellner's point was that the subjective noise or nonsense accompanying 'nationalism', laughable, deplorable or dangerous as it may be, is quite objectively determined.

But why couldn't the 'people above' (in the eighteenth-century phrase) respond to such earth movements by adaptation and reform? Why did the older order of multi-national state–nations and dynastically founded empires have to shatter so dramatically, and relatively suddenly, into the crazy paving of today's nation-state world, where the number of independent polities has accelerated to nearly two hundred, and shows no sign of slowing down? And why was this fragmentation process so antagonistic, so overflowing with resentment, hatred, vengefulness and warfare? Gellner's answer here was to point to what he called the 'uneven' nature of the process.

No one planned Progress as a whole. It simply erupted. Had planning been involved, 'development' in what became the standard twentieth-century sense would presumably have been launched from the largest, oldest, most solid and culturally equipped of world cultures, China. This is surely what any inter-galactic navigator approaching our planet a thousand years ago would have expected. The space-vehicle probes would have informed him, wrongly, that the Chinese imperium was most likely to take over all other habitable territories, thus constituting a single societal culture with which (eventually) civilised communication might be possible.

Actually it happened the other way round. Industrialisation erupted among remote, squabbling, hirsute tribes of the extreme periphery, and spread out from there amid warfare and mayhem to reach the great world imperium last of all. Accident, unevenness and conflict may not inhere in 'development' as such, but they have undoubtedly structured the way it happened. This is why the rough edge of nationalism was inevitable. Because the breakthrough occurred in one population rather than another, it could not fail to give a developmental edge or lead to that population, including all its distinguishing marks of language, customs, faith, etc. (ethnic traits, as they were later labelled). Had any leading-edge gang from the Atlantic backwoods possessed, or developed, the capacity to impose itself on the others, then I suppose, at least for some time, that would have been that. The ancient Chinese-style business of empire would have been taken over, consolidated and 'improved' by one or other New Imperialism. This is in fact the sombre dystopia which Gellner evoked at the conclusion of his 1964 essay, pointing out how 'universality' could then so easily have meant universal oppression or even a global apartheid system. Grim though that vision was, it has become amusing in retrospect: we know what has actually happened to South Africa since 1964, when apartheid appeared irremovable. A beauty has been born, and not so terrible either: democratic black nationalism has shifted the course of history, Cape Town has become the favourite place for white capitalists and crooks to migrate to.

1984-style dystopias were prevented because those populations unblessed by the initial accident of scientific and economic breakthrough have been able to react in time. Appropriately generalised after the impact of the American, French and industrial revolutions, it was this reaction which injected the '-ism' into nationhood. Wilful and occasionally crazed symbol-operators came everywhere into their own. Educated, half-educated, self-educated, heroic and ineducable alike, they opted for development on their own terms: progress with reference to the interests of the (thus far) unblessed, potential or actual *déclassés*, those menaced with backwarding and marginalisation, the supposedly hairier, smellier and less washed. Noble or ignoble, savages learned to demand their own rights. Such demands had to be couched in collective terms, not simply the individual ones which the more liberal growth-metropoli were quite happy to grant. It was always obvious to the unwashed that the impositional side of progress was itself collective in nature, meaning in practice the triumph of Parisian *moeurs*, Manchestertum, Aryan-Teutonic spiritualism, Muscovite communism, or whatever. Hence resistant or alternative mobilisation required the constitution of equivalent identities, along whatever fault-lines were available. These were in most cases provided by nationality, which was now construed, reconstrued or 'discovered' (enemies in Paris, Manchester, etc., liked to say 'invented') as actual or potential nationhood. Our state is needed in order to prevent their imposition, as well as to give this particular population its chance at development.

In our own day, the generalisation of 'identity politics' and its popularity in the USA have made it fashionable to stress the multiplicity and fluidity of identification. Homo sapiens members are (the normal implication is: 'and always were') familial creatures, worshippers, stamp-collectors, music groupies, blacks, rugby-club subscribers and homosexuals, as well as possessors of passport appellations like 'Irish', 'Serbian' or 'Burmese', etc. Hence nationality is but one identity among many – and what's so special about it? Gellner's answer was that it became the operative, dominant form of identification under the circumstances of modernisation; for it, rather than they, represented effectual adaptation to the weather of industrialisation. That 'weather' was essentially a storm, one almost violent enough, after the invention of nuclear weapons in the 1940s, to destroy societal culture itself. Constructing breakwaters against such conditions demanded a certain scale, rigidity, cultural concrete and political armour; in most cases nationality could provide these, and alternative solidarity modes could not.

The possibilities of adaptation were limited, therefore, and appeared as 'given' rather than chosen. Contrary to Kedourie's strictures, and even if sometimes the decisive identity-mode was 'made' or helped to appear, it seemed a determination of nature rather than the will. Admittedly, this was 'nature' rather than nature: a transmitted inheritance rescanned, as it were, within the novel circumstances of modernisation, and so placed within quotation marks. None the less, certain factors of transmission ('ethnicity', the reconfigured past) remained central to the process, giving it the seriousness and the actual salty bite everyone recognises in nationalism. In his famous passage about Paul Klee's painting *Angelus Novus*, Walter Benjamin wrote that the appalled Angel of History, who seems to be contemplating in dismay modernity's piles of wreckage upon wreckage, 'would like to stay, awaken the dead, and make whole what has been smashed'.[4] But through nationalism the dead are awakened, this is the point – seriously awakened for the first time. All cultures have been obsessed by the dead and placed them in another world. Nationalism rehouses them in this world. Through its agency the past ceases being 'immemorial': it gets memorialised into time present, and so acquires a future. For the first time it is meaningfully projected on to the screen of futurity.

Critics love fulminating about the distortions and phoniness which so frequently blight such transpositions, forgetting the hopeless or totally daft mythologies which held all previous *mentalités* down into status clamps. Nationalism tends to produce B movies or cartoons, quite true. No doubt these are inferior to the epics which modern technology and research are making possible; but they were a great advance on the timeless folk-tale and the endless folk-poem. Did no one ever fall asleep sitting through the 200th rendition of Homer (albeit creatively modified by local bard, touches of homely colour added, etc.)? Given an opportunity, folk themselves have invariably voted for the movie-house, the tabloid and then the home TV screen.

So the cankered, one-off, lop-sided, ham-fisted, half-baked, one-eyed trajectory of actual modernisation led to rough justice. That was still better than what preceded it – no justice whatever, and forever. It also led to an ascriptive equality of pasts: the Irish, the Serbs, the Tibetans, the Inuit and the Micronesians will not be left out, and stake their claims like everyone else. Sometimes these are invented or preposterous, because they fear disappearance. Modernity made such fear more alive and real, but has also made it contestable. Having been startled into memoriality, they are damn well not going to subside again. Before industrialisation this happened all the time: cultures, peoples, traditions would just 'go under', leaving a few puzzling bricks or stones behind if they were lucky. Even at the very end of the twentieth century, metropolitan blueprinters come out every other week with new plans for improved or graceful subsidence in the best interests of 'everyone'. Damn 'everyone', goes the logic of nationalism: everyone is us, time is now, and that's it. Given the once-and-only chance of modernisation, we mean, with whatever help can be extracted from the dead, to stick around, remain awake for good, and have a say in colonising the future.

The point here is so deep it goes better into poetry than stilted theoretical terms; but of course this has been done too. In fact a lot of modern poetry is about it. In Scotland the deepest voice on such themes is Douglas Dunn, who has said it better than I ever could in 'Going to Aberlemno'. Aberlemno is a site in Tayside which holds a celebrated Pictish stone, commemorating a Dark Age battle about which practically nothing is known.

> By archaeologies of air,
> Folkways of kirks and parishes
> Revised by salty haar,
> You reach the previous
> Country.

The country is that of the Pictish people who once inhabited north-eastern Scotland, were defeated by Agricola's legions in the first century AD and later on 'merged' (whatever that meant) with the incoming Scots. It is approached via 'industry's ill-starred inlets, a breaker's yard, a ruby sore of rust' – like so much of post-industrial Scotland – until

> Here four roads intersect
> Beside the tallest oak
> And the best hawthorn
> Where every step you take
> Breaks on an acorn.

In such idyllically 'timeless' woodland stands the great, mysterious stone proclaiming victory over some other forgotten king and people (probably an Anglian or Northumbrian army), echoing a tongue and dynasty long since condemned to an oblivion like that of the stars:

> Through astral solitude
> A Pictish dialect.
> Above a bridged Firth, cries
> For lyric nationhood,
> And horsemen, in a stone disguise,
> Ride through the Pictish wood.

– alive millennia beyond their stone effigies, in fact, and still riding on through the dreams of those who cross the Tay bridges today. The wood was never timeless: once Pictish, it has become Scottish, and in the successor country of the latter poets like Dunn go on summoning up the dead and trying to make whole what has been smashed in the breaker's yard. But with a crucial difference. Piles of wreckage are indeed strewn everywhere, with this old mystery at their heart. But in the poet's own time, differently from that of the Picts, nationalism can try to redeem a particular time and wood, and make them whole.[5]

The great achievement of Gellner's 'modernisation theory' was recognition that all this takes place as a manifestation of modernity, and not a mere reaction against it. Past time is remobilised in order to confront the future, but in an essentially new way. Any universalism which fails to encompass this is itself phoney – the voice of 'Megalomania' (as he enjoyed putting it) perennially and selectively thundering against the atavism, romanticism, narrowness, selfishness (and so on) of 'Ruritania'. Its Enlightened indignation forgets all about the decisive role of Megalomania in engendering such sinfulness. At bottom Megalomanians feel they are the world. All the miserable Ruritanians want to do is join the world. They want to get in on Universality before they are forced to join the Picts.

'Primordialism'

A great amount more could be said in exposition of modernisation theory. But we must go on, and go on to see that, seductive and successful as it has been, this theory is itself very one-sided. It did see and first explain how industrialising modernity was a necessary condition of nationality politics. The way Atlantic-based – one might also say, peripherally launched –

development actually occurred brought about a 'second nature' of human-kind. Because of its, at first sight, arbitrary and uneven character, nationalism became an inescapable feature of that new or second nature. And yet, a necessary condition is not a sufficient one. Science-led technological development may have made the series of changes we call 'modernity' possible, and shaped a good deal of them. However, a *sine qua non* is not a cause – although it may end looking like one if too much attention is paid to it. The complete aetiology of the transition should acknowledge different levels of causation and range the causative elements in some kind of order. Only then will it be a sufficient or comprehensive explanation of things being as they are.

Although it redeemed nationality theoretically, the distinctive bias of Gellnerism was in fact always towards perceiving it as an effect. A necessary effect, perhaps, which gains some causative force from its generalisation and political momentum; and also a fortunate effect, better than any all-conquering alternative we can imagine. But still an effect rather than a motor, a chain of resultant phenomena rather than an originating or causative impulse. From 1964 onwards he nearly always couched this argument in the form of a standard put-down of naïve-nationalist belief.

Nationalist enthusiasts, he enjoyed pointing out, invariably claim that their nation was always there, waiting around to be reborn, and it is all too easy to debunk any mythology of this kind. One of his favourite examples, as a Czech, was that of a neighbouring people, the Slovaks. Slovakian nationalists like to think they have always been part of nature in the Tatra-Danubian homeland, at any rate since the general migration of the Slavs into Eastern Europe (about the same time as the Scots moved into Scotland). Hence there 'has always been' a Slovakian ethno-cultural entity which assorted previous empires and alien rulers all failed to acknowledge, dismissed, scorned, trampled underfoot, etc. This entity and unrecognised *Geist* were transmitted down the ages, until conditions were right for their emergence. Then transmission turned into communication – Slovak became a written language, acquired poetry and the endorsement of the Pope, generated intellectuals, showed restlessness about oppression, demanded rights and so on, until complete independence was attained in 1992.[6]

The distinctive modernist note has been to deny the naturalness or inherent fate of this trajectory: only commerce, industry and their many accompaniments made the transition possible, and without these 'Slovakia' would, like Pictland, have vanished somewhere in the longer *durée* – a process less than wholly unwelcome among the neighbouring and more 'advanced' (Megalomanian or quasi-Megalomanian) peoples of Austria, Bohemia, Hungary, etc. It may then be noted, with some relief, that inevitable destiny has nothing to do with Vladimir Meciar. History could have managed without him. Yes, but there is of course something else lurking in the background here. Certain discourse protocols have been established by successful nationalism (and finally assumed the caricatural and Teflon-coated form of Political Correctness). These mean a broader question is rarely if ever put these days (it was once quite common): couldn't history have managed quite well without the Slovaks? Slovak intellectuals of course still feel it hanging about in the air, even unvoiced.

Well, it may be true that modernisation–industrialisation could probably have unfolded across Central Europe without the reconstituted Slovak *ethnos* (and probably without Austrians, Czechs and Hungarians too). But there is a deeper insight which also remains valid here – although we can now see that it undermines some of Gellner's own arguments, as well as such shallow, though alas ever popular, conclusions. The process could not have unfolded as it actually has without the exacerbation and promotion of diversity. Any one nation may have dubious antecedents, which have had to be 'imagined', reforged, etc. But nationality's general lineage is in no sense either dubious or dispensable. In counter-factual histories, therefore, any particular population may be imagined as irrelevant or dispensable. Yet we know that as a whole the factual unfolding of history has depended absolutely upon clashes and contrasts among particular peoples. No particular particularity may be essential; but particularity as such was inescapable, and inescapably promoted by the real conditions of modern development.

To recapitulate a little at this point: progress had to be launched somewhere, not everywhere, and much of it was a series of accidents, rather than a God-like prescription dispensed from some global capital. Ironbridge Gorge, Lanarkshire and the suburbs of nineteenth-century Liège set the machinery in motion, not Peking, Vienna or the philosopher's stone.[7] From such contingent origins sprang the storm of impacts and further accidents which so far compose 'modernity': the world of nation-states and nationalism. What the 'ism' in the latter partly registers is the general consciousness of this, something shared from the later nineteenth century onwards by Slovaks alongside everybody else. This is what they mean by claiming Slovakia as a sleeping beauty or a soul in embryo, waiting around to claim life by way of poets, patriotic *intéllos*, ethno-purists and Slovak-Firsters. Their *ethnie* may in truth not have been asleep, lovely, destined to bedazzle or more genetically endowed than anybody else's. But neither was it less worthy than anybody else. And in the global Homo sapiens universe which Progress took by storm – six (or was it more like eight?) thousand tongues, conflicting faiths, assorted colours and physiques, divergent and irreconcilable customs – this comes to be what counts.

What does 'counts' mean here? Well, it implies bidding for new life, and paying for it with whatever past credentials can be scraped together. However, to get into the bidding a people or community must surely already exist and be alive. This is the thought which has increasingly preoccupied the main body of Gellner's critics over the past generation.[8] These critics are customarily grouped together as 'primordialists', and their common characteristic seems to be unease about the ascription of quite so much generative power to the modernisation process itself. They have tended to argue that the pre-modern, and above all 'ethnicity', must have contributed more, and much more positively, to whatever it is the storm has brought out. In some sense, surely, nationalities must indeed have been there, and must have been conscious, semi-conscious, or at least not 'sleeping'. Hence the variegation of humanity should not be conceived as merely a passive 'given', the patchwork of ethnic 'raw material' which happened to be around when the modernisation lightning struck. All research in social anthropology (including Gellner's own early work in North Africa) shows how un-passive 'traditional' society actually was, even if its restless dynamic was largely recycled and contained.[9]

Coupled to this was the suspicion that modernisation theory was simply over-rational and 'bloodless' as an explanation for processes in which so much unreason is typically manifested, and so much literal blood has been spilt. It leaves too much out; it accounts for the material or vested interests in nationalism rather than its 'spell'. It is articulated around high-cultural politics rather than low-cultural glamour and popular identity.[10] But all the actual experiences of mass nationalism from the American Civil War down to the second wave of post-1989 suggest there must be 'more to it' than the characteristic idiom and emphases of modernism allow. Unevenness came to be the name of the game – the only game in town. Yet that game did not itself originate unevenness, or diversity. In W.B. Yeats's 'Second Coming' shapes 'with lion body and the head of a man' find their hour come round at last, rough beasts who 'slouch towards Bethlehem to be born' again, and encounter the second nature of modernity.[11] Did first nature bring nothing – or nothing which really mattered – to this encounter? The in-built temptation of modernisation theory has been to suggest just that. It reacts against earlier nonsense about nationalism being a tale of Dark Gods and resurgent tribalism by stressing how much of it is novel, unprecedented and forced from the press of modernity. Correct as this is, one may doubt whether it is sufficient for analysing the resultant brew.

Resurgence of 'the Blood'

'Deep is the well of the past', says Thomas Mann's narrator at the beginning of *Joseph and His Brothers*. Modernity has all come out of it, and drawn constantly from it to make the surrounding landscape. There has to be more to the view than modernisation doctrine allows: but what? The most obvious answer remains 'the blood', in the familiar metaphorical sense of transmission or inheritance from the past, in either a biological or a socio-cultural sense. But of course this at once poses damned awkward questions. Since the 1930s, and including the period in which modernist theory took off (from the 1960s to the 1990s), everything associated with 'the blood' has stood in extremely bad odour, for extremely good reasons. For around a hundred years various forms of scientific or, as we now know, pseudo-scientific racism appropriated this mode of discourse and made it into a justification for domination, oppression and occasionally extermination. Industrialisation led to New World slavery as well as to literacy, democracy and a higher standard of living. Similarly, the emancipation of Darwinism led, via 'Social Darwinism', straight into new ideologies of inherent superiority and inferiority which, pursued with the logic and the means of modern industrial culture, could justify almost any cruelty and barbarity. Not much is known about what happened to Douglas Dunn's Picts; but it is all too easy to imagine what fate might have overtaken them had they survived into the nineteenth or twentieth century and been put down as 'genetically' third-rate, defective, inferior, dangerous and so on.

Certainly, as ideology all this was defeated alongside the Third Reich in 1945. As scientific explanation it has been repeatedly and utterly discredited by one revelation after another. None the less, its black shadow still affects all speculation in this area and for a long time more or less prohibited serious rethinking. That inhibition affected modernisation theory. It probably conditioned its crystallisation in the 1960s and has certainly preserved its hegemony longer than it deserved, ending by turning it into something of an orthodoxy. Primordialists wishing to stress ethnicity, for example, were compelled to make it clear from the outset, and repeatedly, that they disavowed all connection with the old nonsense about race and inbred inequalities. Hence ethnic distinctions had to be interpreted quite differently, as being themselves cultural artefacts, hence decipherable, learnable, reprogrammable and so on. Nationalism may be preluded and underpinned by ethnicity, went the argument; but ethnicity itself could never be 'nature' in the final-determinant sense beloved of Gobineau, Confederate slave-owners and Hitler. It too had to be 'constructed'. It was to be understood as sociology, not as biology.

Well, possibly – but if this is so, then does not a certain 'bloodlessness' overtake primordiality as well? In a disconcerting manner, it is as if all native beings turn out to have been in some unsuspected way modernists – or maybe even post-modernists – *avant la lettre*. If such ancient and indelible-seeming differences can seriously be viewed as 'invented', then the construction of modernity itself becomes less surprising, less of a shock. Yet the whole point – the positive input of sociological modernisation philosophy – had seemed to be the shock of the new, the transformative convulsion brought about by science and industry. Now suddenly everything becomes in retrospect suspiciously reasonable and transparent: the very thing of which modernist theory stands most commonly accused. Anderson's 'spell' ends by being exorcised in the deepest historical retrospect, as if there had never been anything but 'identity politics'. This tendency has been especially prominent among the Scandinavian theorists of ethnicity who have played such a prominent part in this stream of theorisation, like Frederick Barth and Thomas Eriksen.[12]

If, on the other hand, peoples have not been able to help being like that (inventors of cultural contrasts, antagonistically differentiated, etc.), then what is to prevent blood and accursed 'human nature' coming into their own once more? In that case, doesn't atavism appear to reassume its rights? To the general pleasure of conservatives, descent, transmission and the unconscious appear to reassert themselves over decision, communication

and individuality. The resurgence of nationality politics within the globalisation arena becomes more comprehensible, if in a thoroughly depressing
way. In Gellnerian theory, it was a combination of ethnic fault-lines and
uneven development which occasioned the rise of nationalism. But the same
conjuncture can be read in a less liberal way too. It could be argued that
the very thing which thus motivated the creative reaction to industrialisation,
and destroyed all modern imperialist projects, may mean that antagonistic
fragmentation is fated to continue. Gellner was a non-conformist; yet he
retained a powerful underlying conformity with Enlightenment traditions
by wanting to think of antagonistic differentiation as an episode in history,
as something likely to diminish once industrialisation has become sufficiently widespread. If the role of primordial human nature was greater than
his theory allows, however, then may it not be that what saved us may also
be condemning us to an indefinite futurity of differentiation?[13]

'Human nature': yes, here is the traditional vantage point to which the
continuing study of nationalism returns us. The reason why the dispute
between modernists and primordialists is not resolved in contemporary
debates is because it is irresolvable. That is, irresolvable within the given
terms being used by both sides. What it has tended to mean in practice is
something like a courteous difference of emphasis, like that presented in
the last live debate between Gellner and Anthony Smith at Warwick
University.[14] The terms are inadequate: in other words, there is as yet no
theoretical framework capable of bearing the argument further. The
paradigm created by Gellner has had its positive effect, but also shown the
limitations to which primordialist critics point. No successor paradigm has
yet been constituted, however, so that it looks as if the theory of nationalism
is currently at a moment of forced transition or development. The old
philosophical presuppositions of modernism are losing their hold; but no
one is quite sure what new ones will replace them. Events since 1989 have
returned us squarely to the problem of 'blood' – the inherent and
irreconcilable diversity of 'human nature'. But there is not yet a post-End-
of-History theory convincing or plausible enough to impose itself as a new
paradigm of explanation.

Angles of Approach

I don't have one to hatch out here and now before your startled eyes. But it
may be useful to conclude by looking at some angles of approach towards
such a new framework of theory, in order to help us see just where we are.
We don't know what that theory will be; yet it may be possible to guess, at
least, what sort of a theory it is likely to be.

Modernisation theory was a version of philosophical materialism. In fact
its basic assumptions were surprisingly similar to those of the 'historical
materialism' linked to Marxism, and so to the ideologies of the state-
imposed communism which encountered its come-uppance in the later
1980s. Gellner was a conservative liberal who detested political Marxism,

and spent his last years back home in Prague, trying to ensure nothing like that would ever happen again in Central Europe. None the less, his diagnosis of modernisation rested upon the notion of economic or socio-economic forces as responsible for modernity. Although made possible by early natural science, and the application of scientific ideas as technology, the transition was essentially, as I suggested earlier, 'blind' in the sense of producing a novel or unexpected array of societal forces and pressures whose meaning and possibilities – among them, nationalism – only became conscious, or self-conscious, much later.

The philosophical opposition to this approach had come traditionally from idealism. Kant, Hegel and their successors maintained that the blindness was apparent only, since history was driven at a profounder level by ideas – God's ideas, perhaps, to which we may have no direct Freephone line for explanation or justification, but which none the less must carry an intrinsic meaning. This meaningfulness functions as a guarantee against human existence being a cosmic accident. It also seems in principle accessible to our own limited awareness, in the sense that the Creator's ideas, although frequently inscrutable, must be fundamentally of the same stuff and hence divinable if only one thinks hard and long enough about it. Religion is both reinterpreted and relegitimated by this approach, so that a spiritual aura attaches to whatever conclusions emerge out of such thinking. For example, may it not be that different peoples, nations or races manifest differing 'ideas' through history and bear one or other of these to justified dominance in some kind of recognisable pattern? First prospected by Hegel in his philosophy of history, this view was later to assume the disastrous forms mentioned before, social Darwinism and Aryan racism.

Sociological modernisation theory emerged in the wake of the steep nose dive inflicted by World War II on this German-based idealism. Though politically opposed to Marxism, it could not help incorporating something of the enemy's philosophical assumptions – Marx's famous 'inversion' of Hegel's ideal dialectic into the concept of materially social forces as the determinants of history. As soon as Communism materially collapsed, however, there occurred a striking reinversion of outlook towards ideational thought. This post-1989 *Leitmotif* was struck most impressively by Francis Fukuyama's hugely influential *The End of History, and the Last Man* (1989), which moved straight back into Hegelian philosophy for its key categories of explanation. Stripped of political clothing and importance, socio-historical materialism achieved instant dismissal from every conceivable think-tank and was packed off downstairs to join phrenology and astrology in the basement museum of exploded relics.[15]

I think this punishment will turn out to be excessive. Any new paradigm is much more likely to represent a synthesis of materialism and idealism in these traditional and sacrosanct forms. I know this sounds rather Hegelian itself, yet doubt if there will be much the great philosopher of Prussianism would have approved of in the conclusion. Disputes as profound as that between modernism and primordialism never result in 'victories' for one side or the other: rather, both views turn out to be right, and wrong in ways unforeseeable when the initial theories were formulated. The most probable arena for such a fusion of perspectives is, surely, that of what one has to call 'life science', in a sense which extends from the new genetics, via 'bio-sociology' and palaeo-anthropology, to the sociology which Gellner and the modernists chiefly relied upon. Any new paradigm depends, in other words, on establishing a more plausible link between biology and kinship on one hand, and the world of political nation-states and resurgent nationality on the other.

This link will of its nature transcend materialism and idealism, in the encrusted traditional sense. Since the 1950s, with the discovery of the intimate structures of living heredity by Crick, Watson and others, and the subsequent world-wide research into the patterns and movements of pre-historic population now incorporated into the Human Genome project, we understand the materiality of descent in a way simply not available to any previous generation. That alteration is absolute, and final in the sense that nobody can now go back on it or 'rediscover' older or better ideas (as Fukuyama thought he was doing with the resurrection of Hegel, for example). In this area, each new student begins by learning things Charles Darwin was completely ignorant of at the end, not the start, of his career. Much of Darwinism and practically the whole of 'social Darwinism' were founded upon simple ignorance. But now that ignorance is over in principle, and when the Genome project is completed some time after the year 2000, it will be over in scientific fact as well. The geneticist Steve Jones has put all this quietly but brilliantly in the Preface to his book *In the Blood*:

> Genetics is, at last, like Germany, ready to stop apologizing for its past. My title *In the Blood* turns on the widespread conviction that destiny is inborn. That belief began long before science. The term 'nature' itself derives from the Latin *natus*, that which is born, 'nation' from the same root.[16]

His point is not that the huge advance in understanding genesis itself 'explains' nations and nationalism. Quite the contrary, it shows how there can be no straightforward explanation of that sort: the dreadful simplicities of racism and ethnic nationalism all derived from delusions of this sort, which from now on do belong in the basement reliquary. But to be certain of that is itself a great liberation. It means that the parameters of the material have been genuinely drawn, and metaphysics exiled from another important zone of speculative thought.

Instead, 'primordialism' must be focused upon the social. That is, on the pre-history and evolution of the kinship (literal and metaphorical) which effectively links *natus* to nation and then, under modernity's impact, to nationalism. Under the grander umbrella of sociology, there would seem to be two ways of approaching the study of the linkage. One lies of course with palaeo- and social anthropology, and with archaeology, concerned with examining what remains of pre-modern or early-modern social formations and speculating on how these could have originated and become so diversified.[17] Modernist theory perceives language functionally, as the required cultural instrument of industrialisation. Tongues must be reconstituted and elevated into 'high cultures', in order to take their state-worthy places in the steam-engine universe. Yes, but was their original constitution and variation of no importance for grasping the way things then evolved? The 'spell' of community always depended not just on language but on the proliferation of tongues, which always entailed incommunicability, privacy and falsehood, as well as understanding, common sense and truth.[18]

Logically following from the centrality of speech is another key area – fairly obvious to common sense, yet so far largely absent from the academic array of disciplines touching on nationalism: psychology. This can be interpreted in the first place as 'social psychology', naturally, which gives it a more immediate relevance to what nationalism seems (mostly) to be about. In fact all existing theories of nationalism have deployed notions of social or collective mentality, and spoken of community or 'communal' responses or reflexes (usually to equivalently generic 'forces', 'changes', etc.). However, I'm not sure how important this distinction really is. 'Social' does not here exclude 'individual'. Psychology in the sense most relevant to this discussion can be taken as denoting small-group, familial and even personal mentality and reactions.

The reason for that is simple. In dealing with what 'underlies' the manifest phenomena of nationalism – collective actions on a certain scale, and often on a huge scale – I argued that we are forced back on to 'human nature'. Though partly this can be construed as the pre-history and history of human society, we can be reasonably sure that all too little will be literally discoverable there, and nothing comparable to the great leap forward in genetic science. *Bones of Contention* is the appropriate title of one important study in the field of palaeo-anthropology, and its sense can all too easily be generalised.[19] In his conclusion the author points out how the search for origins has been inseparable from 'questions of self-image':

> Paleoanthropology shares with all historical sciences the limitations of trying to reconstruct events that occurred just once. It also shares with all sciences the truism that science is an activity done by people, and is therefore subject to the unavoidably personal and erratic nature of intellectual progress. But paleoanthropology alone operates within [a] dimension where humanity's self-image invisibly but constantly influences the profession's ethos.

However, the 'personal and erratic' progress can be read somewhat differently. There is, after all, a good reason why humanity's self-image evolves unstoppably and generates such acrimonious disputes: every new generation and in a sense every new individual is 'humanity' and has a share in the self-image. No one can help recapitulating the story in question; hence the story – or part of it – is reproduced in each episode, unconsciously but also to some degree consciously or, for theorists, self-consciously.

Historical materialism and sociological modernism employed primarily a discourse of impersonal forces and movements, partly to establish their social-scientific credentials. Yet among the most vital credentials may be what tends to be omitted or sidelined by this approach: the psychological structures of both adhesion and dissent, of 'belonging' and repudiation or innovation.[20]

On this terrain all are in one sense alike, sharing an origin in awareness as well as in genetics and societal history. This has been very well described by Conor Cruise O'Brien:

> There is for all of us a twilit zone of time, stretching back for a generation or two before we were born, which never quite belongs to the rest of history. Our elders have talked their memories into our memories until we come to possess some sense of a continuity exceeding and traversing our own individual being. The degree in which we possess that sense of continuity, and the form it takes – national, religious, racial or social – depends on our own imagination and on the personality, opinions and garrulity of our elder relatives. Children if they are imaginative have the power of incorporating into their own lives a significant span of time before their individual births.[21]

An unkind critic might interpret these remarks as heedless endorsement of one of the most noticeable features of nationalism study: the powerful conviction held by each student that he or she knows something about this subject – probably a good deal more than the panjandrums, and quite possibly of very special significance. But the point here is to recognise how every 'twilit zone' does mean something, as does the imagination and culture subsequently put into it both by the environment and the individual's effort of incorporation. We do all have a stake in the underlying sense and form of 'continuity', which itself reaches backwards from twilight into darkness, and forward into imagined light – and hence, an 'interest' distinct from those material or socio-economic concerns figuring so prominently in modernisation theory.[22] It may be true that the latter's influence renders the former much more alive and acute. Does it follow that prior to the modernisation impact there was merely a 'potential', or relatively insignificant latency? More crucial still: why should the heightened liveliness diminish or lose its sting once modernisation has accomplished its work?

It will be obvious to any student from remarks made earlier, for example apropos Benjamin, that religious belief is one of the things which flows into and helps configure nationalism. It plays virtually no part in the modernisation theory. Rather, that tends to locate faith as an alternative form or surrogate for national identity – as in Ireland and Sri Lanka, say, or in some new East European conflicts. This problem grew more acute after the emergence of Islamic fundamentalism in the 1970s, as it became evident that the Age of Faith (let alone that of Nationalism) was anything but over and done with. A lot of Gellner's effort in his last years went into reconsideration of political Islamicism and its meaning.

Mass, traditional religious beliefs were nourished by a general socio-economic context – the predominantly rural economy, life and routines which prevailed in most of the world until far into the twentieth century, long after the initial episodes of industrialism and urbanisation. Capitalism's 'world market' – the supposed matrix of modern politics and culture, and hence of the nation-state – encountered and convulsed a largely agrarian universe. The latter's reluctance to change, then sometimes its abrupt or forced spasms of change, all affected the resultant process. In retrospect 'uneven development' seems a pathetically inadequate way of trying to cover such varied and occasionally cataclysmic shifts. But that pathos derived from in-built bias: over-emphasis upon the factors of leading-edge alteration resulting in understatement of everything behind the edge – what actually forced its way through the 'fault-lines' to lay down the successor landscape we inhabit.[23]

Coming to better terms with nationalism calls for Perry Anderson's 'more differentiated approach' all right. But my God, how differentiated? Genetics, archaeology, linguistics. psychology, different styles of anthropology, religion, peasant studies: is there any end to the spectrum of post-modernist concerns in this subject area? We have not even got to 'culture' in the usual senses anyone would see as relevant to understanding nationalism: ethnic or folk-culture, manifestations of national identity in the arts, or the bizarre trajectory of twentieth-century nationalist ideologies in relation to aesthetic modernism. Yet if one reached that shore – which I will not try to do, as I feel the swimmers tiring, including this one – it would only be to find others beckoning one reproachfully. How can a theorist deal with popular culture and political nationality, for example, yet ignore the colossal weight of sport upon that culture? If pre-nationalist countries tended to be configured by gods, 'tribes', rural myths and localities, their contemporary successors are analogously affected and influenced by sporting identifications and contests. Any survey of such a strongly inter-disciplinary theoretic zone threatens to dissolve into an endless book list, the kind of interminable non-reading lists often dispensed at the start of university courses (naming no names).

But the only genuine answer to Anderson's question is 'no': there is no end to it, once the boundaries of modernisation theory are challenged. Most things are bound to seem 'relevant', and it would be futile to rule out this or that in advance. Modernism was itself a sort of ruling-out-in-advance: it made its extremely effective point partly in just that way. Yet once the point was established (between the 1960s and the 1990s) we find ourselves returned into the grander arena of 'human nature' and history for a fuller, more comprehensive understanding. At the same time, I don't think the return necessarily implies futile diffusion or mere floundering about. Philosophy is returned on an altered plane, after all, one advanced by the very achievements of Gellner and sociological modernism. We know that in post-Enlightenment times the complex of things denoted by 'nationalism' did not become so central and commanding by accident or disaster. 'Dark gods' and blood atavism were not the cause – these were, as Gellner argued, themselves among the legends of early modernity. But 'human nature' is another matter. The immense perturbation of modernity threw into relief features of human community and diversity whose characteristics and relationships social science is still struggling to encompass. The 'national' has now proved to be by far the most persistent and ineffaceable of the nodes in this area, beyond all earlier predictions: it remains the forger, rather than the forged artefact, of modernity's storm-ridden domain. There was a crabbed, resentful strain in Enlightenment thought, present in Max Weber and still discernible in Gellner: fear of the world's imminent 'disenchantment'. Disenchantment be damned: as Steve Jones notes acidly in his Preface to *In the Blood*, we dwell 'At a time when three and a half million Americans claim to have been abducted by aliens and many more believe in the literal truth of the Book of Genesis' and when, therefore, there is need for rational analysis of such matters. Far from dissipating the enchantments of antiquity, the nationalist world has amplified them into the vast cacophony of the late second millennium.

So – returning to my original suggestion – the true subject of modern philosophy is nationalism, not industrialisation; the nation, not the steam-engine and the computer. German philosophy (including Marxism) was about Germany in its age of difficult formation; British empiricism was about the Anglo-Britons during their period of free-trade and primitive industrial hegemony; American pragmatism was about the expansion of US democracy after the closure of the Frontier; French existentialism mani-fested the stalemate of 1789 Republicanism after its twentieth-century defeats – and so on. What philosophy was 'about' in that sense has never been just 'industrialisation', but rather the specific deep-communal struc-tures perturbed or challenged by modernisation in successive *ethnies*, and experienced by thinkers as 'the world'. Although Gellner's critique of modern British empiricism was itself a brilliant example of such analysis, it seems to me he always feared its implications.[24] He feared a descent into a helpless relativism where each and every parochial ideology might *vaut une autre*, and the Enlightenment's crude yardstick becomes completely useless. But here we have another story, one which, you will be relieved to hear, I cannot embark on today.

Part I
The Internationale

Questions of Rootedness

For reasons constantly restated here, nationalism is a universal condition of modernity. The more unified world of 2000 AD has emerged from transcending, rather than repudiating, the diverse and quarrelsome past of humanity. The transition has made particularity itself a universal condition, but it has achieved this through the reproduction or reinvention of diversity, rather than by simple effacement or a subordination to common standards and values. Finally, in the age of information technology, the enchanting powers of Joseph's 'coat of many colours' in the Christian Bible appear magnified rather than diminished. Thomas Mann described the moment of the original garment's unfolding in *Joseph and His Brothers*. It carries the whole folk-memory of humankind:

> The lad stared in amaze ... The metal embroideries glittered in the lamplight. The flashing silver and gold blotted out at times the quieter colours as the old man held it up in his unsteady arms: the purple, white, olive-green, rose-colour, and black of the emblems and images, the stars, doves, trees, gods, angels, men and beasts, lustrous against the bluish mist of the background.

Later, when Joseph is cast into the pit and sold into slavery, this is the wonder which reappears soaked in blood, evidence of his degradation and supposed death. Then Jacob himself terrifies the family by tearing and stripping off his own clothes in protest at the horror, at that ultimate shame felt 'when the primitive breaks through the layers of civilisation ... the abasement of man to mere creature'.

When, around 1989, the worst shadows of the pit were dissipated, many commentators mistook the pains of release for those of deeper abasement. In December of that year the French author and columnist Jean-François Revel gave an acid description of the panic in the air – the fear of destabilisation which immediately prevailed among Western leaders and intellectuals. Under the old conditions of glaciated blocus they had at least known where they were. Not any longer. Gorbachev had represented their ideal formula, someone who still might reform communism from above without too much fuss and upheaval. True, supporting him did mean urging the peoples of his imperium (and by implication everybody else) to stay in line. No upheavals, please, until responsible all-round Progress has been authorised by the proper authorities. Irresponsible revolt might lead to nationalism, break-ups, new frontiers and embassies, and even to fighting. Nuclear winter and the untimely extinction of humanity were no longer threatened; but there might be some fighting.

Revel underlined how utterly surreal this position had become. 'Balkanisation may be a problem', he pointed out, 'but far less of one than the Gulag ... Democracy is always accompanied by some instability. And surely the re-democratisation of Europe may be worth a bout of sea-sickness.'[1] Over this whole period Revel had also consistently emphasised how striking and irreversible the development of democracy had become. Echoing Francis Fukuyama's estimate in *The End of History*, he wrote in his *Le Point* column in 1993:

> Twenty years ago 44 of the 184 countries now represented at the United Nations were democratic, and in 1983 there were still only 57. Today there are 99 ... Have we forgotten that twenty years ago three members of today's European Community were still dictatorships! So was almost the whole of Latin America. The democratisation of South Africa seemed quite unimaginable, and that of South Korea or Taiwan most unlikely. Marcos still ruled the Philippines.[2]

Democracy's new lease of life seemed unstoppable. For many years Revel had been a sharp critic of Western failure and half-heartedness against communist totalitarianism. No one denounced more forcefully than he the sneaking collusion with authoritarian attitudes so often discernible among both the politicians and the intellectuals of societies which had taken democracy too much for granted. Now, it was becoming clear how such postures were persisting beyond the disappearance of the 'totalitarian temptation' itself. Incredibly, *nationalism* was already perceived as more of a threat than state socialism had been – a threat to the Proper Authorities, that is, to an order and stability for so long encrusted in place by decades of Cold War. Democracy was desirable, but secondary. No longer dispensable, it was surely postponable to a 'proper time' in the future when people had 'matured' or been prepared for the exercise of power. What was absolutely indispensable was that things should not get out of hand: a matter for the local *responsables*, benevolently assisted by their equivalents in the West.

The underlying attitudes reiterated in the Introduction to this book (pp. 1–17) are close to those of Revel, and some of them explore the theoretical hinterland of the absurd cramps which he has so effectively mocked. The idea of internationalism, for example, as a sacrosanct short cut from division into unity. Joseph did not stay in the pit. He went on to traverse the real world symbolised in the dream coat, without forgetting or renouncing his roots, and returning at length to his own. However understandable, Jacob's lamentations were mistaken. There can be no transition without the risk, and sometimes the disaster of breakdown or failures. Some of these are also dealt with here. But it was Empire alone – the negation of diversity on a deeper plane – which risked rendering such failures permanent, by locking them into an inescapable atavism.

1

Internationalism: A Critique

For over a century, a noble spectre has haunted the whole development of socialism.[1] Like Hamlet's father, he appears on the battlements at every important psychological moment, pouring out a familiar mixture of admonition, reproach and prophecy. We all carry a bit of him inside us, of course. He is the great common ancestor of all parties, sects and fronts, a more or less irreproachable father-figure to both vast socialist states and diminutive socialist cults. He wears a long, rather ragged beard which, in our common dream state, merges indistinguishably into those of Lenin, Engels, Marx and God himself.

This well-born ghost, 'Internationalism', probably deserves more critical scrutiny than he normally receives. Like War and the Generals, Internationalism is too important to leave to the internationalists. It has been clear since 1871 that he is not the body of socialism. He is not the intelligence either, though the collective guilt he embodies has certainly influenced our reasoning. But people do behave as if he were in some way the Soul of socialism, or communism. That is, the unchallengeable, exalting Moral Presence one may occasionally forget, but must never renounce. It is known that he unleashes a fatal moral thunderbolt upon all those who abandon him, dooming them to chauvinist perdition and reaction.

In what follows I would like to pose some questions to the Old Man, mainly from a nationalist point of view. Can we do without him? Is there a rational kernel inside the awesome robes of semi-sacred piety? Why is he a perpetually grumbling ancestor, rather than our hopeful child? Can we hope to reappropriate our Soul one day, and live with it rather than be haunted by it?

Internationality

One ought to start with an elementary distinction. Internationalism means what the word says: we are discussing a creed that has been articulated (not necessarily very consciously) into an '-ism', with a systemic nature of its own. Like others, this conceptual system has its own logic as well. I hope to explore some of the mildly amazing peculiarities of this logical structure later on. But to begin with it is indispensable to distinguish the '-ism' from international reality.

The term 'internationality' is not in common use, at least in the English language. However, it will do well enough for my purpose here. Ironically enough, the first example of it given by the *Oxford English Dictionary* comes from 1864, the year of the founding of Marx's First International. 'Of course, a French racecourse is not like an English one. Internationality is not yet so perfect', commented the *Daily Telegraph*, striking to perfection that absurd note of scarcely veiled Great Nation chauvinism which, as the years passed, was to constitute such a notable part of the internationalist chorus. But I anticipate my own argument. The explicit rather than the implicit is what matters for now. Racecourses are growing more alike, the world over, as material civilisation advances. So are factories, shops, towns, transport, farms and even people.

Internationality denotes simply this growing tendency, deriving from the formation of a capitalist world-wide market, the diffusion of the new industrial means of production, and all the social relations of production which followed them – in particular, obviously, the constitution of the universal modern class structure, the capital-based bourgeoisie and its proletariat. All the things that were so conspicuously hymned in *The Communist Manifesto*, in short, and perceived as the material basis for the coming international struggle and its *dénouement*, the international revolution.

Lenin took up the hymn in his own way later. Marxism, he wrote, must always 'advance internationalism, the amalgamation of all nations in the higher unity, a unity that is growing before our eyes with every mile of railway line that is built, with every international trust, and every irresistible tide of economic development, bearing standardisation and conformity with it, and demanding larger and larger spaces to operate in'.[2] Hence a growing interdependence of peoples and nations, and a growing sameness of racetracks and other phenomena; hence the futility of any sort of old particularism which gets in the way and tries to hold things back. Lenin's term for that was 'medieval particularism', against which it was invariably the sacred duty of the class-conscious proletariat to fight. This was because socialism had to transcend capitalism, and could never merely undo it. Capitalism needed 'the largest and most centralised possible states' for its success; but so would socialism, with its even larger, more centralised plans for putting things right.

I make these references because I am mainly interested in socialist internationalism. But there is, naturally, nothing left-wing about inter-nationality. It is bourgeois, capitalist Progress incarnate. There is no need here to pass the stages of Progress in review, from the era of Manchester free trade to that of the 'international trusts' and their present-day, more powerful successors, the multi-national corporations. The message has always been much the same, whether given as hymn or curse. 'For business purposes', declares Mr Jacques G. Maisonrouge of International Business

Machines, 'the boundaries that separate one nation from another are no more real than the equator. They are merely convenient demarcations of ethnic, linguistic, and cultural entities. Once management understands and accepts this world economy, its view of the marketplace – and its planning – necessarily expand.'[3] Socialist purposes too have always been expanding their view. And, one must add, all those ethnic and other 'entities' less than delighted to see their boundaries treated like the equator, whether by typewriter manufacturers or revolutionaries.

Internationalism is not the simple ideological manifestation of inter-nationality. There have merely been constant recurrent, simplistic arguments which employ the undeniable facts of internationality as a spurious justification of internationalism. Those suspect of sympathies with medieval particularism have always been belaboured with this stick. How can such nostalgic fogeys get so out of touch with the obvious? That is, with the fact that every extra mile of railway line turns them into History's extras and small-bit players (or even understudies). Internationalism is only common sense, for capitalists and socialists alike. Because of the nature – cumulative, objective, irrefutable – of internationality.

I mention this mode of argument only to dismiss it. The only interesting aspect of it is the fact that it is so commonly employed, not exclusively by corporate hacks or mouthpieces of the Soviet state. However, this is a fact of ideology, not the real world, and it is as such that I will return to it later. As for reality, all we need do is remember that the overwhelmingly dominant political by-product of modern internationality is nationalism. Not the logically prescribed common sense of internationalism, but the non-logical, untidy, refractory, disintegrative, particularistic truth of nation-states. Not swelling 'higher unity' but 'Balkanisation', a world of spiky exceptions to what ought to have been the rule. The exceptions have become the rule. This is the point. And if we allow historical materialism the smallest influence upon our theory of it, I fail to see how we can avoid thinking that 'Balkanisation' must be the necessary, inevitable translation of all those miles of railway line and business machine salesmen. Not a dispiritingly endless chain of accidents, in other words, but the process itself; not doomed and mindless resistance to advancing reality, but the reality in action.

The spurious, giddy leap from internationality to internationalism is over this truth. Looked at from one angle, indeed, internationalism is a con-spiracy to avoid recognising it – a conspiracy with distinct motives and methods, sinking very deep indeed into the Western intellectual world-view. No one in his senses is going to deny the increasing interdependence of the global economy, the economic rationale of larger productive units and markets, the growth of state intervention, the role of multinationals, or any of the other fetishes. But no automatic, 'logical' rendition of these factors into political or historical internationalisation has in fact occurred. Hence it is grotesque to employ them so automatically as a foundation for the ethical or political posture of internationalism.

An obvious analogy may help at this point. The relationship between international realities and 'internationalism' is in truth not unlike that between nationality and 'nationalism'. In neither case does the '-ism' spring automatically or straightforwardly from the real historical entities which it represents. There were, and are, nationalities without nationalisms. It is an elementary thesis of theories of nationalism that peoples and nations only began to evolve 'nationalism' at a specific stage of their history: broadly speaking, from the later eighteenth century onwards. One can find any number of precursor phenomena in earlier times, which seem (in retrospect) to prefigure the age of political nationality. But in truth there was no systemic character – no '-ism' – attaching to all those forerunners. The generalisation came with the Age of Improvement and Progress, as those were thrust upon the world by the great bourgeois revolutions and empires.

'Nationalism' is a complex, multi-faceted response to such general alterations of course in modern and contemporary history. It is not 'natural' to ethnic communities or peoples but (in a longer time perspective) highly novel and artificial. It has evolved an ideology of naturalness, certainly. However, this is part of a necessary self-image, rather than of the inherent nature of these peoples.

'Internationalism' is another reaction of the same general kind – and to the very same general circumstances. Like 'nationalism', it is far more ambiguous and complicated than the self-image in which it lives. Capitalist internationality generated both nationalism and internationalism, in fact, and since the rise and fall of Napoleon's French Revolutionary Empire these political world-views have existed in permanent, uneasy tension with one another. In ideological terms, nationalists invariably point to a separate history and an ethno-linguistic patrimony as the basis for their creed of independent development; internationalists show us the railway lines, the ever rising tide of Coca-Cola, corporate or state mega-structures, the 'same problems' everywhere, and so on. But what are they actually doing with these displays?

Internationalism

Internationalism is an organic part of the conceptual universe of nationalism. Both creeds derive from the modern epoch of industrialised development and empire, plainly. But there is no doubt which has been generally dominant. Ever since the vast, multi-ethnic recoil against French conquests it is the principle of political nationality which has emerged and re-emerged, as the apparently inevitable form of almost all new states and international state settlements. So, internationalism has to be seen as a function of this principle's victories, rather than vice versa.

This is why internationalism bears only a somewhat tortured and distant relationship to universalist beliefs of the past. It is quite easy to see resemblances between these spiritual doctrines of man's nature and the sort of preaching internationalists go in for, of course. But I doubt if they take us far. The great religious verities are counterposed to sin and evil, in the framework of an essentially unchanging universe. Internationalism is set over against the never ceasing, endemic betrayal of a shifting world – the world of revolt, upheaval and failed restoration brought in by the combination of industry and democracy. Its Devil is far more powerful: contingency, particularism (medieval, feudal, tribal, ethnic, etc.), the brutish, reasonless darkness which does actually triumph, over and over again. Priestly evil was installed by a deity who, even amid the worst disasters, always remained there as referee and final arbiter. Internationalists were never so lucky, and their fortune keeps dwindling.

There is not a very strong rapport between internationalists and 'cosmopolitanism' either. The latter reflected the circumstances of a pre-industrial elite, convinced that they were the vanguard of a civilised internationality fed in from above. For it, as Edmund Burke noted, there existed 'a system of manners and education that was nearly similar to all in this quarter of the globe', such that by the later eighteenth century, 'no citizen of Europe could be altogether an exile in any part of it' and no one 'felt himself quite abroad'.[4] Sometimes internationalists may fancy themselves as cosmopolitans, and quite often they are accused of this rootless vice by aboriginal spokesmen. But there is not much substance to such fantasies. Enlightenment high society provided the last semi-international social caste that could furnish a kind of foundation for the ideal. But most of this drained away in the nineteenth-century world of national states and wars. After that, only marginal, dislocated groups and intellectuals – and notably Jewish intellectuals – provided any basis for it.

Though connected in tangential ways with these predecessors, internationalism is mainly as new, and as different, as the national-identity world which it inhabits. It is the permanent, polemical denunciation of certain essential aspects of that world, and the permanent if defensive affirmation of certain counter-values – the values attributed to internationality. Those inter-nation or supra-nation attributes have been awarded varying contents, naturally. Liberal internationalism saw them as traits inherent in the capitalist or free-trade scheme of things, if only the system was allowed a chance to evolve properly. Proletarian and socialist internationalism see them as principles to uphold against that system: a democratic-popular heritage constantly being sacrificed on the altars of profit and bourgeois conflict. But for both forms, internationalism is clearly at once antithesis and imagined transcendence. A fallen world stands condemned, in the name of values really present and active which have, as yet, failed to take charge. One day they shall. This is what counts in history.

Exit or Entry

Internationalist philosophy asserts that between ('inter') national or ethno-state realities there lies a common higher ground, and our most sacred duty is to struggle on to it. But this terrain is – obviously – difficult of access.

Some historical trends may be carrying us up to it; others block the route, ever more threateningly. Since relatively few actually arrive there, it is legitimate to ask what the function of the belief is for the rest. What does internationalism actually stand for, in this world where the centre never seems to hold long in the face of ethnic anarchy?

Internationalists have often been great reducers. Their refrain has been that nationality is a secondary, illusory dimension. National struggles are (e.g.) class struggles in disguise. If only people would face up to their real problems, they would see these were the same as everybody else's, and so on. It is tempting to reduce internationalism in the same way, by suggesting a single covert, animating purpose. This would be unfair. Internationalism is also something of an umbrella term, and its ideas are pluri-functional. However, it does seem reasonable to insist upon one such covert function, if only because it is so remote from the self-justification of the *Weltanschauung*.

Internationalism poses a moral alternative to the way the world has actually gone, since the Franco-Prussian War, the end of the First International and (more emphatically) since 1914. Because this option has been so rarely and partially translatable into practice, one must ask whether the apparent aspiration was always the real one. There has been small chance of making that sort of exit (or transcendence) from our fallen world. But on the other hand there has also been an unremitting need to come to terms with it – to enter the shambles, as it were, without being suffocated by the stench and trampled underfoot. Internationalism has been an admirable way of adapting to such realities, especially for socialists.

Adaptation does not mean recognition, or assent. It can mean quite the opposite, in a vital inward sense. On an individual level, after all, people frequently adapt to unspeakable intrusions by outward plasticity and inward excommunication. Their whole behaviour becomes governed by the intruder – an illness, a rival, a loss – while internally it remains quite unreal for them. Their lives may come to be organised around what they go on understanding as a mere accident, a temporary setback. Inward acceptance comes later, often slowly and grudgingly. But it comes more tolerably, and more may be saved than face. Sanity or even the capacity for living may be preserved by the exercise – the ability to fight another day, not necessarily in quite the same cause. And this (clearly) can be seen as of supreme importance.

There can certainly be a farcical side to operations like this. I don't want to over-stress it, but the fact is too blatant to anyone who has been involved in a national movement to be simply ignored. Nationalism can yoke the sublime and the stupid together in one movement; so can internationalism. Although a priestly veil seems often to be cast over this possibility, there can be internationalist idiots as well as heroes. At its worst, far distant from its best, internationalism may be little better than face-saving abdication. It can be aimed at conserving the sanctified bones of a revolutionary creed, rather than keeping the strength to do anything. Indeed, it may easily turn into a way of avoiding doing anything – a permanent defence of the ossuary against nationalist vandals, therefore, blind to the element of delinquency in all actual revolutions.

At moments of maximal bitterness, I have been tempted to see all our internationalists in Scotland in this light. They remind me of Jacques the Father in Ionesco's play *Jacques ou la soumission*. This has a patriarch who is continually scandalised by his son's betrayal and egotism, rather as our old Left has been by the rise of nationalism. So he is forever 'walking out' on his own family, shaking with indignation:

> You dare show yourself unworthy of our common forebears. Murderer! Praticide! I will not stay here one more minute. *I* mean to remain worthy of our eggcestors.

However, this total rejection carries him merely into the adjoining room, and an empty ritual of bag-packing:

> Come what may, I have resolved irrevocably to leave this place to its fate. That's it. I'm off to pack my bags next door, then you will never see me again. Except at mealtimes, and now and then in the course of the day, or the night, for the odd cup of tea or an occasional snack.

Jacques the Son is unmoved by all the fuss, and the oppositional charade subsides, inevitably, into equally hollow reconciliation. Nationalism is not so terrible after all. There may even be something to be said for it, and one certainly has to put up with it. Finally the aged guardian of principle is blinded by the revelation that his offspring does after all like jacket-baked potatoes :

> My son, with due deliberation, let me embrace you (*He does not embrace him*). All over and done with. I take back what I said about disowning you. You are back in the family again, back to tradition, wholesomeness and whole potatoes. (*To Jacqueline*) But he's still got to learn belief in Regional aspirations.[5]

Spluttering intransigence turns into weak-kneed acceptance, then a search for compensations. How often has this routine been gone through in the history of the Left! Whether it is comical or serious depends upon just what is being defended, and by whom. This is not so simple either, as I will try to show later. There is as much room for false consciousness in the mansion of internationalism as under the tents of nationalism.

Dignified, stage-by-stage adaptation to the irresistible eruption of political nationality, and conversion from the non-national idea world of socialism: this is surely what internationalism achieves in practice, as distinct from what it proclaims in theory. But there are other functions as well, which I need only refer to briefly here. For instance, although the world literature foreseen in the 1848 *Manifesto* has never arrived, it is undeniable that most modern culture is highly international in character. Virtually all art is produced in a national idiom, of course, but the mutual contrast and impact of other cultures is vital to it. There is mercifully little to be said for the ultra-nationalist notion of purely home-grown novels, pictures and ideas. Internationalism can be an ingredient in this indispensable cross-fertilisation.

More widely, it can simply be a way of taking other peoples and their experiences seriously. Unlike the cosmopolitans, most people live in back-yards. Non-elite political and cultural existence was inevitably cast in these moulds. Internationalism, understood as a systematic outward-looking and inquiring attitude, an imaginative search into the meaning of other experiences, is the most valuable way of counteracting the disadvantages of this truth. Without it, it is not only culture that gets lost. People can only comprehend their backyards properly through some degree of comparison and inter-cultural perspective.

Or again, taking the principle from a more ethical point of view, few but the most indurate reactionaries would deny that internationalism has always provided the foundation for useful action to help other people: victims of natural or political disasters, the deprived or unjustly imprisoned of foreign countries – and so on. Liberal, Christian and socialist internationalists share much common ground here – sufficient to indicate, surely, that such fraternal attitudes derive from no particular reading of the gospel.

I mention all these somewhat self-evident facts, because any critic of internationalism is automatically put down as an uncaring fascist cabbage. In reality, while such indispensable outward-looking processes may get encouragement from internationalism in the more pietistic and strict observance sense, they do not depend on it at all. To appreciate the distinction, one need only remind oneself of the damage which the more 'ismic' form of the creed may accomplish, in the same circumstances. Remind oneself (that is) of artists who believe they can leap straight out of their backyards on to the clouds of the international style, thinkers who convince themselves that the truth can be imported in containers for home application, and activists who end up substituting the 'international struggle' for doing anything next door. In short, there is an internationalism which functions as a dialectic, and a more rigid, priestly variety (I am tempted to call it 'all-the-sameism') which does nothing of the kind. I am mainly concerned with the latter here.

So here is the essence of the dark, misshapen side of modern inter-nationalism. A traumatic defeat transformed it into a much more rigid, fetishised creed than it had previously been. But then, once the defeat was over, in the decade after World War I, the circumstances of world history did not lead to any demobilisation of these hardened ideas. On the contrary: this was the period when Marxism broke up into Stalinism and anti-Stalinism. The former usurped Internationalism into the service of the Soviet Great-Russian state, inevitably in still more theocratic terms; the latter responded to this and the other betrayals of the Revolution either with distance and pessimism (like some Western Marxists) or with even greater idealisation of the international idea. The tide of revolution did not merely retreat; it was overtaken by fantastic nationalistic parodies, counter-revolutions with mass support. At a certain level of consciousness, therefore, 1914 was continued until 1945. And its long-term effects have not disappeared – obviously – up to the present. Only a successful First World or Second World revolution with international repercussions comparable to those of 1789 could have undone such a powerful and fossilised structure.

Internationalism and Class

On Sunday the 24th of November 1912, in the afternoon, all the bells of the venerable Cathedral of Bâle rang out together. They were ringing in honour of the brotherhood among all men of good will, through the old arches which had once resounded to the voices of the Bishop Princes of Bâle, proud of their liberties and rich lands, and later seen the turbulence of the iconoclasts, and Erasmus's flight from the city to safety in Fribourg-en-Brisgau. Now, in this late autumn, they rang to salute the International Socialist Congress which was due to meet with one single motion on its agenda: 'The international situation, and agreement on action against the war.'[6]

The motion was soon to be defeated by the facts of 1914. But Humbert-Droz's account of this and many other events of that period reminds us that internationalism was still a living faith for great numbers of working-class people.

The same point was made to me by the late Neil Williamson, in a review of *The Break-up of Britain*.[7] He accused me of placing too much emphasis on 1914 as a revelation of the underlying real trends, and too little upon what followed only three years later – the Russian Revolution, with its initial belief in diffusing the cause and the widespread support this evoked all over the world. In the response to 1917 one could still discern 'a universalist consciousness which extended far outside the ranks of intellectuals or party cadres. These were not dreams, illusions of an impossible order (but) tangible and viable building-blocks in the construction of a socialist society.' Their reality was visible in the history of our own country. Working-class Scotland was the scene of a violent revulsion against the war after 1917, and this insurrectionary mood continued into the 1920s. 'When Countess Markiewicz (a heroine of the Easter Rising) spoke at the Glasgow May Day parade in 1919, there were 150,000 workers there to listen to her, but this level of popular mobilisation was only reflective of a genuine political sophistication incredible by today's standards. Discussions around Constituent Assemblies, principled support for self-determination, opposition to imperialist war and militarism were actually commonplace in the immediate post-war period.'[8]

What followed later – Williamson concludes – was a 'regression' from this high point, represented by the capitulation of the Scottish proletariat to Labour Party reformism in the later 1920s and 1930s. None the less, 'It is the possibility of working class people regaining that type of elemental consciousness which Nairn cannot fit into his theoretical universe.' From the error of taking 1914 as the key turning point there flows an over-estimation of the power of nationalism, and a consequent general pessimism about socialist development; while if one looks instead to 1917 hope will revive, and remain constant. Betrayal and regression there may have been; but sell-outs can in principle be revenged, and lost time be made up for.

He was right to criticise my over-emphasis on 1914. But that stress was itself polemical in nature, and derived in fact from what appeared to me as the incessant and usually quite uncritical focus upon 1917 in wide sectors of the Left. Indeed, such a focus has been for several political generations almost synonymous with the title 'revolutionary'. Williamson's restatement of the 'revolutionary' line had – as usual – the merit of trenchant clarity, and laid its own emphasis on the function of internationalism.

It is undoubtedly true that a more universalist outlook was common among the European working classes from the period of the First Inter-national up to – at least – the moment when the Third International became an instrument of Soviet state power. And this was accompanied by a sophistication, and an educated self-reliance, which do seem remarkable compared to the standards of (e.g.) today's British Labour Party. But these things reflected, surely, specific circumstances of working-class develop-ment: roughly speaking, the terrain upon which the recently constituted proletariat had to undergo its experience of maximal alienation from, or even hostility to, the societies that had given it birth. Though ultimately tied to nationalism, internationalism had preceded it as a creed, in the first half of the nineteenth century.[9] As an ideology it had a headstart, and strong though narrow foundations among Enlightened intellectuals and the artis-anate which preceded the rise of the contemporary working class. Hence there was a prolonged transition era when workers subscribed actively to a non-national philosophy, and looked after their own interests instead of expecting the national state to do so.

Though inevitable, the nationalisation of the proletariat took a long time. In peripheral regions like Scotland or Catalonia, marked by strong ethno-cultural differences as well as the miseries of rapid industrialisation, it took longer than elsewhere and left room for the savage upheavals of 1917 and later. It is in this longer perspective that the 1914–17 dilemma deserves to be viewed. The collapse of the Second International was brought about by underlying processes inseparable from the real evolution of the 'social relations of production'. Both tragedy and real gains may have been implicit in the fact: but the national form these relations assumed was necessary, and worked at a deeper level of the personality and culture than universalist ideology ever realised. Hence, it is an apocalyptic rather than a materialist interpretation which perceives 1914 primarily as the great betrayal.

There was neither betrayal nor regression in this sense. That is, in the absolute (and consequently mythical) terms prescribed by the international-ist world-view. Once the myth is abandoned, there is of course no reason to expect a great revival or revanche proving it right all along. No reason, therefore, to persist in interpreting history in its light, rather than the other way round.

However, mighty and understandable efforts were made from the very beginning to save it. Lenin's is the most famous, and influential. But Rosa Luxembourg and countless others did the same thing, with the same fatal underlining of the factor of conscious leadership and willpower. Because the collapse was essentially betrayal, it could have been averted if only some people had behaved differently. There is a section of Herman Gorter's *Der Imperialismus, der Weltkrieg und die Sozialdemokratie* where this is put exception-ally clearly. 'How is it that the proletariat can so totally deny its own interests?' he asks. 'If we look for the reason, our first finding will be that the proletariat does not yet know how to intervene against the bourgeoisie as a single international entity. And our second will be that the proletariat does not yet know how to fight for major, long term objectives. It did not know what to do.'[10] So he continues for pages on end. Why did they not know? Because the wrong, self-interested leaders had taken charge and in practice fostered nationalist tendencies among workers, by making them 'busy with the fine plans drawn for them by the reformists. With their national insurance and taxation proposals, and electoral legislation and the pensions that the liberals were to help them obtain.' So what should be done? Make sure they know next time, by returning to the true principle of internationalism. That is, to the founding moment when 'A genius went before them, a sower went through the countries of Europe and America. They had one programme and one executive, sending them the addresses that issued from Marx's brain and which lit up the path of the future like bright torches; one executive to give them leadership.'

In Williamson's critique (sixty-two years later) the same emphasis emerges as the claim that the 'dramatic regression' of class consciousness 'was fought out by self-conscious agents, for there was nothing inevitable about it'. The same kind of self-conscious agents – it goes without saying – will lead people back to the more 'elemental consciousness' of an internationalist world-view. The term is an interesting one. It entails that internationalism is not a construct which might be slowly built up in the future, but something we had in the past – an outlook more natural than nationalism, therefore, and standing always to be redeemed. There is more to this than saying internationalist conceptions preceded nationalism: the Enlightenment did come before the romantic-national era and its mass popular culture. But its priority is existential, so to speak: metaphysically fundamental and forever open to salvation, if only . . .

What alternative story can be told about the social-class basis for inter-nationalism? It is already written between the lines of the orthodox version. While this universalising consciousness may be a mode of mass mobilisation for a certain period, under certain transitional conditions, it is only ideologically essential *to intellectuals*. They invented it, mainly out of pre-modern materials, to cope with the modern age of revolutionary change, and when its grip slipped they had to save it. This is not to say or imply that they were acting solely 'in their own interests', like a narrow clique of egotists – the kind of sorry picture which the internationalist set has usually painted of nationalist intellectuals, in short. No: the point is that 'their own interests' did actually coincide with the heroic maintenance of an increasingly moral and exhortatory universalism. A tradition of genuine grandeur, great and irreplaceable values, was indeed at stake. But they were not the only values, and they were defended by social groups of persons, not angels, whose defence was an inevitably faulty, increasingly rigid and double-binding reaffirmation of an original (and limited) credo.

Internationalism was inflected by this fearful effort into being a philosophy of defeat. As the diagnosis of Lenin, Gorter and the rest took root amid the war's catastrophes, and then seemed briefly justified by the events in Russia, it acquired a markedly closed and self-reinforcing character. The open, expansive beliefs of the previous century – the torches lighting up future paths – now hardened into dogmatic vicious circles. The new, more weapon-like belief structure may have arisen partly out of failure to 'know', to understand the full dimensions of the nationalisation of the proletariat. But Gorter's epistemological drama had really been among the intellectuals. It was the self-conscious agents who were lacerated and haunted by it. Subsequently the ideology had to become a quite systematic way of not understanding the realities in question. That is, a way of repressing them out of the acceptable ideal world, by means of the infinitely extendable and quasi-demonic category of 'revisionists' ('reformists', or simply 'traitors', etc.).

Many familiar psychological dilemmas descend from this. Who does not know the internationalist sectarian, sternly weighing distant triumphs of the Movement against the humiliations of home? His national proletariat is a permanent disappointment and reproach. Unable to dismiss it, he is compelled none the less to make the situation more palatable by an exaggeration of the distant view. The Revolution is always in better form somewhere else. Remote peasant peoples are doing more for the Emancipation of the Human Being than the (so-called) 'advanced' workers. Not many take this road to its logical conclusion: national nihilism at home and the romanticisation of everywhere else (roughly in proportion to increasing psychological distance). But everybody can recognise these poles, and their influence upon left-wing feelings.

Unfortunately, internationalism in this reverential form encourages such schizophrenia. As all-the-sameism, it is a standing invitation to the notion that 'I' (the Subject of International Revolution, not the unshaven native of Aberdeen or Neusiedl-am-See) am better engaged supporting the Revolution where it happens to be at rather than where I (unshaven native) happen to be located. Fleeing from the inexplicable and leaden contingency of home I (Revolutionary Subject) discover necessity – the meaning of history, hence of myself – wherever that necessity discloses Itself. Darkness enshrouds me, Reason thrives elsewhere. So it is only too easy for me (u.n.) to live an essentially vicarious existence, through my (R.S.) unceasing 'solidarity' with these foreign triumphs. By this 'solidarity' of the pilotfish with the shark, internationalism still keeps one foot in Hegel's grave.

It is this same World-Spirit side of the credo – a mysticism of defeat – which explains the oscillations of internationalists. Determined that all movements imbued with medieval particularism (which can mean simply: all movements) must be denounced as such (other things being equal), in the name of the Revolution, they then discover that this, that or the other upheaval has some redeeming features. However, it is not easy to issue a certificate of World-Spirit-worthiness half-heartedly. Once awarded, such honours tend towards the absolute. So in practice a leap is forced from black to white. Last week the Ruritanian revolutionaries were backward-looking revivers of barbarism; this week they are noble protagonists of an undeservedly oppressed people. Then they were shown no mercy. Now they are permitted no blemishes, all their ethnic spikes suddenly 'understandable'.

The truth must be plainer than this. It is more likely that they (and all other national movements) were, and are, both things together. Nationalism is an inspired vehicle of ambiguity. However, the clumsy spectacles of Internationalism (one lens dark grey, one rose-coloured) permit no such critical or constant judgement. Once he has put them on, the wearer can only zigzag forward, staggering one way or the other depending upon which lens he happens to be looking through: a drunk man's street-theatre version of the Dialectic.

The only genuinely logical escape from this dilemma is furnished by anarchism. Because the principle of anarchism is that all state forms whatever are an inhuman curse, nationalism becomes irrelevant. Marxists cannot take this course of sublime evasion, since whatever their faults they think politically, and admit that the Revolution will have to take the form of a state, at least for some time. Hence the problem of the state (national or otherwise) remains crucial, and anguishing. Half a century after 1914 they have to go on arguing, as in the essays of *Marxismus und Nationalismus*.[11] 'Only the anarchist Idea remains clean', wrote Hersh Mendel in *Erinnerungen eines judische Revolutionär*[12] because it does not base itself upon any theory of economic development. 'Pure human morality' is its sole foundation, and only by faith in this purity may we be sure that we are entering into the epoch of authentic social revolution.

There is a deeper history to this turning point, beyond that of the social democrats, the war, and the Second and Third Internationals. It must lie in the wider river from which the stream of 'proletarian internationalism' was derived. By the very definition of their cultural antecedents, Western intellectuals tend to view themselves as agents of universalism. Christianity and Judaism, the reinvented message from Antiquity and then the final laicisation of the Enlightenment – all these make up the grammar of their language. And yet, capitalism's actual advent was a progressive dissolution of this language into dialects. The Nationalist Babel was to threaten and strain all its deep structures. Modern intellectuals are the living actors of cultural reproduction, who had therefore to struggle with this contradiction in their own being. Although this broad dilemma affected Christian or liberal thinkers as well as the socialists, there is an obvious reason why it was likely to affect the latter most acutely. Because, through Marx's notion of the universal proletariat, they carried the most clear-cut formula for redemption around with them.

Believing (wrongly) that its failure might mean the disproof and rejection of historical materialism, as well as of socialism, they were impelled towards a panic-stations defence of internationalism. Something important in all progressive thought was elevated into an absolute, an inflexible mixture of command and taboo. In political terms this came to mean Lenin's theory of the world revolution, led by a 'world party, strongly centralised on a global scale, with a semi-military discipline and rigorous ideological unity'[13] – the only way of fighting off the demons of revisionism, and preventing repeats of 1914. Theoretically, it led to two closely related forms of hysterical blindness. One was the refusal to penetrate into the world of the enemy, nationalism, and obtain a firmer grasp of its ambiguities and contradictions. Devils must be by nature unambiguous, and also joyously free from contradiction. The other was unwillingness to perceive what 'leaders', 'self-conscious agents', ideologically regulated 'party cadres' (etc.) actually signify, materially speaking. Until Gramsci there was scarcely the beginnings of any materialist theorisation of the intellectuals (and that could not be pursued further until the 1950s). Too much had been pinned on them. If the chance of socialism as against barbarism rested exclusively on their frail shoulders, they could never afford to be less than angels.

Lenin and Self-non-determination

The way towards the distortions of contemporary internationalism had been paved by Lenin, in the years between the turn of the century and 1915. I quoted above from *The Right of Nations to Self-determination* (1914), one of a whole series of vivid polemics on the subject which have been turned into canonical texts. But I left out one important phase. What he said was: 'Other conditions being equal, the class-conscious proletariat will always stand for the larger state', combat medieval particularism, and so forth. The entire structure of argument rests upon the conception of 'the absolute primacy of class over all other historical categories'.[14] The bigger and more econ-omically developed the state, the more important the class struggle is likely to be, clearly. However – as Lenin and most other Central and East European socialists knew only too well – those other conditions are very rarely 'equal' in the relevant sense. The whole evolution of socialist thinking in the twenty years up to 1917 took place against a backdrop of increasing nationality struggles, both against Tsardom and the Habsburgs, and in the newer colonial empires of the West.

People were vigorously asserting their particularism all over the world. They were helping unseat imperial tyrannies, which was fine. But at the same time putting nation before class, which was not. Those reared in the internationalist orthodoxy of the First and Second International movements found this an anguishing and inscrutable dilemma. It was impossible to ignore or deprecate revolutionary movements which were actually going on, as distinct from the one in the blueprints. After all, they might even destabilise things to the point where the Revolution was possible. Yet the dominant ideology, the leaderships, and much of the immediate effects of these upheavals were anathema to Marxists.

Lenin invented a brilliant way out of the dilemma, which has informed most thinking about it since. It is normally referred to as the Leninist principle of the absolute right of all nations to self-determination. However, the title is itself ambiguous and misleading, and not in an accidental or secondary way. Quite the opposite: these are the essence of the position. To put it crudely – what orthodoxy required was a plausible way of both supporting and not supporting national movements, at the same time. It needed an agile and imposing non-position which would keep its options permanently open. That was what Lenin supplied.

'You people have, of course, the absolute, inalienable right to self-determination!' declares the Leninist. But before one has time to smile one's gratitude, he adds (nervously or with relish, according to temperament): 'Of course, we do not advocate asserting the right in this particular case.' Mastering one's infantile annoyance at having a sweet dangled and then snatched away, one inquires why not. It then transpires that particular circumstances are always vital in determining the actual bestowal or recognition of the inalienable right. 'Inalienable' can also mean 'inexpressible'. One must be a patented case of progressive National Liberation Struggle for the full licence to be issued. Without the permit one remains alas an example of narrow, bourgeois and tendentially reactionary nationalism, blindly asserting particularism in the face of the larger international struggle.

Hence the general principle is that all nationalist struggles and movements are bad; however, special and pragmatically identifiable circumstances may make them good – though only for a time, and in a highly qualified fashion. These circumstances have normally to do with sufficiently gross forms of imperialist oppression. An adequate quota of suffering alone serves to legitimate a national struggle. As long as that goes on it impedes the 'normal' development of the subjugated society along lines of class awareness and healthy internationalism. 'Get rid of all that just as soon as you can', snaps the Leninist, briskly rubbing his hands, 'and then we can get on with the real revolution'. One can only be 'progressive' for a minimal and cautionary time period. After that the certificate is snatched away, and it becomes one's duty to oppose the (newly formed) national elite and march onwards to the 'amalgamation of all nations'.

It was all rather like marriage and divorce, Lenin explained in 1914. 'To accuse those who support freedom of self-determination, i.e., freedom to secede, of encouraging separatism, is as foolish and hypocritical as accusing those who advocate freedom of divorce of encouraging the destruction of family ties.'[15] Everyone has the absolute and incontrovertible right to break up his or her marriage ties. But, other things being equal, in a reasonably constituted world, the less that right is exercised the better. Marriage remains the rule, conserved and indeed strengthened by such allowable exceptions. We have the right to opt out; but only so that as soon as possible (and Lenin believed this future was close at hand) we should all opt in for good. The transient era of secession and ego-affirmation will close mercifully soon, as international revolution brings us to a better time of free, permanent and healthy unions.

Since other things and conditions are so rarely 'equal' – unevenness being the condition of capitalist development – there have been far more exceptions than Lenin or the others imagined seventy years ago. The world is covered with them. More are threatened every day. In a recent defence of Leninism, Eric Hobsbawm conceded that Marxists have had to continually 'widen the category' of national movements recognised as progressive (or progressive-for-a-time, or not-so-bad, or with-redeeming-aspects). Indeed, the category has become baggy enough to include 'the great majority of 20th century national movements' – even such inherently implausible candidates as the French and British reaction to Nazi aggression, where it was plainly also true that varieties of armed imperialist chauvinism were in conflict.[16]

Thus, the internationalist stance began by seeking pragmatic reasons for letting a few nationalisms into the drawing room, and ends by looking nervously around for any that may have got left out. It is just as well there are always a few irredeemably bad boys, like the Croat exile movement, who will never be allowed in.[17] Meanwhile, Balkanisation marches on. The United Nations, Hobsbawm concludes morosely, 'is soon likely to consist of the late 20th century equivalents of Saxe-Coburg-Gotha and Schwarzburg-Sondershausen'. Jacques *père* has fulminated so frequently, and to such miserably small effect, that one wonders how he keeps going at all. But actually he is sustained by a remarkable truth. The principle being defended is, as a matter of fact, completely unscathed by this avalanche of exceptions, anomalies and compromises. It never will be swept away by them. Hobsbawm does not say so, but one may be sure that proletarian internationalism and the primacy of the class struggle will be as passionately defended in the newly independent Coburg-Gotha as it used to be under the Tsars and Habsburgs. This is of course a truth of discourse, rather than of material reality. What it reflects is the peculiar logic of Lenin's adroit reworking of internationalism, and not anything mysterious about either national or class struggles.

I referred above to the closed and self-reinforcing nature of post-1914 internationalism, set up around a sacralised principle. Such delaicisation occurs when the generalisation or law in question is implicitly removed from direct contact with reality, for its own protection. But this implies it must become more than simply non-disprovable. The quasi-demonic categories supporting it turn each exception into a form of proof, not disproof. Where a principle remains in open relationship to reality, and a sufficient number of exceptions or negative examples have happened, it is dropped (or simply forgotten about). But when it has been translated up to the level of the sacred, these may become so many further illustrations of a fallen state. The greater the Fall, the more precious the Truth. Each new tragedy of Balkanisation serves to underline the ever fresh principle that only the international class struggle can prevent this sort of thing – if only the revisionists and narrow nationalists can be stopped, next time.

An Internationalist *Bestiarium*

If internationalists were simply the valiant defenders of a lost ideal world, fighting on in the hope of seeing things suddenly come right, their philosophy would be more sympathetic, but less important. But that is rarely if ever the whole truth. Failure to notice this may stem from a conceptual blank – that is, from unwillingness to perceive that internationalism and nationalism are, in a curious way, perfectly twin ideologies. They are parts of a single, overall, modern thought-world.

According to the customary image socialists bear with them, Nationalism is the Mr Hyde of that world. He is the Id of modernity, our revived and delirious archaism, the seductive yet dangerous fellow from the forests whom Marx pilloried back in 1843. 'Germano-maniacs', he called them, 'seeking our history of freedom beyond our history, in the primeval Teutonic forests.'[18] 'Let us leave the ancient Teutonic forests in peace', he concluded, and concentrate upon the thoroughgoing revolution, that purely social movement of events where (thanks to the proletariat) the emancipation of the German is the emancipation of the human being'. Alas, the forests were not so easily disposed of as that, either in Germany or elsewhere. Nor are nationalists allowed to forget the fact.

But what about Dr Jekyll? This is the real question I am putting here, and it is all too rarely posed. We – 'on the Left' – are assumed to be on his side. We disregard his oddities. He is a strangely Protestant figure, forever tensed up in an irreproachable piety punctuated with terrible nervous tics. The slightest forest odour sets his forefinger wagging. Though he takes two baths a day to preserve his demeanour and sense of smell, the world remains permanently unsatisfactory. This must be – one can hardly help feeling – because there is something unsatisfactory inside him somewhere, of which he may be only obscurely conscious.

And so there is, usually. There is a Hyde in most Dr Jekylls, just as there is a Jekyll in the vast majority of Mr Hydes. All this reflects is the underlying interconnectedness of the modern world-view which they occupy different floors of. Even the most berserk chauvinist is a sort of 'internationalist' – a fact recorded in the 'ism' of his nationalism. Nationalism is the raising – or anyway, the attempt to raise – his own forests up to the general plane of international recognition, acceptance and reality. It means joining the grand mainstream, even though one has to fight one's way out of some larger yoke to get there. While, equally inevitably, internationalists are in mundane truth always the trees of some particular forest or other.

This point is vital for seeing how the whole apparatus functions. There is something else Hobsbawm forgot to mention about the future Saxe-Coburg-Gotha. Within the new mini-state there will of course be a Gothan secessionist tendency demanding restoration of the rights of the ancient dukedom, with the usual arsenal of ethno-nationalist arguments. But over in Coburg this agitation will be indignantly refuted, most notably by the (principally Coburgian) leaders and thinkers of the CPSCG, the CPSCG (ML), the IVth International (SCG Section) and so on. In the heady metropolitan atmosphere of the Coburgian capital all these internationalist rebuttals will go down naturally enough; but from the Gothan angle, the other side of the truth will be more visible – these are, after all, just so many Coburgians justifying their own status quo and particular interests (which include continuing to strangle Gothan aspirations).

Coburg is bigger than Gotha. Profound spiritual implications arise from this tediously geographical and demographic fact. Because a vital part of the definition of the modern 'metropolis' is that it is where intellectuals concentrate, and function from. So, when it is decreed by internationalist gospellers that the ambitions of this or that region or minority must be firmly subordinated to the General Movement, or the International Class Struggle, or simply The Revolution, it goes without saying that the only place where such trends can normally be charted is up there – amid the libraries, colleges, political gatherings, through the echo chambers of lively journalism, in the cafés, salons, etc. The capital city, in this sense, is a device for transforming humble aboriginals into universalist steam-pressure. It encourages the fatal conviction that one is no longer a so-and-so (a Coburgian, a Frenchman, a United States American) but a Special Agent related to Superman and the *Zeitgeist*, semi-apotheosised by contact with Olympians.

From the heights, it looks as if the grand sweep and significance of History can be discerned through the mists arising from the valleys of medieval particularism. From down there, alas, all one can see is bands of unwitting Great Power chauvinists at their usual antics. Seen from the particularist swamps, 90 per cent of what is trumpeted out as internationalism is veiled, thinly veiled or occasionally full-frontal metropolitan self-interest and aggression. The 'metropolitan' culture is one which functions by instilling the notions of centrality and responsibility, assumptions never so prominently on display as when (e.g.) somebody says 'Speaking not as an American but as a socialist'.

How could it be otherwise? It is the whole of modern history since the revolutionary Fall which reiterates its own nature in this dialectic. The

French and English launched the process, with their conviction that they were exporting not their own imperialist power to the rest of the world, but (respectively) the Revolution and Industrial Progress. The particular peoples centred on Paris and London could hardly help apprehending themselves as missionaries of civilisation – their merely aboriginal nature sublated into the international. But actually (and in the long run fortunately) no one loses his aboriginal nature: a central if neglected truth of historical materialism. The truth was of course grasped in practice if not in theory by everybody who found themselves with a French or English boot on their windpipe.

Internationalists reject imperialism, naturally. But their problem is that the post-1914 orthodoxy remains fixated in a highly metropolitan form, that lends itself quite systematically to Great Power prostitution. The grossest example of this was the appropriation of the internationalist creed by the Soviet state after the triumph of Stalin and 'Socialism in One Country'. From then onwards – in the words of a contemporary Soviet document – 'The underlying sense of internationalism is that every Marxist-Leninist party, especially if it is in power, must be conscious of its responsibility for the movement as a whole. Devising specific "purely national" roads to socialism and denying the common laws of socialist construction may jeopardise the cause.'[19]

'The movement as a whole', 'the common laws', 'the cause' – all things so much more discernible from the capital of the Motherland of Socialism than from out in the wilderness. The Third International became the instrument of the ruling class of an actually existing Great Power. But there does not have to be such an actual metropolis for the metropolitan illusion of internationalism to function. Internationalists who have no Paris, Moscow or Peking to sustain their act carry round a kind of spiritual metropolis with them. This accretion of alienated universalism – the deposit of (socialist) humanity – is still quite sufficient to excommunicate foolhardy specifiers and nationalists. The Revolution to usher in emancipation of the human being is, after all, centrality and responsibility incarnate – Marx's 'decisive somersault' (in Marx's own words) out of the woods of particularism. Without knowing where or by whom it will occur, one can still be sure a priori that it is simply out of the question that (e.g.) the Welsh, the Basques or the Gothans could lead the way towards socialism through queer, specific little revolutions of their own.

Trotskyists and others have the habit of speaking with disdain of the appropriation of the internationalist scrolls by Moscow or Peking. Their picture is that of a Holy Virgin taken by force and violated, wholly against her better judgement, by the latest wave of chauvinist traitor revisionists or Great State bureaucrats. It is time they saw that she lends herself to the fate, rather more than half-heartedly. Great nation chauvinists slip into these robes because they fit so naturally. There is the same crypto-imperialist streak in the proletarian internationalist ideology as there was in the liberal and free-trade dogmas that lent themselves so well to Anglo-Saxon empire.

Non-metropolitan Internationalism

In Amsterdam each 25 February thousands of people gather and form a long, patient queue round the side of Waterlooplein. Their destination – which it often takes hours to reach in the bitter cold or rain – is the statue commemorating the city's general strike of protest against the deportation of the Jews, in 1941. Eventually they reach the memorial by the old synagogue, where flowers are laid, and there are blazing open fires for them to warm hands and feet by. The figure itself is of a docker, hurling defiance at the occupying power. Astonished by the strike's effectiveness, the Nazis proclaimed an immediate state of siege which was to remain in force for the rest of the war. From December 1941 onwards it was reinforced by the 'Dead of Night Decree' (*Nacht und Nebelerlass*) permitting indiscriminate action against suspected 'terrorists'.[20]

This simple ceremony is worth more than all of Europe's Establishment rituals put together. What it remembers is more important than Concorde, the Helsinki Agreements, or the new European Community Parliament. I am obliged to say this (though there are plenty of other examples I could have employed) because strict-Sabbatarian internationalists assert that criticism of their dogma entails indifference to such truths. This is not the case. Rigid anti-nationalism was an ideology of armoured defence invented by the (principally) Marxist Left to cope with the terrifying threats of the 1914–45 epoch. Though used as an aggressive weapon by the Soviet Union and other (big and small) metropolitan or crypto-metropolitan centres, it remained essentially defensive in structure. But its aim, the preservation of non-national, class-based revolutionary thought, was only attainable under those circumstances at the cost of drastic deformation. Internationalism could be 'saved' in that sense solely by sacralisation and simplification. Uplifted from apparently betraying realities for its own protection, it ceased to enjoy live and fertile relations with the continuing world revolution – a process continuing in predominantly antagonistic and highly nationalistic forms. The logical (in truth theological) structure of its doctrine betrays these origins by demonological traits like the view that history would have followed the Plan, if only traitors had been thwarted, the police had not persecuted internationalists so successfully, Stalin had not gained control (etc., etc.).

It may be argued historically that this armour was indispensable, and the only way of saving something out of the disaster. I pointed out earlier how, after all, it has functioned as an adaptive cushion, a tolerable way of getting used to the inevitable. Without prejudging this issue, however, I think one may claim that now conditions have altered so as to make the ideology rethinkable. There is a double edge to this change. Nationalism has become even more important on the world stage, making theoretical blindness on the subject more crippling than ever. But it has become less of a threat to civilisation and reason themselves. Present-day imperialist doom wears a more impersonal, quasi-rational countenance; it menaces the literal liquidation of culture, not that metaphorical regression to barbarism which made the walls of the old internationalist spirit go up.

It is of course characteristic of the theme that one must speak of 'losing faith' in internationalism. But, semantics apart, there is no reason whatever why losing such faith should compel anyone to lose either his head or his reason. In a world where revolutionary communist states and movements have begun to wage nationalist wars with one another, the contrary is the case. Only by shedding a bit of faith may one aspire to recover one's nerve, and keep on reasoning.

Recovery from blindness is difficult. In this case, perhaps, both very simple and – in all its implications – very hard. The Lenin-inspired orthodoxy put its historical emphasis in the wrong place. It argued that on the whole, in relation to the general motion of history (other things being equal, etc.) nationalist or secessionist trends were regrettable lapses. 'On the whole', they are not: the revolutionary movement ought always to have welcomed and encouraged them, even when not led by hallmarked socialists, rather than grumblingly and belatedly opened the door to a disheartening succession of *faits accomplis*. A general prima facie attitude of principle was needed. Internationalism was, and still is, the wrong one. But it would be crazy to believe that no international attitude, politics, spirit or organisation was possible without the 'ism'.

A different, more open, tolerant and inquiring posture towards the great twentieth-century tide of national movements would not have been mere 'surrender to nationalism'. All principles invite exceptions and have to explain them. Reactionary, regressive, chauvinistic trends have of course also informed much of that tide. The point is surely that these 'exceptions' would not simply have been occluded from the rule, by that bizarre logic I have attempted to describe. We would not then have ended up with (almost literally) a world of exceptions and a pristinely useless 'rule' good only for the political equivalent of Sunday prayers.

But the implications remain pretty indigestible. It was not only handsome characters like International Solidarity who were sheltered by the walls. Fundamental fetishes were there too. It was (for instance) impossible to go for a more genuinely open and pragmatic approach towards nationalism and continue subscribing to the absolute primacy of class, at the same time. However, if the latter went, so did the complex philosophical apparatus associated with that primacy. In the canonical formulations the theory of capital was tied, apparently inextricably, to a conception of relations of production as the exclusive essence of modern social developments. Both the past and future of class struggle, the motor of change and revolution, seemed inseparable from this web. Hence, to concede even the equivalence of ethnic-national factors with social-class ones in the new struggles amounted to a victory of the 'contingent' over the essential. The thought that the former could be more important than the latter, generally speaking, for a prolonged historical era – that was no better than the general foundering of philosophy.

Philosophy is not easy in an era of general, accumulating reaction. There is still a temptation on the Left to cling even closer to the elements of fantasy in its *Weltanschauung*. When all the particular 'models' have crumbled, a perfectly abstract internationalism may become more appealing rather than less – one moving ever closer to Mendel's anarchist moralism mentioned earlier. However, this need not be so. The alternative is simply to understand nationalism better in theory (which entails a complementary understanding of its alter ego, internationalism). And then, in an old and quite undiscredited phrase, to translate that understanding into practice, the better to change the world.

2

The Owl of Minerva

There is no doubt about the new spectre haunting Europe.[1] *Granta* advertised a recent special issue on Europe by claiming to unmask 'the ugly, ugly face of nationalism'. Nor has it been alone in this ambition. Few days have passed since last autumn without a sonorous contribution from the now over-subscribed league of unmaskers. One minor example: two weeks ago the *New Statesman*'s front page read: 'Nationalities are on the loose ... Can Europe avoid chaos and civil war?'

At the same time professorial justifications of paranoia are appearing, like Eric Hobsbawm's *Nations and Nationalism Since 1780*.[2] This new four-lecture exorcism of the bogey ends with assurances that – though apparently in boisterous form – nationalism will pretty soon be on the ropes. Even Minerva's Owl is mobilised for the cause. Do the 1990s look like bringing 'a triumphant world-wide advance of "the principle of nationality"' (p. 163)? Don't worry: in Vilnius, they can't have known that the Owl says otherwise. 'Historians are at least beginning to make some progress in the study of nationalism' (p. 183). The very fact that they are now circling the subject so intensively, and croaking out so many bitter footnotes about it, suggests that 'the phenomenon is past its peak'.

Although enjoying no special relationship with Minerva, I doubt whether her pet would suggest anything of the kind. Hegel's use of the metaphor (in the Preface to the *Philosophy of Right*) appropriates a phrase from the Devil in Goethe's *Faust*:

> My worthy friend, grey are all theories,
> And green alone Life's golden tree ...

I am happy to take the Devil's part here. The grey-painting theorists, Hegel wrote, usually make their advances 'only when actuality is mature', when some process or phase of development has evolved sufficiently to demonstrate its substance and so be apprehended 'as a whole'.

This is not the same as saying it's dead yet, or even moribund. Nationalism as a mode of political development may indeed have advanced enough for its nature to be approximately visible. It does not follow that it's on the way

47

out. Doubt on this score must be reinforced by the fact that metropolitan pundits have been wishing it away (or at least, imagining the worst was over) for most of the time since 1780. But the tree has grown in spite of them. Minerva's owl should be left sleeping in its branches for a while longer yet – at least until the last great empire has been Balkanised, and a new constitution for Europe been worked out. In typically caustic manner Ernest Gellner made a similar point at the end of *Nations and Nationalism*:

> I do not believe ... that the age of nationalism will become a matter of the past ... [and] it would seem overwhelmingly likely that differences between cultural styles of life and communication, despite a similar economic base, will remain large enough to require separate servicing, and hence distinct cultural-political units, whether or not they will be wholly sovereign.[3]

This is not to say that nationality politics will never change. Truisms apart, it may be that the 1989 events point a way forward to some kind of mutation – to changes which a certain style of wishful thinking interprets as 'the end of nationalism'. However, it is very unlikely that nationality will be less important as a result. It may have a different sort of significance (and I would like to suggest what it may be); but whatever that is, the new age of nations will be a lot more than ugly faces and chaos.

Internationalism on the Rocks

National-ism is only an umbrella concept which acknowledges the systematic nature of nationality in modern (post-eighteenth-century) development. The general process of industrialisation has consistently rendered all the factors of nationality (ethnic, linguistic, physiognomic, sometimes religious) more, rather than less, important. In one sense, all 1989 showed was that this is continuing: command-economy failures in the East have generated an overdue reaction which like others before it has to assume a primarily nationalist form.

In other words, nationalism is not now and never was in the past a deviant or accidental departure from what 'should have happened'. It is no counter-current or side eddy, interfering with the majestic mainstream of Progress: nationalism is the mainstream, and it's time we recognised the fact.

The anational Progress blueprint, by contrast, has only been a sustained cultural reaction to that mainstream. International-ism originated among the Enlightenment elites, and has been transmitted down from one intelligentsia to another as the idea of a rational quickstep into Utopia. It has always been the ideology most consonant with their location and class interests.

According to this monochrome creed inherited diversity was supposed to fall away: anthropological débris would find its proper place in museums (some the size of whole countries) as people grasped the advantages of modernisation and mutated from mere Bretons, Sards, Balts, etc., into fully grown men (or as feminine-nationalist usage now prefers, persons).

In practice, this ideology has of course served the big battalions. It was the French, the English, the Russians (and so on) who, in virtue of their numbers, cultural facilities, economic advance or (sometimes) brute force, could most plausibly lay claim to personhood and civilisation. As that kindest of liberals John Stuart Mill put it in his *Utilitarianism*:

> Nobody can suppose that it is not more beneficial for a Breton or a Basque of French Navarre to be a member of the French nationality, admitted on equal terms to all the privilege of French citizenship than to sulk on his own rocks, the half-savage relic of past times, revolving in his own little mental orbit, without participation or interest in the general movement of the world.

There is a simple way to readjust the focus on 1989: for Breton read 'Lithuanian', for French, 'Soviet', and for general movement of the world insert 'the general Triumph of Scientific Socialism'. Note, too, the harmless-sounding phrase Mill slipped into the middle of the metropolitan argument: 'on equal terms'.

Metropole persons never perceive any problem here: *ça va de soi* – the minor, really rather technical, matter of their becoming for all practical, progress-related purposes like us. After all, they can folk-dance at weekends. Stalin loved folkum much as the Windsor monarchs love kilts: Kitsch contentment signals, exhibiting a reservation at peace with itself and (more important) with the general movement of the world.

Much of the terrible truth can in fact be read off from Mill's three-word phrase: the rise of nationalism, internationalist delusions, the irredeemably (but also fortunately) crooked and double-edged character of real development – and, finally, the great return to reality of 1989. There is no such thing as 'equal terms'. No such thing (i.e.) as a general condition, a prevalent climate of change. Perhaps some circumstances were better than others, and perhaps they will – in a very long *durée* – become more even. But on the whole they have been cruelly unequal. It is this inequality which has been the living marrow of actual development.

Had humankind remained more equal, or been less varied in a social-anthropological sense, then modern history might indeed have assumed the different forms forecast by big-battalion liberalism and socialism: a supposedly benevolent *rayonnement* from centre to rock-folk, gradual dispersal of their ethnic sulks (with or without tearful backward glance) in the course of uplift to general-movement status.

Terms of Separatism

But the material possibility for this did not exist. The quaint old creed of 'historical materialism' used to teach that underlying socio-economic conditions 'determined' the overall direction of events, including what sorts of

ideas and leaders were likely to gain control of states and political movements. Belief in this seems largely to have evaporated from *Nations and
Nationalism since 1780*. This is odd, and a pity: because the study of
nationalism, above all, should persuade one that there is still much to be
said for it.

'Development' (industrialisation and the associated social structures of
modernity) began in specific places: in Europe rather than in Asia or Africa,
and within certain zones of Europe rather than others. These zones
acquired a multiform ascendancy over the others. This different kind of
empire brought about in turn a new sort of subjection – the provinces or
colonies of an advancing world, of a general movement into which all would
be sooner or later compelled, rather than invited.

The sheer unfairness of all this penetrated one little mental orbit after
another. Although with a 'backward' side to them (all peoples have is what
is behind them) the resultant ethnic sulks were not in the main retrograde,
or attempts to cop out of modernity. They were (and still are) overwhelmingly demands for modernisation on different, less disadvantageous terms
than those offered by the existing development-controllers. By (that is) the
'great power', majority-run state, or heartland people who have, in a
significant and ancient phrase, 'stolen a march': that is, redefined the
moving frontier of development to suit themselves.

The 'sulks' have not really been about ethnic purity, rural bliss, ancestral
Gemeinschaft or ineffable idiom truths. As Gellner has so convincingly
suggested, these are only instruments of self-defence, mobilised by nationalists as part of a broader strategy. Their strategic purpose is better defined as
recovery of the march – redefinition of the development frontier in
favourable (or at least less unequal) terms.

In this sense, it is the general process of modernisation which creates
nationalism; from the system climate of nationalism particular national
movements and claims then arise. Only some of these manage to build
states, true. Gellner made a lot of this failure factor in *Nations and
Nationalism*. But what really counts is that the number has always been
sufficient to keep up a momentum of differential growth – to keep green
the ideal of 'independence', or (at least) of a growth separate enough to
contest intolerable forms of subjection.

There is no sign that this ideal is turning grey. Indeed, a quirk of
developmental fate made an unprecedented number of nationalisms rise
from what had been considered their graves during the six months or so
which elapsed between Hobsbawm sending in his manuscript and publication day. 'If I believed in God', writes a Lithuanian philosopher with due
irony, 'I would say that during the last 18 months He had remembered
Lithuania again . . .'[4]

Development could only be uneven; the unevenness could only generate
a continuing reaction, the politically driven mobilisation of those excluded,
'left behind', colonised or sentenced to become heritage trails. Such
mobilisation is primarily along ethnic rather than class lines for another

reason too. Although professedly universal in intention, the heartland motors of progress have already assumed powerfully ethnic shape in practice. In spite of the big-city broadcasts about the common good, allowing time for development perestroika to work (and so on), that shape is usually unmistakable to outsiders – to the press-ganged peasant conscripts of growth, as it were, rather than the begowned and medalled General Staff (all from the same foreign school, and all addicted to the same insufferable jokes about savage relics).

Middle-class Triumphs

It couldn't have been otherwise. Nor should it have been otherwise: for the other development paths proffered by history's various hearts of darkness since 1780 would all have been far worse. The alternative to antagonistic, ethnically biased development was never in fact cosmopolitan growth or 'internationalism'. It could only have been one form or another of empire. As Ernest Gellner also pointed out long ago, whatever the disasters of nationalism past and to come these remain infinitely preferable to the 'global South Africa' which imperialism might have (at least for a time) created.[5] In 1940–42 it very nearly did so, in a German-speaking version.

Hobsbawm mistakes that era for 'the apogee of nationalism'. Though founded upon an exacerbated nationalism of defeat and revenge, Germany's 'place in the sun' in fact turned rapidly into a universalist crusade: a world domination which, if successful, would have put all ethnic objectors and minorities indefinitely in their place as either puppet states like Vichy and Croatia, or slave labour. It was not a 'logical implication' of the post-1918 Wilsonian attempt at a nation-state Europe, but the result of that effort's failure: the climax of what Arno J. Mayer has described, much more coherently, as the epoch of generalised counter-revolution – Europe's second 'Thirty Years War'.

I will not try here to discuss Hobsbawm's many particular arguments, as the book has been reviewed separately in the *New Statesman*. There are indeed almost too many to cover, in any but an over-extended review: a determined and erudite empiricism pushed so far (with so 'much more to be learned' in every direction) that the overall line of explanation often vanishes from sight, reappearing only when the reader has been thoroughly footnote-battered. During such episodes, a kind of acrimonious distaste stands in for the general view: anything good about national movements turns out actually to derive from some other source or inspiration (quite often internationalism); everything bad is disdainfully highlighted as typical, suspect or ominous.

However, one question worth concentrating on here – since it carries us forward very much into the European present – is that of nationalism's class nature. Few can have failed to notice the ascendancy of intellectuals and middle-class professionals within the leadership of Eastern Europe's post-1988 national movements. The nomenklatura's swift (if sometimes feigned) rush to the plug-hole of history has left an array of classically nineteenth-century figures at least temporarily in charge: teachers, writers, journalists, musicians and representatives of the old bourgeois families which had survived socialist development.

Marxism had a steely term for these – 'petty-bourgeois intellectuals' who, incapable of embracing proletarian discipline, often fell into bad nationalist (or 'chauvinist') ways before selling out to the big bourgeoisie. Hobsbawm rediscovers them in *Nations and Nationalism*, naturally. 'Provincial journalists, schoolteachers, and aspiring subaltern officials . . .,' he remarks grimly, 'the socialists of the late 19th century period who rarely used the word "nationalism" without the prefix "petty-bourgeois", knew what they were talking about.' Indeed, nationalism in what was to be the twentieth-century sense was (he suggests) effectively forged by this stratum, which inflected it permanently into a narrow, right-wing and exclusivist mould – the very template of fascism, nationalism's high point in history.

Why, then, is a recognisably similar petite bourgeoisie now in charge of Eastern Europe? Including ex-Soviet republics determined, with obvious mass support from the ex-proletariat, and connivance by ex-bureaucrats, upon narrow-minded exit from the Russian imperium? In the USSR this stratum did not have to fight for the nationality of station-masters' jobs or the right to use its own language (those bones of contention under the Habsburgs and the Tsars). It was manifestly not in terror of a communist revolution, against which chauvinist frenzy was once considered to be a baleful substitute or diversion. So what's it doing here at all, liberating nations a century late? How dare it, in fact, when for decades now perfectly clear Minervan verdicts have been delivered upon the futility of 'so-called national liberation' (in a new world of blocs, multi-nationals, etc.)?

One crass yet appealing explanation is that nationalism must be more important, more recrudescent and above all of a nature other than what big-battalion theorists have wanted to believe. It is a Protean and poly-functional developmental phenomenon whose uses may themselves develop and alter – but which (like that other candidate for early immolation, the state) is very unlikely to wither away.

The Eastern Question

Eastern Europe is as much of a test-bench for these conflicting views as we are likely to find. For forty years its national development was frozen in an imposed supra-national mould. The ethnic-linguistic factors of national identity were preserved there by an elaborate system of reservation culture: all that was decreed healthy about nationhood, minus the political '-ism' (i.e. the pathological side, beloved of provincial journalists and subalterns). This was supposed to satisfy national aspirations once and for all, and permit general-movement advance to the Higher Things.

In fact, the moment the key was turned in the lock, every single reservation-*ethnos* has made straight for the *dépassé* lower things. Showing, surely, that the genuine point of national identity is not possession of one's own folk-dance academy but government – or anyway, the attempted government – of one's own affairs. There is simply no substitute for that '-ism'. Or if there is, the unspeakable *Mittelstand* no longer believes it (and is supported in scepticism by the majority of its *Volk*).

The pathology is included in the '-ism', and therefore in the kind of mass return to nationality politics which we are seeing in the East. This has caused much fulmination, and is behind a lot of the current 'ugly face' mythology. Renewed ethnic feuding, anti-Semitism and irredentism have accompanied the reversion to nationhood and the installation of democracy. At a recent conference I attended, another leading left-wing historian was heard to state – with ominous candour – that he had just returned from Vilnius, where he had actually heard Lithuanians making positively racist remarks about Russian and other nationals.

Hobsbawm is quite right to point out there's little new here. In the USSR, one journalist wrote:

> Even to suggest a remedy of nationalism without warning of its possible side effects is an act of some irresponsibility [where it] is so commingled with virulent chauvinism and jingoism . . . However odious the tyranny, potentially uglier strains of obscurantism and hatred lurk below its surface.

That was George Feifer, in *The Times* of August 1974. He was rebuking Bernard Levin, whose 'perniciously misleading' column had suggested the previous week that the Soviet nationality question might quite soon become more significant than the American racial one.

'In melancholy retrospect', chips in Hobsbawm, a great achievement of communism was 'to limit the disastrous effects of nationalism'.[6] What nationalities suffered under the knout was nothing to what they will now suffer from one another. Bring back *le frère aîné* as Hélène Carrère d'Encausse called Big Brother in her *L'Empire éclaté*[7] – 'With Stalin . . . the egalitarianism once officially upheld disappeared in favour of the idea of a community of nations organised around their elder brother, the Russian people, tutor and guide to all the rest.'

In less nostalgic retrospect, something else is worth adding. The stable elder-brother world which abruptly crumbled a year ago was governed by fear of quite a different kind of disaster. No doubt glad to be rid of it, opinion seems none the less to have forgotten that fear in an astonishingly short time. The 'essentially bi-polar world organised round two super-powers' worked in fact on a basis of blackmailers' dread. It was kept going by the idea that a super-power conflict might bring about the near-extinction of the species.

Now – incredibly – we are invited to feel that the new world of liberation chaos must be worse than this. Border problems, mob violence, discrimination and vendettas pursued with hunting-rifles are decreed more vexing than the 'order' of the Bomb. 'Such ethnic reactions', concludes

Hobsbawm, 'do not provide in any sense an alternative principle for the political restructuring of the world in the 21st century.' 'Political restructuring': a sonorous phrase, and best left to the hallmarked notables of Paris, Washington or even London. These matters are not for sulky rock-dwellers. Yes, sooner or later we shall get Brezhnev and Reagan back again, and deserve them: nationalist folly will see to that, as it did last century after the short-lived Springtime of Nations in 1848–9.

The Ecology of Development

If this is true, Europe will really be in trouble. But there is, surely, an alternative to merely projecting such melancholy retrospect forward forever. It is to argue that the new wave of nationalism does (or can be made to) furnish, precisely, an 'alternative principle' of political restructuring for the twenty-first century.

Nor (anticipating an obvious objection) is this a matter of declaring that the ills and evils of nationalism 'don't matter', or that some new omelette will demand a few more eggs be broken. We suffered enough idiot ruthlessness of that sort during the Age of the Bomb. The true point at issue here only echoes the one made earlier: on the whole (as in the past) any other alternative would be worse.

As an inescapable system, nationalism has to sort out its own reborn structural ailments. It may be difficult to work out blueprints for that. However, the difficulty is overshadowed by another – that is, by the fact that we now have the most long-drawn-out (and long-suffering) grounds for believing that super-power and multi-national elder brothers never will. Big-battalion order carried the world to the very edge of oblivion. Though any smaller-scale internationalism is inherently harder to figure out in advance, one can be fairly sure that it will save us from that direction.

It seems to me we also have some grounds for optimism within the specific area of these new nationality struggles. The first of these is democracy. Mainly through reaction against the great Big Brother freeze-up, the world is now far more deeply democratic than it was at previous moments of nationalist advance, like 1848 and 1918. As long as democracy continues to inform and arbitrate liberation conflicts, their damage will be limited.

In this sense the reason for supporting Baltic secessionist movements is not (or not just) their right of self-determination, or Stalin's 1940 land-grabbing. Nor is it because such movements are more angelic and resentment-free than their predecessors. There is nothing surprising about Lithuanians and their Baltic neighbours feeling ethnic or even racist-style resentment about their Soviet-Russian occupiers. What is surprising is that this has not been universal, or (so far) expressed more brutally. 'Not surprising' does not imply condoning, either: in itself reactive racism may be no better than what provoked it. However, unlike its progenitor, it does not intend to (and lacks the power to) last forever.

Baltic and other freedom movements are better because they stand for genuine democratic preference, against a state, a president and an army that (as yet) manifestly do not. Democracy is no automatic solution, of course. The Russians might eventually vote in their own government on a law-and-order platform including the repression of 'unconstitutional' ethnic dissidence. In Yugoslavia the Serbs might decide to have it out with the Croats, the Slovenes and others rather than permit another round of de facto Balkanisation. Yet this is only to say there can be democratic errors (even disasters) as well as the higher level of compromise and moderation which democratic practices ought generally to secure. In a freer world, no new formula will ever guarantee short-term or 'inevitable' victory of the latter over the former.

By contrast, what would guarantee all-round regression and the reanimation of ethnicity's rabid side is the resurrection of the old formula: *frère aîné* and his pals, the decision that 'enough is enough' wrapped up in the mummy-cloths of supra-nationalism or one-worldism. However briefly gratifying to nostalgists of the post World War II *ancien régime*, these would be truly useless expedients. The acute new phase of uneven development provoked by Eastern Europe's return to capitalism is likely to make short work of them.

As well as democracy, a second order of reflection may also now begin to cast a more optimistic light over nationalism's future. Though still far from Minerva's flying-order time, political nationalism has now been around long enough, and reasserted itself often enough from assorted graves and refrigerators, to suggest to us something which as soon as suggested has the merit of sounding fairly obvious.

As Gellner surmises in *Nations and Nationalism*, nationalism may be not just 'inseparable' from socio-economic advance (like a shadow, or a family black sheep) but also necessary to the more conscious and humane development lying (we have to hope) beyond primitive industrialisation. The latter should have taught us some more things about 'human nature'. And one of these may be that nationality and ethnic discord (with a degree of cacophony) are indeed part of human nature – but not (or not only) in the sense of Dark Gods and tribal mysteries of the Blood. They may in fact be part of that same forward-looking, self-emancipating and generally sanguine nature to which internationalists have traditionally appealed.

The appropriate analogy here might be with the rise of Green or environmental political movements. These too represent the beginning of a willed transformation of 'nature': the recognition that an inherited natural world can no longer be merely assumed, or (in the old sense) 'exploited' like an inexhaustible reservoir. Development has destroyed too much of our reserves. It can't go on: nature has to be in a sense redefined, less to be 'preserved' than to be more consciously cultivated, in order that more tolerable development can continue.

But arguably the most important natural inheritance is humankind's own ethno-linguistic variety: ten thousand languages where (in glumly rationalist perspective) one might have done perfectly well; the coat of incomparable colours and contrasts handed down through everyone's blood, from the over-abundance of time past. Such 'destructive prodigality', in George Steiner's phrase, is too much of what we are to suffer replacement by any monoculture. And yet, he goes on in *After Babel*:

> Living languages are themselves the remnant of a much larger number spoken in the past. Each year so-called rare languages, tongues spoken by isolated or moribund ethnic communities, become extinct ... Almost at every moment of time some ancient and rich expression of articulate being is lapsing into irretrievable silence.

'Development' in the modern sense (the cause of all the trouble) began where there was most forced contrast, not least – in the world's bear pit of cacophony, Europe. It has wasted a lot of ethnic communities, but happily provoked others into continuing protest at being silenced. The most valuable parts of modern culture derive from the resultant culture clash – that is, from antagonisms and syntheses dependent not upon the museum conservation of variety, but upon the latter's political will to exist.

Enough variety has survived the Age of Empires to suggest that future evolution should proceed only along this route. Nationalism has always been invention after nature: perhaps its 'greening' ought to be the phase in which such invention is more consciously and radically legitimated (or sometimes insisted upon), as the most tolerable way of preserving the species. The big battalions in permanent retreat: wouldn't that be a better sort of internationalism, and one more at home with democracy?

3

Demonising Nationality

Two and a half years ago *Time* magazine published a special exposé about the future of the world.[1] 'Being on the cover of *Time*' has always been an American honour (something like a knighthood) and on this occasion *Time* did not let readers down. The cover of 6 August 1990 obliged with a portrait of ... Nationalism.

An elementary tombstone-shaped visage of plasticine, or possibly mud, glowers out from an equally rudimentary map of central Europe. One primitive, soulless eye is located near Vilnius. Beneath the emergent snout a hideous, gash-like mouth splits the continent open from Munich to Kiev before dribbling its venom down across Yugoslavia and Romania. No semiotic subtlety is needed to decode the image, since closer perusal shows the teeth inside the gash read simply 'Nationalism'. But in case anyone failed to register that, the whole image was crowned with a title in 72-point scarlet lettering: 'OLD DEMON'.

This was two and a half years ago. Hardly an in-depth retrospect, therefore, more an early, apprehensive glance during the first round of the ex-Soviet and post-Yugoslav tumult. It was, in fact, what most Western or metropolitan opinion really expected, on the basis of these early stirrings. Some time before either the Baltic peoples, the Ukrainians or the Georgians had actually established their independence, when virtually all Western diplomacy was still devoted to shoring up Gorbachev and Yugoslavia, there already lurked a pervasive sense of doom in the North Atlantic mind. It was summed up in a *Guardian* leader of the same vintage: 'Don't Put Out More Flags!' This editorial did become famous enough to endure mild mockery but only because it was characteristically over the top, exaggerating what most readers instinctively felt.

What they felt was that if enough new national flags were put out the Old Demon would, unless severely dealt with, wreak havoc with the New World Order. The second springtime of nations was, in this glum perspective, already turning to winter, and a bad one at that.

Now, anyone could see from the outset that there were at least three principal strands in the gigantic upheaval against Communism. There was a popular, democratic rebellion against one-party autocracy and state terror.

There was an economic revulsion against the anti-capitalist command economies which for forty years had imposed forced-march development on the East. And thirdly there was the national mould into which these revolts were somehow inevitably flowing – the new salience of the ethnic, or (as in Bosnia) of the ethnic-religious in post-communist society.

The *Time–Guardian* perspective on this triad is that the third element will most likely end by confining, endangering or even aborting the first two. And I suppose what I am primarily objecting to tonight is that perspective itself – the instinctive notion that number 3 on the list is somehow an atavistic revenant, there by unfortunate accident, the bad news which has resurfaced alongside the good, an Old Adam who refuses to let the Angel of Progress get on with it.

The conclusion to the *Time* article by John Borrell accompanying the front cover puts this point as well as anyone else, in terms which, since then, have been echoed thousands of times in tones of mounting hysteria: 'Not since Franz Ferdinand's assassination have conditions been so favourable for an enduring new order to replace the empires of the past. With a unified Germany locked in the embrace of democratic Europe, and the Soviet Union re-examining its fundamental values, the way is open for an era of peace and liberty – but only so long as the old demons do not escape again.'

But escape they did, alas, notably in what used to be Yugoslavia and especially – as if some truly profound irony of history was working itself out – in and around the very town where Franz Ferdinand perished in 1914. The general view or new received wisdom soon became set in concrete: nationalism is upsetting everything. It has ruined the End of History, in Fukuyama's sense. History has come back like some evil shade, mainly in order to ruin the State Department's triumphal victory celebrations.

There were always serious difficulties in store in the East for both democracy and capitalism, of course, and no serious commentator has ignored them. But what has made these insoluble is the return and dominance of the third force – the atavistic, incalculable force of the ethnic revival, compelling peoples to place blood before reasonable progress and individual rights. Three years ago it already felt as if this might be the story: mysterious unfinished business of Eastern nationality wrecks any 'enduring new order'. And so it has proved. We (in the West) now face a prospect of interminable Balkan and post-Soviet disorder, where forms of demented chauvinism and intolerance risk arresting progress altogether. Putting out too many new flags, having too many liberated nations, leads only to *etnicko ciscenje*, 'ethnic cleansing'.[2]

Unless civilisation intervenes, they may end up by replacing naissant democracy with forms of nationalist dictatorship like those prefigured in Gamsakurdia's Georgia or the Serbia of Slobodan Milosevic. As for economics the consequences can hardly be anything but intensified backwardness.

Old Stories

You are all over-familiar with this dreary tale. If I have taken up too much time reminding you of it, it's mainly in order to stress one neglected aspect of it. What 'civilised' news coverage of Eastern folly perceives is primarily a re-emergence of archaism. It rarely occurs to the editorialists or reporters concerned that this enlightened, liberal perspective on the great change may itself be archaic.

Yet I believe it is. Whether or not old demons are returning to haunt anyone in Bosnia and Ngorny-Karabakh, there can be no doubt that old theories – the conventional wisdom of the day before yesterday – have come back to haunt and distort Western interpretations of what is happening. This wisdom is easily dated. One need only turn to the nearest available library shelf groaning beneath a copy of *Encyclopaedia Britannica*. Turn to 'Socio-Economic Doctrines and Reform Movements' (vol. 27, pp. 467–71), and the signature, 'H.K.' – Hans Kohn, a prominent and prolific writer on the political history of nationalism in the 1940s.

The thesis which Kohn argued at that time rested mainly upon a distinction between Western and Eastern nationalism. The former was original, institutional, liberal and good. The latter was reactive, envious, ethnic, racist and generally bad. Undeniably, Western-model nation-states like Britain, France and America had invented political nationalism. But Kohn argued that these societies had also limited and qualified it, linking it to certain broader, more universal ideals. Nationalism may have been a child of Western Enlightenment. But that very fact enabled the original enlightened countries to at least partially transcend it – to confine and then pass beyond the demon's potency (as it were). As time passed, in spite of various imperialist adventures, a measure of tolerance and internationalism came to compensate for such original sin, and to moderate the crudity of Anglo-French nationality.

Not so in the East. By the 'East' I think Kohn really meant the rest of the world, but typified by Central and Eastern Europe. He was talking about all those other societies which from the eighteenth century onwards have suffered the impact of the West, and been compelled to react against it. That reaction bred a different kind of national spirit – resentful, backward-looking, detesting the Western bourgeoisie even while trying to imitate it, the sour and vengeful philosophy of the second- or third-born. It was this situation (he claimed) which generated genuinely narrow nationalism.

Countries were hurled into the developmental race without time to mature the requisite institutions and cadres. Hence they were forced to mobilise in other ways. The intellectuals and soldiers who took charge there needed an adrenaline-rich ideology to realise their goals, and found it in a shorthand version of the Western national spirit. This was of course blood-based nationality, a heroic and exclusive cult of people and state founded upon custom, speech, faith, colour, cuisine and whatever else was found available for packaging.

Though originally drawn to the West, the Germans had ended by succumbing to an Eastern-style package. Developed into a form of eugenic insanity, it was their blood cult which threatened to drown the Enlightenment inheritance altogether after 1933. This was mercifully (though only just) defeated in 1945. However, out of it came the experience which stamped a lasting impression of nationalism's meaning upon both the Western and the communist mind. Nazism may in truth have been a form of genetic imperialism – in its bizarre, pseudo-scientific fashion universal (or at least would-be universal) in sense – but its nationalist origins were undeniable, as well as keenly felt by all the victims. So its sins were inevitably visited upon nationality politics as such. Since the largest, most important ethnos in Europe had gone mad in that particular way then the ethnic as such must remain forever suspect.

Such is the mentality which the post-1989 events have brought again to the surface. Instead of prompting a new search for theories to account for this extraordinary transformation of the world, these events have by and large resurrected the old ones. There are some important exceptions here (to which I will return in a minute) but on the whole it seems to me that theory has contributed astonishingly little to understanding of the New World Order (or the New World Disorder as – like nearly everybody else – Ken Jowitt calls it in his interesting if eccentric 1991 study[3]). The greatest revolution in global affairs since the epoch of world war is currently being explained almost wholly in terms of *Time* magazine's Old Demons. Somehow a new age seems to have been born without any new ogres: all we have are the old ones, the Old Adam of atavistic Eastern-style nationalism thawed out from the Cold War icebox and on the rampage once more.

World of Nations

Actually, we were frozen up by Cold War circumstances as much as they were in the East. They have been brusquely thawed out since 1989, but a much gentler, more protracted thawing-out process is still going on at this end of the continent. Such is the sad dilemma that underlines the task of this and any similar conference today. Of course all meetings about ideas look for, and usually find, ideal tasks awaiting their attention. But in this case they seem to me to be really screaming for attention, rather than waiting patiently for academics to get round to them. It is not a pity but a scandal that theory has had so little input into the ongoing political and media debate about nationalism.

These creaky old ideological vehicles trundled out to cope with the post-Soviet and Balkan upheavals explain nothing whatever about their subjects. Their gore-laden pictures of ethnic anarchy, of the Abyss and the Doom to come start off by obscuring what is, surely, so far easily the most significant feature of the new world disorder.

Since 1988 the post-communist convulsions have drawn in about forty different nationalities and a population of well over three hundred million in an area comprising about one-fifth of the world. Thanks to the holding operation in Tienanmen Square they did not embrace an actual majority of the world's population (but it's surely reasonable to think that they will still end by doing so).

Now, when this scale and those numbers are kept in mind, the most impressive fact is surely not how much the transformation has cost in terms of either life or social and economic destruction. It is how astoundingly, how unbelievably little damage has been done. In one of the few efforts made at countering conventional hysteria the *Economist* did try last September to estimate loss of life in the ex-Soviet empire, and published a map showing that probably about 3,000 plus had perished, mostly in Georgia, Tajikistan and the war between Armenia and Azerbaijan. 'Fewer than most people think', it concluded, and far less serious than what was happening in one small part of the Balkans. Social and economic disaster had been brought about by the collapse of the old Soviet-style economies, but though aggravated by the political breakaways and national disputes these were certainly not the cause.

This impression must be reinforced if any concrete time-scale or historical memory is brought into the picture. The Old Demon mythology is essentially timeless – a dark or counter-millennium of re-emergent sin. In actual time the reflorescence of ethnic nationhood has followed a forty-year period during which humanity cowered in the effective shadow of imminent extinction. The demonologies of that epoch (anti-capitalism and anti-communism) at least rested on something real, in the sense of an array of missiles and other hardware which any serious clash between the empires – or even any sufficiently serious accident – could have activated, with the genuinely apocalyptic results everyone now seems (understandably enough) to have exiled from recollection.

But the old frozen mentality did not vanish with the missiles. Instead it has found the temporary surrogate – Devil of Nationalism. Another End of the World has been located – Armageddon has been replaced by the ethnic Abyss. A pretty feeble substitute, in fact, in the obvious sense that, even if some worst-possible-case scenario were to unfold – a prolonged 'Third Balkan War' in Misha Glenny's phrase, a Russo-Ukrainian war over the Crimea, the break-up of the Indian state, and so on – the consequences would not, by the standards of 1948 to 1988, be all that serious. Nobody would have to worry about taking refuge on another planet.

Anarchy and Method

Almost by definition there is a great deal of anarchy in the New Disorder, and no sign of its coming to an end. But there is (I would suggest) no abyss save the ideological one in metropolitan craniums. As Ben Anderson says in another of the more critical contributions to the debate (also entitled 'The New World Disorder') the key misconception is that what's going on is essentially, 'fragmentation' and 'disintegration' – with all the menacing, pathological connotations these words bring with them. This language makes us forget the decades or centuries of violence out of which Frankensteinian 'integrated states' such as the United Kingdom of 1900, which included all of Ireland, were constructed ... Behind the language of 'fragmentation' lies always a Panglossian conservatism that likes to imagine that every status quo is nicely normal.[4]

But as Anderson and anyone else making this kind of objection knows all too well, the immediate result is bitter recrimination. One is at once accused of apologising for savagery, or of indifference to the escalating Balkan wars. An appeal to Western governments and the Secretary-General of the United Nations was published in last week's *New York Review*, demanding that the world take action to stop the Yugoslav wars: 'If democracies acquiesce in violations of human rights on such a massive scale they will undermine their ability to protect these rights anywhere in the post-cold war world. And then, when, as has happened many times before, an armed hoodlum kicks our own doors ajar, there will be no one to lift a finger in our defence or to raise a voice.'[5]

In this climate, to suggest that on the whole the nationalist course of history after 1989 may be preferable to what went before, and may not be treatable by any recourse to the old multi-national or internationalist recipes, is to risk virtual excommunication. One must be lining up with the armed hoodlums. One is either a dupe of Demons like Tudjman and Karadzic or some sort of narrow nationalist oneself (I'm not clear which of these is considered worse).

Well, no: it does not follow, and the point at issue is really a methodological one. Though obvious, it usually gets ignored in the new fury of the ideological times. Both anti-nationalism and pro-nationalism are extremely broad attitudes or principles – the kind of important yet very general rules which are needed as signposts or reference points. But signposts do not map out or explain the journey which they indicate. Although by no means empty or meaningless, attitudes on this plane of historical generality are bound to have – indeed, to demand – hosts of qualifications or exceptions. 'On the whole' inevitably leads to 'but ...' What they 'mean' in any actual situation isn't, and cannot possibly be, just a deduction or a blanket endorsement or rejection. Exceptions don't exactly prove rules, but they are the lifeblood of useful principles.

This was blatantly true of anti-nationalism. Both in its standard liberal or Western form and in the socialist or Leninist versions which used to hold court in the East, it was always acknowledged that occasionally, reluctantly, a few more flags had to be run up. This was permitted in cases of hallmarked national oppression. Emphatically colonial or imperialist dominance gave legitimacy to nationalism, at least for a time. 'Great-power chauvinism' could morally underwrite small-country national liberation, though only up to the point of independence, when universal values were supposed at once to reassert themselves.

So, the very least a pro-nationalist can say is that he or she is as entitled to exceptions as *that*. That political and economic nationalism is, very generally, a good thing does not mean there are no blots, excrescences or failures on the increasingly nationalised map of the world. Recognition that only a broadly nationalist solution will be found for the succession to the Soviet Union, Yugoslavia and Czechoslovakia does not entail apologising for the bombardment of Dubrovnik or the political rape of Muslim women in Bosnia. Insistence that the small battalions are likely to be 'on the whole' better than the large – particularly the multi-national large – does not imply there can be no pathology of the ethnic, or no cases where nationalists are wrong.

I must say too that it seems to me that since 1989 the pro-nationalist is justified in a measure of sarcasm. He or she can also observe that, however many pustules and warts there turn out to be in the new world of nations, the small-battalion principle is unlikely to end up consisting of nothing but exceptions. Such has of course been internationalism's fate since 1989. The seamless garment always had to make room for occasional, supposedly temporary, tears and patches; but after 1989 it come to consist of almost nothing except empty holes, which no amount of lamentation or wish-fulfilment will repair.

For the first time in human history, the globe has been effectively unified into a single economic order under a common democratic-state model – surely the ideal, dreamt-of conditions for liberal or proletarian internationalism. Actually, these conditions have caused it almost immediately to fold up into a previously unimaginable and still escalating number of different ethno-political units.

The European Enigma

Why has the one produced the other? Why has globalisation engendered nationalism, instead of transcending it? This is, surely, the fundamental problem of theory that the last three years have thrown up. It goes far beyond what has become the obsessive question of Yugoslavia, and what should be done there to stop or lessen its crimes and cruelties. I hope that the conference doesn't get diverted into this, so that – as it were – thinking up by tomorrow night a formula for saving Bosnia becomes the yardstick of progress on all other fronts.

This may require some psychic effort of disengagement, but I suspect that is necessary. It is necessary, above all, in Western Europe – inside the countries of the European Community. Hans Kohn's theorisation of Western liberalism reposed (as we saw) on a distinction between West and East (or the West vs. the Rest). Unfortunately, this distinction was not simply resuscitated in 1989 but in a sense fortified.

The reason for that was what seemed to be taking place in the West End of the continent at that time. Innumerable people couldn't help feeling, and repeating with varying degrees of self-satisfaction, 'Just look at the difference!' They may be breaking up and disintegrating, but we appear to be doing the opposite – to be integrating, getting over at least some features of nationalism, pooling sovereignty, looking rationally outwards, and so on.

Thus, extra complacency about the North Atlantic dangerously fortified the old prejudices about the East, and made it appear even less urgent to search for new explanations. If Western advance and superiority were the explanation, why waste time rethinking history with elaborate theories about the comparative conditions of development? I suppose the worst single incident of that phase was the day Boris Yeltsin turned up at the Strasbourg Parliament in 1991, and found himself (as he put it at the time) being harangued like a backward school-kid by Socialist MEPs. Why couldn't he be more like Mikhail Gorbachev, they indignantly demanded, what did he mean by being so nice to all those would-be separatists, could he not see that breaking up the USSR would be a disaster?

This outburst of daft parochialism was perhaps the most humiliating moment in the history of Strasbourg; but it was also a symptom of a phase destined rapidly to pass. Maastricht and the Danish and French referenda were not far away, and were soon to produce an abrupt change of climate. The sense of inevitable and uninterruptable progress towards post-nationalist light gave way to the doubt and uncertainty of the present. It is (at least) not now so clear that never the twain shall meet, and also that they represent fundamentally diverging forms of development.

At the same time other important blows to Western confidence have been dealt by events in Canada and Czechoslovakia, especially the latter. This was the central, linking country between East and West which after its emancipation from communist rule was generally expected to follow a Western route and act as an example to less fortunate neighbours. The fact that it has chosen the (supposedly) Eastern route of division, civilly and without excessive commotion or animosity, is something whose significance has not been allowed to sink in. Four weeks ago the birth of two new democratic republics in the heart of Europe was greeted here with a torrent of bile, commiseration and preventive accusations. Every single birthmark was seen as presaging doom. How dare they! Not only out of step but going in the wrong direction, they'll learn, they'll soon be fighting like the rest (and so on).

Liberal-capitalist complacency has been replaced by the mood, darker but also more realistic, which Etienne Balibar conveyed in a 1991 talk about racism and politics in Europe. 'Es gibt keinen Staat in Europa' was his title, a remark originally made by Hegel: there is no real state in Europe.

Before there can be any serious analysis of racism and its relationship to migrations, we have to ask ourselves what this word 'Europe' means and what it will signify tomorrow (he argued). In reality we are here discovering the truth of the earlier situation, which explodes the representation that we used to have of it. Europe is not something that is 'constructed' at a slower or faster pace, with greater or less ease; it is a historical problem without any pre-established solution.[6]

The evaporation of frontiers has not – or not yet – been replaced by the new definitions and boundaries of a European state, one capable of establishing the social and political citizenship so crucial to migrants. In a curious way, Euro-development has led to another kind of under-development in this key area. So that (he goes on):

> All the conditions are present for a collective sense of identity panic to be produced and maintained. For individuals – particularly the most deprived and the most remote from power – fear the state but they fear still more its disappearance or decomposition.

I'm not sure about his description 'identity panic', but I agree the complacency of 1989 has been overtaken by identity concern, often coloured by anxiety and by a sharp disillusionment with the older European formulae. These features were certainly prominent in both the Danish and the French referenda over Maastricht, and they are also important in the much more smothered, inchoate argument now limping along in the United Kingdom.

However, identity alarm can be read positively too. It is surely not wholly bad that this has replaced Western (and notably Britannic) identity somnolence. These circumstances creating the new sense of dislocation and doubt may also prompt new initiatives and departures. Of course, ethnic closure and brutal self-defence is one response to a loss of familiar horizons and signposts. But not the only one, and not one predestined either to return everywhere, or to an easy triumph where it does.

Grander Theory

This returns us to that larger plane of theory I alluded to before, and on which I would like to conclude. To understand the difference, to retain and cultivate a wider, more balanced perspective on the post-1989 transformation must be the task for serious theorists in this new world. Why has the End of History carried us forward into a more nationalist world? Why is a more united globe also – and almost at once – far more ethnically aware, and more liable to political division?

In mentioning theories of nationalism before, I hope I didn't give the impression of nothing having been done in the field. Far from it – the years before 1989 were actually ones where very significant advances were made in both the history and the sociology of nationalism. The central weakness of Kohn and liberal theory had been its neglect of economics, its failure to place the rise of ethnic politics within a more substantial framework of development. This failure was remedied by the important work of Ernest Gellner,[7] Anthony D. Smith and others from the 1960s to the 1980s.

They showed, to my mind conclusively, that nationalism was inseparable from the deeper processes of industrialisation and socio-economic modernity. Far from being an irrational obstacle to development, it was for most societies the only feasible way into the developmental race – the only way in which they could compete without being either colonised or annihilated. If they turned to the past (figuratively to 'the blood') in these modernisation struggles, it was essentially in order to stay intact as they levered themselves into the future. Staying intact, or obtaining a new degree of social and cultural cohesion, was made necessary by industrialisation – even (as in so many cases) by the distant hope, the advancing shadow of industrialisation. And *ethnos* offered the only way of ensuring such cohesion and common purpose.

The strategy was indeed high-risk, both in the sense that the blood might take over and drown them, and because they might never really catch up. However, that risk was itself unavoidable. It arose from the conditions of generally and chronically uneven development – the only kind which capitalism allows. The only kind, and the kind which has finally, definitively established itself since 1989 as the sole matrix of further evolution.

In this more rational but insufficiently appreciated perspective, national-ism is therefore as much a native of modernity as democracy and the capitalist motor of development. It is as inseparable from progress as they are. In his earlier work Gellner in particular stressed how vital was the function of nationalism in resisting over-centralised and monolithic devel-opment. Without 'fragmentation and disintegration' some type of Empire would long ago have appropriated industrialisation to its own political purpose.

Earlier on I mentioned the standard triad of categories used to read the post-1989 changes: democracy, capitalism and nationalism, the third repre-senting some kind of ghost or retreat from reason, an upsurge of atavism interfering with the other two – with the reasonable adaptation of the East to modernity. This is itself a piece of superstition. But unfortunately a superstition which has grown so popular that today it has come partly to define (or redefine) the task of nationalist theory. It seems to me that anti-demonism is the prerequisite of getting anywhere with a debate about ethnic issues and their future.

I don't have time to spell out further a theoretical perspective which, in any case, everyone here will be familiar with. But it may be important to reflect just why we have to remind ourselves of it. The fact is, for all their weight and intellectual superiority to the old commonplaces, studies like Smith's *The Ethnic Origin of Nations* (1986) and Gellner's *Nations and Nationalism* have not become acquisitions of the wider culture. They have had very little influence on common perceptions of their subject. Hence, when the whole world was abruptly compelled to focus on it again, an older common sense – the embedded theories of generations ago – took over and explained it all in terms of demons, resurgent fascism or the irrational side of human nature.

There is an interesting reversal at work here which you will already have detected. Once upon a time (before 1989) the protagonists of international-ism tended to be over-rational creatures, professorial politicos who occasionally displayed noticeable nervous tics. Apologists for nationalism were supposed to be hirsute, romantic souls who took folk-dance too seriously and were liable to get carried away (especially by rogues). I can see little of this in the arguments today. The shocked, semi-hysterical response of the West to the Eastern rebirth has plunged it into the style of unreason once supposed typical of wild-eyed chauvinists and patriotic poets.

By contrast it must be up to the defenders of nationality politics and *ethnos* to assume a cannier, more balanced point of view on the emergent world. It is they who should assume and develop this perspective, on the basis of the enduring theoretical and historical work I indicated. It's they who must look for the broader view, and the longer historical perspective, taking their distance from the metropolitan virtual reality being pumped out in London, Paris and New York.

That perspective is one which I hope will be welcome in this conference. It ought to find as natural a home in Glasgow as (say) in Kiev, or Ljubljana, or Riga – the newer centres of a more varied, more emphatically nationalist world which, in spite of all those pessimistic titles and notwithstanding the abscess in Bosnia, will turn out to be more than just disorder and atavism.

The promoters of this occasion were kind enough – for which I must thank them – to include a quotation from something I wrote years ago about 'The Modern Janus', likening nationalism to the two-headed Roman deity who couldn't help looking backwards into the past as well as forward into the future. Since then the whole world has come to resemble him more rather than less. But with an important difference. I believe that, on the whole, the forward-gazing side of the strange visage may be more prominent than it was in 1977. Perhaps because today the forward view is that much more open and more encouraging than it was then.

Part II
Faces of Nationalism

Part II

The Modern Janus

In an unpublished manuscript of the 1970s, referred to at the end of Part I, and called originally 'The Modern Janus', I put forward an idea about the essential ambiguity of nationalism which the title was meant to echo. Its two-facedness arose from the underlying dilemma of modernisation, which compelled one population after another to desire progress. There was no escape from the compulsion, given the planetary scale we inhabit and the inherent expansiveness of the phenomenon. Over the two hundred years 1789–1989 it reached everywhere: Tibet, the Antarctic, Greenland, Amazonia. The same expansiveness had a further consequence: modern empires – polities in some ways like those of earlier history, yet now infused with the far greater power of science and technology derived from industrialisation's core areas. Whatever their official claims, medieval and earlier empires were actually limited in power and ambition. There was very little chance of the Chinese, Persian, Mogul, Habsburg or Ottoman polities attaining a literally 'world empire'. Modernisation changed this: it became at least conceivable that Napoleon, the British Crown, German Aryanism or Soviet Communism could achieve just that.

Nationalism was the effort by one 'backward' culture and people after another to appropriate the powers and benefits of modernity for their own use. Having been redefined as backward, they aspired to move forward. However, this motion occurred partly against the tide coursing over them from the central domains of industry and urbanisation. The pressure wave was mainly imperial (arrogant, ethnocentric, homogenising and armed to the teeth) as well as gift-bearing. In order to appropriate the gifts without enduring the imperial wrappings, overborne populations had to assert 'their own terms' – that is, political and cultural independence. This implied that, in most cases, the terms had to be 'discovered' via scrutiny and vindication of their own past history. There seemed no way for nationalities to become nations without such new retrospect. Hence, modernising ambition and novel cults of a particular past and tradition notoriously co-exist within most varieties of nationalism: the backward- and forward-looking faces of any discrete population or area struggling for tolerable survival and prosperity.

It was a neat theory derived mostly from Ernest Gellner's pioneering

71

work, but ended by posing as many questions as it answered. Some of these problems are tackled in Part II. There are, alas, more than just two general 'faces' mixed up in the great, continuing dilemma.

Part I argued that 'internationalism' was one such visage: that of principled, but also pseudo-universalist, opposition to the very idea of separate (hence 'selfish', antagonistic, etc.) development. 'Civil society' is one of internationalism's progeny, given lusty new existence by the collapse of the communist imperium in 1988–89. I have looked at that below, and also at descendants from the other side: the present-day protagonists of race and inheritance, also reanimated to some degree by the post-1980s turmoil. The two other essays look at aspects of the reconfigured past. The well of the past is not just very deep, but much richer and more heterogeneous than most nationalist, and counter-nationalist, ideology ever admitted. The antagonisms of mainstream modernisation imposed rude and condescending simplicities upon all sides. It was these simplifications which crumbled away after catastrophes like the Cambodian revolution, considered below, the Rwandan genocide, or the Bosnian wars. It seems to me that they force theory to regard the question of persisting rurality more steadily, and critically.

First-phase, or mainstream, nationality politics was unavoidably fixated on rurality. Janus had nowhere else to direct his ideological gaze, in most cases. But this too was an effacement. As Martin Thom has forcefully and creatively argued, the past was always cities as well as 'countries', in the sense inflected by post-romantic development. As globalisation subsumes this evolution, the city returns to its own. The descendants of the city-state may be the city-regions or city-nations of tomorrow, redefining political autonomy, and nationalism, to accord with the altered gravity of the post-imperial world. Some interpretations of this shift have focused on its global or world-order side, even seeing, in Justin Rosenberg's phrase, 'the empire of civil society' as a vindication of metropolitanism and old-fashioned international relations 'realism'. The reader will hardly be surprised to find a different reading of the shift here.

No grand ideological contest of that sort – Primordialism vs. Modernism, Internationalism vs. Nationalism – is ever won, or lost. Reality concludes such disputes by surprising all the old protagonists with new fusions of its own, 'syntheses' drawn from no known textbook or seer-dream but the well itself. Nationalism was itself such a creation, astonishing to its own originators and unimaginable by their predecessors. It reforged the world on the crude template of ethnicity; but only those confusing the process with that primary template can think that nationality politics will be overcome or drowned in globalisation. Human nature has been too deeply changed, and the re-enchantment of its cultural domain has gone too far. I believe species variety is unlikely to have laid empires low in order to succumb to 'Macdonaldisation', Islam or breakfast television. Italo Calvino's *città invisibili* – an imagined proliferation of fantastically different urban-based cultures haunting the future as rural ghosts once dominated the past – may yet be closer to the mark.

4

From Civil Society to Civic Nationalism: Evolutions of a Myth

The philosophical, political and ethical concept of 'civil society' has become one of the most popular and influential ideas of the present day.[1] This didn't use to be the case. Not so long ago 'civil society' was something that figured mainly in academic scholarship, and was discussed by those interested in the factory of origin – the Scottish Enlightenment – or else in Hegel, or in the political ideology of Marxism (including the life and times of Antonio Gramsci).

'The phrase itself had no living resonance or evocativeness', notes the late Ernest Gellner in his last book *The Conditions of Liberty*.[2] Yet the book itself – surprisingly for someone who had such sensibility to living resonances – is a defiant resurrection and restatement of 'civil society'. It had passed, as he went on to explain, in a few years from being covered with library dust into 'a shining emblem' (of something or other). I think this is what appealed to him. He wanted to make a strong ideological statement, one which would resonate above all in the Eastern Europe to which he had returned. Towards the end of the book he even declares that civil society is a more important ideal than Democracy.

As well as trying to analyse what 'civil society' is an emblem of, I should at this point also come clean and confess my own general view of the idea. My contention here will be that the strange resurrection has been on the whole undeserved. The dust should be allowed to settle down again (and in fact it is already doing so). 'Civil society' has been at best a kind of transitional ideology, a way of crossing – though it might be better to say, staggering across – the bridge from the Cold War continent of 1950 to 1989 to wherever it is we are living now. Having got over it the last thing we should do is try to eternalise the circumstances of that passage, as I'm afraid Gellner does in his book. Not – let me hasten to add – that I particularly want to get into disputes about the correct description of the new habitus: post-modern, *posthistoire*, post-History, post-nation-state or post-whatever-it-is that the Professor in question dislikes most.

Gellner saw the reanimation of civil society primarily as a consequence of the fall of Marxism. Disliking the latter so much, he was inclined to like the former – even to like it, perhaps, somewhat against his better judgement. Although actually profoundly influenced by Marxism, in the sense of historical materialism (some would even say – I would myself now say – over-influenced by it) he had always angrily opposed political Marxism, or Leninism. The resurrection of civil society gave him the opportunity to denounce the latter once more, with enhanced satisfaction since this time it was once and for all. But, simultaneously, he had to promote and argue for an alternative. This could only be in practice the one to which he had become personally committed, after his return to Prague and his involvement in George Soros's Central European University. This academic enterprise is of course devoted to fostering civil society or, in Karl Popper's version of it, 'Open Society', throughout post-communist Eastern Europe.

'The central intuition of Marxism is to say: Civil Society is a fraud', he starts off.[3] That is, the notion of a self-standing plurality of institutions 'opposing and balancing the state' is supposedly perceived by historical materialists as a disguise for the effective dominance of other social forces, especially economic ones. It is these which covertly control both the state and all other institutions, reducing their professedly self-standing or independent status to that of a façade for, if not a tool of, the determining influence of property. The collapse in the 1980s of most of the societies founded on this economic and reductionist vision of history led (he argues) to 'a new counter-vision'. This was the emancipating concept of 'civil society'. The primary definition of the term is: 'A set of diverse non-governmental institutions which is strong enough to counterbalance the state and prevent it from dominating and atomising the rest of society.'[4]

The immediate or intuitive validity of the idea arose, naturally, from the way that people in the communist-bloc countries had in fact been dominated and atomised by authoritarian governments devoted to the old Holy Scrolls: vanguardism, proletarian internationalism, omnipotent economic planning and of course the constant and ritual denunciation of civil (or 'bourgeois', or 'petit-bourgeois') society.

Now, without for a moment defending any of these holy parchments or '-isms', it seems to me that Marxists were quite right about 'civil society', or at least, about the sociological concept of 'civil society'. They may have been right for the wrong reasons, and, as Gellner thought, at the cost of encouraging far worse ideas. None the less, it was not mistaken to think that the modern and contemporary resurrection of *societas civilis, la société civile*, is fraudulent in the sense of not denoting what it claims to. More accurately it is a myth. Whether or not there is in general terms something to be said for it, whether or not it is to some extent a benign rather than a malign delusion, and whether or not this belief has had some utility in the recent conditions of post-totalitarian break-up and reform, it does not deserve the grander theoretical and historical place now so regularly awarded it.[5]

The Exorcism of Autocracy

'Civil Society' is essentially a reactive idea. It has arisen and sometimes appealed quite widely in exceptional situations or moments of crisis, as a way of exorcising a certain type of threat. Thinkers from Adam Ferguson up to Gellner, via Antonio Gramsci, to whom I will return later, have striven to describe civil society as an actual or possible state of affairs, a societal reality distinct from and independent of the state. But it seems to me that its real charge is ideological or polemical. The accompanying evocative or inspirational force has always arisen from its direction, its denunciatory and argumentative thrust. 'Civil society' has always been aimed at the contrary idea (normally also the contrary fear and hatred) of an over-centralised, interfering, bureaucratically organised and would-be omnipotent state: the Sovereign State with a capital 'S' on both words, the Leviathan or great political monster which has repeatedly and menacingly arisen over the historical era stretching from the absolute monarchies of the seventeenth and eighteenth centuries up to the post World War II communist autocracies. 'Totalitarianism' was the twentieth-century progeny: Leviathans equipped with new techniques of physical and mental control and ultimately with military technology letting them literally obliterate opponents.

The etymology of terms like this is always important. So where did Leviathan's antithesis, 'Civil society', come from? Here at least there seems to be no doubt. The notion may be cloudy, but its origins are precise. As far as I know, every single treatise, article, political speech and argument about the notion agrees on that. The effective invention of the concept was by an eighteenth-century Gaelic-speaking minister of the Scottish Presbyterian church, Adam Ferguson.[6] He published *An Essay on the History of Civil Society* in 1767. It was an account of humankind's ascent from conditions of rude unlettered barbarism to those of cultivated and legally regulated society, and often reads like an earlier version of Gellner's many accounts of the transition from 'traditional' to modern society.

As the editor of the most important contemporary edition of the *Essay*, Duncan Forbes, points out, Ferguson knew better than most what he was talking about:

> The *Essay* was the work of a man who knew intimately, and from the inside, the two civilisations (for his Lowland friends, of course, there was only one) which divided eighteenth century Scotland: the *Gemeinschaft* of the clan, belonging to the past, the *Gesellschaft* of the 'progressive', commercial Lowlands.[7]

Thus, what was to be the long and distinguished (if somewhat salutary) career of 'Civil society' (both book and idea) began twenty-one years after the Battle of Culloden. Ferguson was twenty-three years old when Charles Edward Stuart's rebellion was finally defeated in April 1746, and along with it Gaelic-speaking clannic culture, the 'traditional society' of Perthshire which he had experienced as a boy. He came from the small village of Logierait, near Pitlochry, within the domain of the area's principal clan chief, the Duke of Atholl. To this day all tourists along the Perth–Inverness road enjoy a view of the splendid Ducal residence at Blair Atholl. Great Britain's last private army is still maintained there, and deployed for parade purposes on festive occasions.[8] But as Forbes indicates, there was nothing festive about it when Ferguson was growing up.

The Fergusons were dependants of the ruling family, since Adam's father was given the living at Logierait by the Duke. He was referred to by a later Hanoverian report on the endemic Jacobitism of the area, in terms requiring no comment:

> The Presbyterian Ministers are the only people we can trust, and to give you an idea of one small part of the country, I mean the country of Atholl, the Minister one Ferguson of Logierait, told me that if you were to hang throughout all that country indiscriminately, you would not hang three people wrongly.[9]

Later the theorist applied to succeed his father at Logierait church, but the Duke turned him down. One biographer suggests that Ferguson's abandonment of the clerical vocation – and presumably his career as an academic and writer – was provoked by lasting bitterness over this disappointment.[10]

Ferguson was better acquainted than most with the military side of the new British regime, though few commentators have thought this of any importance. He became an army chaplain and served for some years with the Black Watch regiment formed in 1737: one of the earlier Scottish contributions to the progress of British empire. He served with them in the Netherlands and took part in the Battle of Fontenoy, returning to England in 1745. Official anxiety about the loyalty of the regiment became acute during the Jacobite rebellion, so the chaplain was asked to explain things to them in Gaelic. He did so while it was still encamped at Camberwell, in a speech fortunately preserved and published in English translation in 1746, under an appropriately portentous title: *A Sermon Preached in the Ersh Language to His Majesty's First Highland Regiment of Foot, at their Cantonment at Camberwell, Translated into English for the Use of a Lady of Quality in Scotland, at whose desire it is now published.*

Ferguson's first publication was dire stuff. His American biographer David Kettler is reduced to remarking on how brimful with 'patriotic fervour' the sermon was: a series of eulogies of the Protestant-Hanoverian way, conventionally counterpointed against stern denunciations of The Pretender, Popery and wooden shoes. Although there is no way of knowing how it went down on Camberwell Common, Kettler admits that – 'All his life Ferguson retained a slightly patronising identification with his Highland schoolmates and comrades-in-arms, while never sharing their enthusiasm for "the good old cause"'.

Ferguson was born the same year as Adam Smith, 1723, and lived until 1816. After his time as a military chaplain he succeeded David Hume as Keeper of the Advocates Library in Edinburgh (the ancestor of the present-day National Library of Scotland). Later he was a Professor in both Edinburgh and Glasgow, and remained 'well-known as a disseminator of Whig views' in the revolutionary era.[11]

Civil Society Moralism

After 1746 both the menace of despotism and the ancient *Gemeinschaft* of pre-civil society disappeared together, leaving the way clear for Hanoverian progress, agricultural enclosure or clearance, and the development of trade and industry. By the time the *Essay* appeared in 1767 these developments had had a chance, and the political Union with England – still widely unpopular in 1745 although it had been set up a generation earlier, in 1707 – was more stable and accepted. Of course some, possibly most, of these socio-economic changes might have taken place anyway under a restored Stuart dynasty. However, that was how they actually occurred, as part of a great reinforcement and extension of the 1688 or Union state, now gaining the upper hand in its prolonged conflict with France.

One of the repercussions of that historical context was 'civil society'. The Treaty of Union set up a unique style of polity, whose dominant feature among the Scots (not of course among the English) turned out to be rule at an extraordinary distance, through the mediation of virtually self-managing institutions that were little interfered with by the state. These institutions were the traditional ones, the bodies of pre-eighteenth century Scottish society before its own parliament and state removed themselves to London after the 1707 merger. Such national institutions were now, so to speak, teleguided by a remote multi-national state. But the telepathy was intermittent and sometimes as open as an Ouija board to creative interpretation: by and large, absence of mind prevailed (and continued to prevail until the arrival of the Welfare State in the twentieth century). The legal system, the school and university system, and the churches were left alone to run their own business. Naturally a host of other things can be put under the same umbrella, like the Advocates Library I mentioned earlier – societies, clubs, private as well as Kirk schools, and associations for this and that.

But as soon as such lists appear, one is at grips with 'civil society', the diffuse assemblage of anything and everything which can be located somewhere in between politics and state power on one hand, and the family on the other.[12] So far, so banal: nobody would deny the existence or significance of such institutions, but in what sense do they compose an overall or corporate entity meriting a title like 'civil society'? In what sense are they self-standing or self-directing as distinct from control by Monarchs, politicians, policemen or administrators? Much justified puzzlement has always surrounded the concept. However, in eighteenth-century Scottish circumstances the answers to such questions were actually fairly clear, and also a matter of daily experience.

This is because they had been spelt out by the Treaty of Union. The new unified British regime was obliged by that very unusual constitutional deal to guarantee and maintain, necessarily at a distance, such a range of institutions and bodies 'for all time to come' – that is, the rights of Scottish sub-parliamentary or extra-political society, including its dispositions on property, local government, commercial and civil law, and so on. So it was relatively straightforward to perceive such an assortment of things both as having a common character, and as autonomous in the sense of not being state-dominated in a day-to-day sense. The common character was national; and the nation was now controlled politically from outside, by a centre most people felt to be remote. Hence the idea could take root of a developed or 'civil' society – an order 'apolitical' with the meaning of distinct from political interference or state-prescribed law and order, yet 'autonomous' in the sense of self-regulating and having a momentum of its own. And, of course, that idea did take root in Ferguson's *Essay*, which became a highly influential Enlightenment text. It was soon translated and studied every-where alongside Smith's *Wealth of Nations* and to some extent built into the mentality of the new political economy.

However, the specific national background was not carried forward with the idea itself, into the broader horizon of Enlightened thinking. Indeed one can almost say it was suppressed. Forbes puts it this way:

> There is no direct mention of the Highland clan in the *Essay*, which is not surprising; there is indeed nothing to suggest the author's origins. The Highland inspiration is clothed in the fashionable garb: admiration of Sparta, the contrast between classical public spirit and modern selfishness, the manners of the American Indian, and so on.[13]

Ferguson reclothed his ideas in the habitual mode of the *philosophes*, in fact, seeing contemporary developments through the lens of Greco-Roman Antiquity and classical literary precedent. In this way, universality was initially bestowed on a highly particular and indeed unique national dilemma.

As history the generalisation was mistaken. There was nothing truly self-standing, autonomous or magically apolitical about Edinburgh's Augustan Age, or its philosophy. Its unusual situation and cultural opportunities were made possible by an imposed state-level arrangement just mentioned, the Union Treaty. The latter was the 'written constitution', in so far as such a thing exists at all, of Great Britain, then becoming the dominant state in the world of primitive industrialisation. The Treaty itself was no emanation of socio-economic advancement: it was one longer-term by-product of William III's invasion and take-over of England and Scotland in 1688, and of his victory in Ireland at the Battle of the Boyne the following year. Even then, its strange provisions would only really be secured by the further, decisive military victory of 1746. The Jacobites remained pledged to repeal the Treaty if successful, and revert to the pre-1707 system of separate kingdoms and parliaments under a common Crown.

Seen in this light, the germ of 'civil society' begins to look much more like an accident: it was associated with the freak development of one national society, in the single generation between Culloden and the drastically new world created by the French Revolution after 1789. Nearly all the diagnoses of civil society's 'rise' or 'emergence' omit that particular history, for the sake of generalisation. They simply link the phenomenon to the familiar data of Enlightenment itself: the formation of an educated middle class, capitalist farming, the beginnings of industry and entrepreneurialism, urbanisation, and so forth. These were noticeable in Lowland Scotland and happened successively in most other places as well; hence, the assumption has been, whatever accompanied them would happen elsewhere too and be, as it were, part of the standard story. But actually civil society did not 'emerge' in the Scottish Lowlands as a natural side-effect of Improvement. What it reflected was a one-off conjuncture: institutional endowment from a previous state; a new, remote and wildly corrupt state authority; and then, after 1745–46, further military defeat and suppression, followed by heady colonial and mercantile expansion. Under such conditions it was tempting, and flattering to the self-consciously post-national intelligentsia of Edinburgh, to think that their society benefited from a peculiar new magic force – that it was self-moving or autonomous, and hence owed little or nothing to the state. In fact 'self-management' owed its being to the state, albeit indirectly: the political violence and counter-violence of the civil wars, the Cromwellian occupation and the Restoration all lay behind the moment of Scottish Enlightenment, as well as the Boyne and Culloden. However, these things could now be forgotten in the period of creative expansion after mid-century.

It may of course be argued that this chain of circumstances was not just unusual, but fortunate, or even blessed. Unionists from Cromwell up to Tony Blair have always believed so, and Ferguson, Smith, Hume and the other literati certainly did. They appreciated being run at a distance by a more or less foreign liberal-parliamentarist government uninterested in Scottish affairs, and strongly preferred that to another native and probably all-too-interested Stuart monarch. However, the point here is a different one. Whatever the temporary advantages in Edinburgh may have been, I am suggesting that comparatively little was really universalisable about the predicament. No other European societies chose to follow it as a developmental path, and indeed none, after 1789, were given the chance of doing so. The only societies in some ways like it, though only in very limited or piecemeal ways, were to be the distant colonial formations of Australasia and Canada.[14] But on the plane of theory and myth things were quite different. There, 'civil society' was to enjoy quite extraordinary luck.

This can be put in another way, in terms of national identity or, ultimately, of nationalism. Scottish society was as 'national' (as differentiated and 'peculiar') as anywhere else, but its odd early-modern political history of Union with a stronger neighbouring state ended by occluding or marginal-ising that identity and fostering the idea (mainly an illusion) of its being 'typical' or universalisable – the first developmental 'model', as it were. Because here institutions were unusually free from political and bureau-cratic interference, it was somewhat easier to go on and imagine institutions generally as totally freed and self-regulating. Social affairs could be per-ceived as regulating or governing themselves by intrinsic accord or mech-anisms inherent in human nature.

The ideal form which accompanied, and in a sense justified, 'civil society' was in fact the dominant moralism of the Scottish *philosophes*. Ferguson's *Civil Society* derived partly from Frances Hutcheson's *System of Moral Philos-ophy* (1755) and Adam Smith's *Theory of Moral Sentiments* (1759), treatises in which mankind's societal nature was analysed as based on 'sympathy' or – in more contemporary terms – as a kind of formative and pre-political bonding.[15] From this standpoint political economy – what became the theory of capitalism – was that much more visualisable. It could be perceived as an emanation of social conditions rather than as an operation of the state. A nationality which had abjured its state by treaty had also renounced – or at least distanced – the ordinary political expressions of particularity and growing developmental concern, such as a petty monarch and court, a resentful and frustrated gentry or intelligentsia struggling and failing to 'keep up with the Joneses', and a military caste diverting wealth into armament and display. These became the normal accompaniments of late-eighteenth-century development and nascent nationalism. There were great advantages in dispensing with them, for the first 'civil society': an odd sort of national liberation, indeed, in which progress seemed emancipated from political shackles and interference. However, this was also accidental rather than exemplary, and in the longer run would produce equally odd disadvantages (to which I will return below).

Anti-fascism to Anti-communism

Once launched in this fashion, the idea acquired its own life and times. I don't want, and anyway I don't have the space, to retrace these here today, through other Enlightenment theorists and on to Kant, Hegel, Marx, Engels and their progeny. But one of the progeny was to be particularly significant for us: Antonio Gramsci, 'the Alexis de Tocqueville of Marxism'.[16] He recuperated the idea in a distinctively left-wing and revolutionary sense, in the Italy of the 1920s and 1930s. 'Civil society' was originally a liberal conception, directed against the threats of absolute monarchy and clerical obscurantism, though often with a socially conservative cast. Emancipation from tyranny was emphatically not intended to bestow citizenship upon the rabble.

However, Gramsci appropriated and influentially redefined the idea to mean something like that. He contended that a revolutionary politics had to have its own, wider vision of non-state, self-standing society, and of the more deeply democratic social conditions under which capitalism and class rule might eventually be transcended. 'Between the economic structure and the State with its legislation and its coercion stands civil society, and the latter must be radically transformed, in a concrete sense and not simply on the statute-book', so that any new state form will rest upon a genuine social and cultural 'hegemony' (*egemonia*), rather than merely upon imposition and force.[17] The attainment of an effective *egemonia* depends upon a long and piecemeal 'war of position' different from the dramatically political or military 'war of manoeuvre' undertaken by the Bolsheviks in 1917. In Western circumstances socialists had to work at preparing hegemony before trying to seize and transform state authority. If they failed to do so they would risk the kind of crushing defeat suffered in Italy in the 1920s – the defeat at the hands of an exacerbated nationalism which had put Gramsci in jail for the rest of his life.

In the 1960s and 1970s this recuperation of 'civil society' naturally appealed to a whole generation of new left-wing thinkers and militants in the West. Those reared within the political stultification and conservative oppression of the Cold War discovered a new icon, an apparently non-dogmatic and anti-economistic forerunner who spoke to them in ironic, frequently sarcastic undertones utterly different from the loud brass of official Marxism-Leninism. Furthermore, his interests were obviously in what they found to be a sympathetic direction: literature, the unexpected undersides of public displays, the minutiae of popular culture and fashion, the world of implications sometimes discernible in small or unpretentious phenomena. All this could not but appeal to a generation undergoing the socio-cultural and lifestyle revolution of the late 1950s and the 1960s. And part of its glamour was the Gramscian representation of 'civil society' as a sphere which not only counted but maybe mattered more than the arid gymnastics of statism, whether in the practice of the East or the aspirations of communist parties in the West.

Sympathetic as the reaction was, it may also have been mistaken. Just as the founding moment of civil-society philosophy had rested on a fruitful misreading of eighteenth-century Scotland, the New Left's twentieth-century reanimation of the idea may have involved misunderstanding Gramsci, the *Quaderni* and inter-war Italy. Part of that mistake involved projecting – or too easily reprojecting – 'civil society' as a universal category. The strange itinerary of the handicapped Sardinian battling against the agonies of belated Peninsular nation-building was converted, over a generation later, into the message of the times. His heroic if cryptic denunciation of Italian fascism became the code for ideal escape from Cold War communism. And one aspect of this leap was again 'civil society' elevated from umbrella term to prescriptive category: it was made over into the standard precondition for socialist revolution in Western, hence in all modern, circumstances.

What this ignored was Gramsci's actual dour view of society. Non-state society was not rediscovered or enjoyed for its own sake, but with an absolutely statist redemption in mind. As Neil Harding points out in the most unsparing account of *Gramscismo* to appear so far, the point of paying such attention to socio-cultural diversity was really to get rid of it:

> It is precisely the pluralism of civil society that must be overcome for the good reason that it generates a plurality of identifiers and perpetuates superannuated ideas. The dense and diverse structures of civil society, far from being admirable bulwarks against the pretensions of the state, represent for Gramsci so many earthworks and defences which must be stormed and sacked in order that a coherent (therefore unitary) consciousness and organisation can be achieved.[18]

The circumstances of censored notebook composition compelled a detour through this pluralism, and the avoidance of an overtly anti-statist, and anti-national, rhetoric. But the point of it was to lay the foundations for the standard proletarian-internationalist state of Third International times: *il moderno principe* or radically Leninist polity within which society would be reconfigured to suit the vision of a commanding elite. Harding points out in conclusion how all Third International dogma was based on the catastrophe of World War I, the moment which had seen 'the fracturing of socialism and the demise of the Second International'. This was when 'the workers flocked to the colours, nation set on nation, fratricide consumed fraternity [and] the class struggle was declared suspended for the duration'.

Such a defeat was explained in terms of 'betrayal'. To ethical betrayal there corresponded a policy of ethical recovery, which demanded a ferocious Redeemer: the modern prince of Machiavellianism reborn. In the collective form of the Party, this radical force was supposed to reinstate the class struggle and render it immune to further betrayals – by putting down firmer roots in 'civil society'.

Alas, the radical force had also translated the Party into the Leader, representing the future but temporarily domiciled in Moscow. Notoriously, Gramsci had his problems with the Leader, particularly during the later years of imprisonment. This too endeared him to us, as intellectuals formed partly through a process of anti-Stalinism. But behind any disenchantment with 'crude' Russian hegemony lay a more powerful will towards, in Harding's words, 'a transcendent tactic and a sublime goal' in the sky of the new proletarian Enlightenment. This tactic may have required more consideration of the civil *differentiae* of society, but would in short order be subsumed into the strategy of a universal goal.[19]

Such universalism is the glory of intellectuals, but also their standing temptation.[20] Here as so often before it had led to the suppression, or at any rate the sidelining, of something vital about the diffuse range of things normally stowed under the 'civil society' umbrella. Societies are different: without plunging into the metaphysics of identity, I think it can be said they differ 'deeply' in the sense that the politico-cultural questions forced upon both parties and intellectuals remain unavoidably various or 'peculiar'. Peculiarity may not be the only universal, but it certainly is one. And one feature of 'peculiarity' is a cluster of things we call the national element. Agreed, 'national' is also a kind of sub-umbrella, which itself denotes untidy collections or families of phenomena. But I would suggest what it tends mostly to cover are those things which have proved indispensable to the actual (rather than the blueprint) development of modernity. They may not be 'more important' than faith, family and nature in any eternal sense; but at least for an historical season – the one in which we still appear to be living – they have proved their centrality. It may not be a matter of fate, blood or divine ordination; but 'nationality' has shown itself to be politically unavoidable. As if the nineteenth and early-twentieth centuries had not been enough, it reminded us of this all over again after 1989.

But I am only echoing Ernest Gellner here. Before he fell back on civil society in *The Conditions of Liberty* nobody had demonstrated more powerfully than he why nationalism had arisen, and why it is likely to go on existing. In this sense – to put it in a kind of shorthand – we should say that differentiation is of the essence of 'civil society'. But then, if we have to speak about 'civil societies' in the plural, might we not as well speak about nations, nationalities or countries, and so be more widely understood?

Fur Collars and Purple Suits

This carries me to my main point. We have seen how 'civil society' was coined in what one might call a denationalised social formation, where the abstract side of Enlightenment thinking found, or could be imagined as finding, an unusually immediate welcome and resonance. There, it was outside the metropolis and yet sheltered from the sort of anti-metropolitan reaction it encountered around the same time in, for example, Germany, and subsequently in Central and Eastern Europe. Yet the shelter was artificial, and temporary. The age which followed 1789 and lasted into the present, gaining renewed life and energy from the events of 1989 and after, is surely correctly labelled as 'the Age of Nationalism' – not as the Age of Ascendant Civil Society.

This is why the dust Gellner comments on had settled so heavily. Civil society began as one way of contesting and exorcising absolute monarchy, but evolved into an occasional or 'emergency' way of exorcising, or at least trying to moderate, the political effects of non-democratic statehood or nationalism (or both together). In the last-mentioned context, the very indeterminacy of the notion has been useful. I don't think that Gellner's efforts to blow the dust off in *The Conditions of Liberty* did much to make it clearer; but perhaps the task was just impossible.

'Civil society' is also a version of 'internationalism'. But the Cold War years had made political internationalism into a very difficult rhetorical property. On the one hand, the Marxian-proletarian version had become intolerably confused with Soviet-Russian ambitions as well as with abusive state autocracy. On the other, liberal-democratic internationalism remained uncomfortably close to NATO, the remains of West European empire and an unpalatably American hegemony. However, the fuzzier and more high-sounding civil-society concept still hung around, apparently recuperable. Could it yet be turned into, so to speak, a fallback position for middle-class internationalists? In this role it recommended itself particularly to all those who had misunderstood Gellner, or read him one-sidedly. That is, to everyone convinced that narrow or atavistic nationalism had become the malefactor-in-chief of the new world order.

It was clearly not enough to preach formal democracy alone as the cure, since democratic majorities were capable of supporting intolerant national-ist parties and leaders. In the ex-Yugoslav countries, as soon as people were allowed to vote freely they voted in the first instance for such parties. It was not in fact clear that they would vote the same way in the second or other instances. Also, their attitude could hardly fail to have been configured by the long preceding experience of an assertively multi-ethnic state which, simultaneously and preposterously, had denied them democratic expression *and* claimed to have resolved all ethnic and national questions. However, these were very knotty issues. A quick-fire diagnosis was easier, and was demanded in the post-1989 rapids. Democracy was lacking something in post-communist circumstances; and this might be it. 'Civil society' gave quite a plausible if hasty interview for the job. Was this not the unaccountably overlooked essence of non-state culture, the social secret required for democratic forms to be genuinely effective? The elixir of autonomous, sub-political civilisation was missing, therefore, but the new dusted-down candi-date suggested that it could in time be supplied, naturally from the direction of the Atlantic. This institutional *Geist* would then be capable of standing up to any new Leviathans, or to nationalist madmen like Milosevic and Meciar. Liberal social trust would take over from blood-based *ethnos* and detestation of the Other.

This takes us back to Gellner's situation in the composition of *Conditions of Liberty*, as part of the Central European University's missionary drive across Central and Eastern Europe. Internationalism has always been conjoined with moral fervour, a posture he was never comfortable with. Scepticism and irony were his normal response to manifestations of it, notably from nationalists. But then he had a convincing theory about nationalism and its capacity for delusion. He did not, unfortunately, have a comparable theory of internationalism and its distinctive perils. It is quite true he would usually cite 'Megalomania' as the rhetorical counterpart of the prototypical new-nationalist land of 'Ruritania' (complete with prophet, paranoia, poetry, policemen and gagged press). However, the sins of the Habsburgs and the Windsors tended in practice to be viewed somewhat more indulgently. These earthly repositories of universalist blather and pretended superiority were judged as being on the whole more favourable to Gellner's enduring touchstone: the earthy individualism of the Good Soldier Schweik. In this sense, I suspect that 'civil society' was for him always really Schweikland, the country where decent tongue-in-cheek dog-catchers were allowed to muddle through, and occasionally get the better of Authority.

This Hasek–Orwell note is equally noticeable in many of the civil-society treatises and sermons which have appeared since the mid-1980s. We saw earlier how 'civil society' originated in a milieu of pervasive moralism and concern over the foundations of human sympathy and trust. These motifs have all duly resurfaced in association with the reborn concept. John A. Hall's book *Civil Society: History, Theory, Comparison*[21] for example, begins like this:

> Civil society was placed at the forefront of public attention by attempts to establish decency in societies where it had most conspicuously been absent. Civil society was seen as the opposite of despotism, a space in which social groups could exist and move – something which exemplified and would ensure softer, more tolerable conditions of existence.

And it ends with Salvador Giner's rather despairing redefinition of this space, as something under siege even in the West itself, from the combined assault of technology and democracy. From this angle, civil society must be understood as 'the sphere of that which is relatively but autonomously private within a modern polity'. But such privacy does not seem secure anywhere. Hence,

> Tomorrow's citizens ought to be aware that often people of power through-out our societies no longer truly believe in its virtues and benefits, though they are forced, constitutionally as it were, to pay their public respects to it. For many of those who still proclaim the need for a flourishing civil society actively help the advent of a bleak universe in which, were they to succeed, there would be no need whatsoever for it.[22]

A dying fall indeed. Having been identified with an essentially non-definable entity, 'decency' ends by threatening to evaporate altogether into a bleak universe of lip service, irrelevance and hypocrisy. After all, in the epitome of Atlantic civilisation's civil society, the United States, half the population doesn't even bother voting. Part of what Giner is warning against, in somewhat coded style, is presumably the New Right belief that formal democracy and market economics alone can guarantee respect for dog-catchers: that is, for autonomy, privacy and the other virtues of a civil society. Yet if its prospects are as grim as that, how can it be promoted with such confidence as the main therapy for East European recovery and progress? If no form of state power can be counted on to uphold decent freedoms and minority rights, then it becomes difficult to do anything except moralise, sometimes with the sense of shouting into the wind.

Well, things are not as bad as this. Without, I hope, resorting to a vulgarly Panglossian position of inevitable or automatic betterment, one may nevertheless suspect that something has been seriously amiss with both the idea and the political deployment of 'civil society'. It was always a polemical metaphor, a tool of earnest argument rather than description. And what it was preparing the ground for, above all in the post-1989 world, is on the whole better, or anyway less inadequately, called 'civic nationalism'. I suggested earlier that 'civil society' was originally and has remained a way of occluding or disregarding differentiation, particularly in the sense of nationality, and 'national character' or identity. Although first directed against the capital-letter State of Absolutist Monarchy, it has been successively rephrased as an ethical critique of both right- and left-wing autocratic statehood – the Leviathans of both 'ethnic nationalism' (including Fascism) and Communism. Since the latter lost trousers, shirt and Leviathan credentials in the 1980s, and nationality politics reasserted themselves instead, it was abruptly inflated into a general remedy or cure-all: the great Atlantic or Western snake-oil treatment which, if only applied with sufficient regularity and sincerity east of Prague, would somehow guarantee the 'transition' to both democracy and a market-based economy there.[23]

The structure of ideas here is that 'formal', state-level, merely political and party democracy provides inadequate defences against 'nationalism', perceived as inherently ethnic, divisive, inward- and backward-looking, atavistic, aggressive and probably not too good for business either. Proletarian internationalism having been such a sensational failure, a different but much subtler version of what Marxists would once have dismissed as 'bourgeois internationalism' was needed. Formal democracy alone was an inadequate standard. Nor would crass free-trade ideology do on its own. The aspiring multi-nationalism of the European Union was, to put it mildly, far from becoming another Megalomania, and not yet in a fit condition for new tenants. America was too far away. But there was always 'civil society', the reified essence of progress, decency, trust, tolerance and all the other 'conditions of liberty' which Gellner's book sought to define.

He was criticised subsequently for placing overmuch stress upon economics and, in effect, agreeing with his political foe Vaclav Klaus that a free market was the principal condition of liberty.[24] But this is not really surprising, since, to be Irish about it, 'civil society' is by definition indefinable. There is no clear or sustainable theoretical distinction either between society (in the requisite 'associational' sense) and the economy, or between society and the political state. Having undertaken to award theoretic location and name to the entity, Gellner found himself driven to a distinctly over-economic rendition of the theme. Having declared nationalism as perilous and democracy as insufficient, he tends to end up with the market as sole guarantor.

In the winter of 1993–94 – around the time when *Conditions of Liberty* was coming off the presses – I commuted regularly to the Central European University's Prague campus in Olsanské Square, where Gellner had his office. For non-Czech-speaking drivers the interminable avenues of rush-hour Žižkov were enlivened by English-language news broadcasts. The unvarying subject of the 8.30 bulletin was the daily achievements of Vaclav Kraus's neo-liberal regime: successful privatisations accomplished in the month of February, promising overtures from Brussels or NATO, granitic stability of the new Czech crown, Western visitors paying homage to Havel in his castle – and so on. The air which had once reverberated to the achievements of the Plan and the transition to communism now imparted – in curiously similar tones – the advent of the market and Bohemia's forced march to freedom. Just below the CEU building (formerly a trade-union hostel) began that zone of narrowing streets I always thought of as 'fur-collar corner', where from early morning BMWs would park illegally in front of shiny new private banks. In the critical essay I mentioned above Charles Turner has a good phrase for this:

> Gellner has no more regard than anyone else for the purple-suited men with gold chains and tennis socks now strutting about the cities of Eastern Europe. But perhaps the sight of them breaks the more precious chain which linked virtue to production by saturating production with virtue.

I admit I never actually saw a purple suit there but that may be a seasonal phenomenon like the tennis socks. More important, this too was the voice of civil society and – without snobbishness or phoney anti-materialism – might indeed be considered a weak, or at least an insufficient, link in the new social fabric. It may have been a necessary condition of democratic freedom and rejoining the wider world, and also a lot better than the old Czecho-Slovak socialism. Schweik would have loved tennis socks and BMWs, undoubtedly. Like my then landlord out by the tram station in Konevova, he would have made the leap from apparatchik dog-catcher to property-dealer in a flash. But I doubt if this was a sufficient condition of either democracy or liberal betterment, as civil-society theorists wished us to believe.

'Civic Nationalism'

In the new Czech Republic as elsewhere, the state alone structures and sustains associational society, even if, as in the original Scottish case, it does so at a distance, indirectly, or by mediated (or even concealed) procedures and institutions. The necessarily differentiated character of the society depends upon an equivalently differentiated state or apparatus of power; not the other way round. In other words, a 'civil' social order (with the sense of 'decency', privacy, individual and group or minority rights, freedom of initiative and enterprise, etc.) depends in the long run upon an appropriately civic form of national identity. The latter can also be called 'nationalism' unless it is insisted that 'nationalism' means necessarily and everywhere, in the last resort, ethnic nationalism.[25] But I think this is simply an understandable conceptual error, derived from the anti-imperial strife of the past century.

It is also too vast a theme to embark on here and now. Instead, let me return to the notion's country of origin. If a certain impatience, or even intemperate annoyance, with 'civil society' has appeared to surface now and then, it is for reasons lying in that direction. This is a field in which everyone has some sort of slant or vested emotive interest, and I would be the last to pretend otherwise. The bias of relativism is never a substitute for the truth, but none the less nourishes the search for it. In a study mentioned earlier, Lindsay Paterson's *The Autonomy of Modern Scotland,* these reasons are very well summed up. 'Civil society' may have originally been a kind of accident, fortunate or otherwise, but the population among whom the accident occurred have now endured it for over two centuries. Alongside David McCrone's *Understanding Scotland: The Sociology of a Stateless Nation,*[26] Professor Paterson's book portrays the history and society of post-Fergusonian Scotland from 1816 down to the present, and compares it to other small nations. These comparisons are by no means always unfavourable to Scotland – on the contrary, McCrone and Paterson show convincingly that the Scots often did very well out of their 'silent way' to prosperity. At least within the British imperial framework, itself a passing accident of history, a marginal 'civil society' flourished rather well without statehood and separate political identity.

However, the silent way could not last for ever. The British equivalent of France's post-war *trente glorieuses* produced restlessness and a desire for liberation among the Scots too. A form of political nationalism appeared in the 1960s. But this was not simply a wish for exit from the United Kingdom: it was, in effect, the desire to escape from 'civil society' and resume business as political society. The homeland of the concept had overdosed on it, in other words, and wanted to grow up. It was, as apologists have invariably said, 'decent' enough all right. Alas, decency was compatible with – and indeed inevitably expressed through – a basically resentful dependence and collective impotence, and the turgid misery of bureaucracy or 'low politics'. On its own, cut off by these strange conditions from normal or 'high politics', civil society itself can amount to a kind of ailment, a practically pathological condition of claustrophobia, cringing parochialism and dismal self-absorption. No one would claim such symptoms are confined to Scotland, of course; sink-bottom 'provincialism' has been a common feature of modern development, frequently pilloried in its literature. However, chosen provinciality is worse – the Siamese-twin condition of nationality linked to abdication, then endured, and sometimes justified, as a kind of fate.

The artist Ian Hamilton Finlay once replied to a TV interview question from Melvyn Bragg that he could never talk about Scotland because it was like 'the shadow on his heart'. The shadow of 'civil society', I feel inclined to add.[27] Apologists of the idea may be right to say that tolerable modernity depends upon something like that: one may not be able to live without it. But the necessary condition will never be a sufficient one. Neither should any society live by it alone, or imagine there can be a magically civil key to trouble-free statehood. Differentiated civil identity seems to be what peoples want; its attainment and maintenance demand modern 'identity politics', the same thing as politicised or state-configured nationality. Finlay's artistic response has been a curious cult of civic nationalism founded upon a graphic and sculptural worship of the French Revolution's most extreme moment, the Jacobinism of Saint-Just and Robespierre. This too is myth country, which I would not defend in any literal sense; but it may be preferable to the Copernican universe of 'civil society'.

5

The Curse of Rurality:
Limits of Modernisation Theory

Northern Ireland, the Basque country, Corsica, Bosnia-Herzegovina, Ngorno-Karabakh: this list of familiar trouble spots is neither complete nor extended beyond Europe, in which case it would be at least eight times longer.[1] Originally coined for Ireland, 'troubles' in this sense have multiplied and become global, notably since 1989. No serious newspaper and few TV bulletins are without their quota of violent trouble items, which often enough make up most of the news.

Under such a barrage it is easy to feel 'trouble' as a climate of the age, and link it to one indiscriminate '-ism' or another. Yet even from the restricted sample quoted something else may spring to the eye, not so easily classified. Most such ethno-nationalist conflicts seem to go on recurring in predominantly rural situations. Nor are these 'rural' merely in the sense of being agricultural or non-urban – like East Anglia, say, or the Beauce plain in central France. No, they are areas where 'rural' tends to mean 'peasant' – that is, where an historical pattern of small landholding prevails, or has until recently prevailed, marked by intense heritable rights, rigid morality or faith, customary exclusivity and an accompanying small-town or village culture.

It is certainly also true that the troubles are not literally confined to the countryside. Thus, Sarajevo was a key site for a good deal of what was, none the less, more accurately described as the Bosnian 'village war'. ETA is notoriously active and supported in the industrial suburbs of Bilbao and San Sebastian, as well as in the Basque mountain heartland. Belfast has undeniably been the focus of much of the Ulster conflict, and witnessed the forced segregation of the contending communities among different streets or quarters, as well as into separate farm-towns or hamlets.

However, in none of these examples did the conflict itself originate in the cities. In Ireland, for instance, it notoriously derives on both sides from a centuries-old struggle over land rights – as Colm Tóibín wrote in his thoughtful travel book about the Northern Ireland frontier, *Walking the Border*, it came out of the 'good and bad blood' generated by violent expropriation, and involved both literal and land hunger. Whatever else it may have become, today's Sinn Féin is also the inheritor of Republicanism's old social ideal: the rural and pious peasant-family utopia which inspired the Irish Constitution, and regulated most of its strategic development from 1922 until Ireland's entry to the European Community in 1975. The resultant generational warfare may penetrate or even take over cities, the urban sites to which extended families of land-dwellers have moved or, sometimes, been expelled. But the violent side of the conflicts appears invariably to have its origin in the peasant or small-town world they have left behind.

Also, such violence may for a time – maybe quite a long time – be aggravated by the transition itself. 'Urbanisation' is the smooth-sounding, impersonal term for what was often an agonising process: the fearful undertow of modernity. During it rural emigrants look backwards as much as forwards, and pass from the remembrance to the often elaborate reinvention of the worlds they have lost. They are helped to do so by other strata without direct connection to the land. Some urban classes have a parallel if different motivation – above all, the intellectuals. They are seeking to 'mobilise' lost-world psychology in order to build a new world, that of the modern nation-state. Eventually this may owe very little to the old rural existence and its folk memories; yet while the original nation-building alliance holds good the debt feels important, and will go on finding expression in myths of rootedness. Hence many traits of the abandoned world may continue to 'haunt' an existence in other ways apparently broken in to city existence and civic conditions.

It seems to me there is another term for such haunting: ethnic nationalism. Ethnic nationalism is in essence a peasantry transmuted, at least in ideal terms, into a nation. Granted, the formation of modern national identities has notoriously involved a multiplicity of other factors, all attended to by different brands of social scientist: states, frontiers, literacy, industrialisation, school systems, symbols and complex cultural artefacts. But it can be read along this other axis too. Underneath all the accumulating paraphernalia of the modern lies a prolonged and massive social Calvary out of peasant subsistence and towards eventual urban inter-dependence. On that level of the *Gemeinschaft–Gesellschaft* journey terrible accidents have been common. Peasantries may be 'reimagined' essentially as a form of leverage, a way of helping to erect the modern nation, and in the end such imagining of communities may turn into green politics and ecology. However, it is not impossible for the instrumental lever to assume a life of its own and, at least for a time, to take over and dominate the processes by which nations are built.

The late Edward Thompson was insistent on how the working class was present at its own birth: it was not only modelled by impersonal forces, he explained, it helped to make even its early history. But most 'workers' originated as ex-peasants. In many parts of the world they for long tried to combine aspects of both fates, and still do so today – most strikingly in the East Asian societies representing the latest round of industrial development. Nor, when it came to 'making', have they operated exclusively in the social,

forward and outward-looking spirit most approved by our century's socialists. Escape or flight backwards or sideways have also figured prominently –
movement away from the rules of a 'progress' whose burdens or sacrifices
came to seem, or were made to seem, insupportable. Occasionally such
flights have taken the form of short cuts to Utopia, a magically foreshor-
tened 'End of History'.

One of the most revealing took place in Cambodia, between 1975 and
1979. There, a significant and concentrated historical attempt was made
literally to reverse the entire process – to abort urbanisation altogether and
forcibly reconstitute peasant society into a different sort of nation, what Ben
Kiernan in his new study calls 'the indentured agrarian state'.[2] Everyone has
heard of the horrors accompanying this attempt. And yet the episode itself
remains ill-understood. In its own day the Cambodian revolution was
interpreted by the outside world primarily in terms of Cold War dogmatics,
as an aberration of Communism or Marxist ideology. But in the longer
retrospect so thoroughly divulged by Ben Kiernan's new book, *The Pol Pot
Regime*, one can see the inadequacy of that prism. Other co-ordinates were
much more important. The Cambodian Hell was more truly an aberration
of nationalist development than of socialism. Hence from the vantage point
of 1996 it appears quite differently: as an extraordinary precursor of today's
ocean of 'troubles'. Twenty years before such crises became common with
the collapse of communist state-power, it demonstrated fully how devastating
the exercise of that power could be upon an explicitly ethnic or racial-
nationalist template.

'In this book I shall show that Khmer Rouge conceptions of race
overshadowed those of class', Kiernan states firmly in his introduction. 'In
terms of population as well as of territory, history was to be undone',
through absolute central control devoted, with ever increasing fervour and
ruthlessness, to what was then not yet known as 'ethnic cleansing'. The aim
of Pol Pot's revolution was a pure-blood and almost entirely rural, self-
sufficient Khmer nation-state. The shadow cast across history by the retreat-
ing peasantry is generally much longer and deeper than most analyses have
acknowledged. And in Cambodia, certain exceptional circumstances let it
attain for four years to an unexampled and murderous darkness. There, the
political instruments of 'revolutionary' modernity were consecrated to the
reconstruction of a nativist countryside – the rooted, Edenic community
that had supposedly existed before the time of cities, social classes and
individual guilt or shame.

A Dark Monkey from the Mountains

His real name was Saloth Sar. 'Pol Pot' – an emblematic title in the tradition
of twentieth-century communist rebaptism – was not disclosed to the world
until 14 April 1976, when he became Prime Minister of the new revolutionary government in Phnom Penh. The Saloth family were peasants all right
(12 hectares, 6 buffalo) but with a difference. They had royal connections.

His cousin was a palace dancer and 'favourite wife' to a king. An elder brother found employment as a lackey, and the future dictator joined him there at the age of six. As Kiernan points out, 'he never worked a rice field or knew much of village life . . . few Cambodian childhoods were so removed from their vernacular culture'.

He went on to a royal monastery and a Catholic school for the privileged. It is still astonishing to recall just how privileged: with a population of about seven million and after nearly a century of French colonial occupation, there was very little secondary education in Cambodia and no higher education at all. When independence was granted in 1953 only 144 Cambodians had the *baccalauréat*. While in France Saloth Sar met the woman who became his wife in 1956, Khieu Ponnary: she was the first Khmer woman to graduate from high school. So it is not surprising that even elite Khmers felt like country bumpkins in the wider world. When he first reached Saigon in 1948, on his way to Paris, Saloth and the other twenty-year-old with him felt themselves to be like 'two dark monkeys from the mountains'.

His scholarship was meant to turn him into a radio electrician, but it failed. He joined the French Communist Party (Cambodian Section) instead, and took part in the exiled independence movement. To avoid persecution the émigré cadres habitually used *noms de plume* like 'Khmer Worker', but Saloth Sar's was unusual: 'khmaer da'em' or 'original Cambodian', an anticipation of that fidelity to native essence which, twenty years later, would turn Phnom Penh inside out and build the skull mountains at Tuol Sleng extermination centre.

Not, as Kiernan immediately observes, that much of this showed on the surface, either in Paris or later. A consensual social view of Saloth emerges from the many careful references in this book: only with some difficulty would butter have melted in his mouth. In public he always displayed the Palace façade – personally 'charming, self-effacing', cultivated, 'genteel' and quite humorous, and rarely showing anger in public. There is one account of Pol Pot's breaking someone's leg in a vicious punishment session: his own Deputy Prime Minister, Vorn Vet (p. 437). But otherwise no record suggests burning eyes, Mussolinian blustering-sessions or *heimatisch* warblings like the lyrics of Radovan Karadzic. In general, the outstanding serial killer of the age shrouded his resentment so well that few could have known what it portended.

This remained tragically relevant for the episode to which many readers will turn in such a definitive volume: the murder of Malcolm Caldwell (pp. 442–50). In December 1978 a small group of independent Western observers were finally allowed into Democratic Kampuchea, as the country had been renamed. They included two American journalists and Caldwell (an academic then teaching at London University), all seen by the regime as broadly sympathetic to its revolution. As well as his journalism, an impressive intellectual record made Caldwell particularly important: in contrast to conventional Marxism, studies like his *The Wealth of Some Nations*[3]

advocated rural-centred development and self-sufficiency as the revolutionary path most appropriate for Third World conditions, and he was just then
working on a development of the thesis to be called 'Kampuchea: Rationale
for a Rural Policy'.

The group was toured round and lied to in the usual fellow-travelling
way, but proved quite stubborn: 'This group is not yet clear on human
rights. Whatever way we try to explain it to them, they refuse to understand',
wrote back the tour reporter. They kept on asking to see people already
slaughtered, which called for an endless parade of unlikely excuses. Armed
overseers and children in rags insistently obtruded on the view, and
Caldwell's diary soon included potentially lethal comments like: 'I have seen
the past, and it works' or 'They've not much to show us in the way of
development projects'. Like many socialist intellectuals of the time, Caldwell's bitter disenchantment with USSR-style development inclined him all
too strongly to favour alternative formulae. But he was also a very honest
man, and less inclined than some others to ignore eye-witness evidence.
This alone was enough to ensure execution in Democratic Kampuchea.

Caldwell may also have unwittingly displayed other credentials which
served to distinguish him from his companions (Elisabeth Becker of the
Washington Post and Richard Dudman from the *St Louis Post-Dispatch*). As a
Scottish nationalist he wrote that he found Democratic Kampuchea's wish
to 'make new things Cambodian' quite sympathetic – and yet, far too
crudely and chauvinistically anti-Vietnamese. This latter sentiment, notes
Kiernan, was 'unlikely to have pleased his hosts'. Unusually among Western
leftists of the era, he also clung to a vaguely neo-Calvinist religious faith,
which made him far too concerned with what had happened to Buddhism
(the near-universal culture of pre-1975 Cambodia). The Buddhist religion
had been proscribed and many of its temples destroyed. In short Caldwell
'understood' Pol Pot's project better than anyone else, including its ideological dimension – yet his conduct on the visit showed he could never be
trusted simply to regurgitate such sympathy.

At the end of the tour an interview was granted with the Leader, described
as 'friendly' and mainly concerned with agriculture. At 1 a.m. the next
morning an intruder broke into the government guest-house and shot
Caldwell dead. Then the intruder was shot dead in turn by guards, who
were themselves almost immediately executed after 'confessing', etc., to
being in the service of Vietnam. A few days later Hanoi did indeed launch
the great military offensive which would put an end to the Khmer Rouge
state. The truth will never be known, since no witnesses survive and Pol Pot
is now believed to be dead as well, though any reader of this book will want
solid evidence of a stake through the heart. But Kiernan obviously thinks
the Vietnamese had nothing to do with Caldwell's assassination. The mild-
mannered despot who looked 'incapable of killing a chicken' knew an
obdurate and unbiddable character when he met one. And the fact that
Caldwell 'understood' so well made him more dangerous, not less: who
could keep tabs on him back in London? The informed criticisms of a

respected sympathiser would be much more telling than the routine anti-communist rhetoric which at that time passed for comment on the Cambodian Revolution.

Living for Death

In a three-hour speech delivered on 27 September 1977 Pol Pot included a few words in honour of the national anthem of Democratic Kampuchea:

> Our national anthem clearly shows the essence of our people's struggle. As you know, our national anthem was not composed by a poet. Its essence is the blood of our entire people. This blood call has been incorporated into the national anthem.[4]

A colossal amount of actual blood was wasted by the Khmer Rouge regime. Kiernan estimates it as about 20 per cent of the previous population, or 'at least 1.5 million. Twenty years before Rwanda, the DK regime was on a genocidal track. There is no reason to believe the killing would have slowed, had it not been stopped by the Vietnamese army.'[5]

However, the anthem (which did in fact mention blood in almost every line) was not exalting mere haemoglobin. 'Blood' in this essentialist sense is the precious, inherited gist of an 'entire people', the secret of a nation passed on in trust from one generation to the next. But 'entire people' should not be read literally either: the meaning was not everybody who lived in pre-1975 Cambodia, and not even everyone 'of Khmer descent' in a certifiable or physical sense. Phnom Penh and the *ancien régime* had been full of traitors and *vendus*, as well as foreigners. These false Khmers had to be got rid of, which could be done only with the assistance of a 'true Khmer' stereotype. Although the Marxist ideology deployed by Pol Pot prescribed 'workers and peasants' for the slot, in practice Cambodia had only peasants. Not just any peasants, however: the well-off ones were no good, since privilege might have aligned them with the enemy. It had to be the poor – or, in terms of ancient piety, the simple – peasants who bore the blood burden of the national soul. This is why they figured so prominently in the hectorings of the Khmer Rouge ideologist Khieu Samphan:

> Did university graduates know anything about the true natural sciences? No, everything was done according to foreign books and foreign standards. Therefore it was useless. By contrast our children in the rural areas have always had very useful knowledge. They can tell you which cow is tame and which is skittish. They can mount a buffalo from both sides. They are practically masters of nature [and] only this should be called natural science because it is closely connected with the reality of the nation, with the ideas of nationalism, production, national construction and national defence.[6]

Such true Khmers had to re-educate their fallen cousins in the meaning of 'national'. That was best accomplished on the spot, close to the soil. Instead of taking peasant brigades to the cities, therefore, the cities were emptied out into the fields. Foreign obsessions and selfish individualism would be beaten out of them there, by a regime of productive if arduous labour which would also raise food production and make Cambodia self-sufficient, or 'truly independent'. This would swiftly bring about 'a clean social system, a new society sound, clean, free of corruption, hooliganism, graft, embezzlement, gambling, prostitution, alcoholism, or any kind of hazardous games'.

All those who could not or would not be cleaned up, died. Betrayal of the slightest unclean impulse meant extinction. Pol Pot and Khieu Samphan were of course influenced by the Chinese Cultural Revolution. That is, they thought the Red Guards had chickened out. After beating up a few *ancien régime* egg-heads they stopped short of serious measures like vacating Peking and abolishing money. Now it was up to Cambodia. The flames of peasant nationalism had been fanned by Mao's Great Leap Forward. But the same fire was far more intense among the Khmers, a small and historically vulnerable people equipped with a relegation complex and an indurate hatred for its neighbours. By harnessing and directing that, the Cambodian Party thought it had the possibility of really forging an exemplary rural-socialist state. For the first time in modern history, 'autarchy' or total self-sufficiency might be realisable.[7] Caldwell had envisaged such a model theoretically, but without imagining its bloody potential.

As we saw earlier, Kiernan believes ethnic purity was one key theme in the resultant Cambodian frenzy. The other was what he calls 'the struggle for central control', or 'the Khmer Rouge Center's unceasing struggle for top-down domination'. However, the one really implied the other. Stereo-typically simple peasants could not themselves plan or organise their new hegemony, or decide who were the incompatible elements and what to do with them. That was the task of the Party. It spoke 'in the name of' the soil-cultivators, of course, as orthodox communists did for the working class. But knowledge of tame and skittish cows did not take it far, and neither did a traditional rankling sense of 'us and them'. Most of the message had therefore to be made up by the revolutionaries as they went along. General Marxist apologetics was too forward-looking to contribute much: however deluded in detail, it was at least devoted to an imminent industrialised future, and to out-producing capitalism in its own unclean terms. The ethno-nationalist stereotype, by contrast, offered significant advantages as an instrument of control and coercion.

Ethnic boundaries are for the most part both murky and alterable. They compose a sign system which lays claim to natural and self-evident status – something like the obvious contrast between, say, a Rwandan Hutu and a Chinaman. But in reality comparatively few signs carry such blatant meaning, and for these the sub-ethnic category of 'race' tends to be employed. Most ethnic markers rely on language (learnable), customs (adoptable or forgettable), faith (acquirable), or still more imprecise configurations like 'national character', common history or memory. One implication is that it often is quite difficult to contradict a verdict about just who is a what. When authority decides the matter, in effect it decrees: so-and-so either was or was not a 'Khmer' or, more to the point after 1975, a 'true Khmer', genetically patented to sustain the revolution of authentic Khmerism rather than to betray it. Mercifully, people do not carry around DNA birth charts or gene tattoos to refute such decisions. In practice contesting them involves something like an argumentative legal battle, with the production and weighing of evidence before a qualified and preferably impartial tribunal. But few are ever really in a position to undertake such procedures – and in the fury of revolutionary warfare, none at all were. Hence the decree was normally immediate, and final. In Democratic Kampuchea the Centre (*Angkar*, 'the organisation') tailored Khmerness to fit the rules of its rural-national Utopia; but as time passed that meant simply to suit itself, or the day's message from the Leader. Central control gains its own momentum, in other words, and, as in post-Yugoslav Serbia, may then turn nationalism into the most malleable instrument of absolutism. This is why, as Kiernan underlines in his too brief Conclusion to his book: 'Despite its underdeveloped economy, the regime probably exerted more power over its citizens than any state in world history.'

A further advantage of nationalism for autocrats lies in its fictive kinship. The idealised nation is perceived as a vastly extended family. This is supposed to bestow a general sense of psychic belonging and community, or, in the Cambodian case, of rural-commune solidarity. In many cases, what it most observably does is to legitimate the actual extended-family behaviour of a leadership clique. As in Syria and Iraq, Cambodian central power gravitated quite naturally into the hands of family relations: the 'people one can trust' from a particular kin network or village area. Nationalism sanctifies nepotism; but also, nepotism can be in a sense exalted by a genetically oriented or ethnic nationalism. As Karl D. Jackson wrote some years ago:

> In essence the concept of collective leadership was infused into the tradition of Khmer family power. Rivals within the Communist movement were tortured and executed in large numbers along with their spouses, indicating the degree to which the Khmer leadership perceived power as flowing along family lines; to destroy an important political opponent it was necessary to root out the entire family.[8]

The 'rooting out' procedure can never be completed. Behind it lies a violent struggle for 'top-down domination' requiring a constant flow of new evidence of the enemy or anti-nation. Since it serves directly to justify power, such evidence must be made visible and catalogued for future time: proof of true descent, as it were, the birth certificate of Utopia. Tuol Sleng's function was to provide this. The agony of its victims was secondary, and their possible repentance unimportant: only seven survived (accidentally) of the over fourteen thousand sent there. The aim was proud commemoration. Their piteous confessions and photographs were filed for the gaze of Pol Pot and his lineage, and much of the archive has survived. In 1996 a BBC television programme, 'The Works', followed the activity of two American photographers in Phnom Penh, Chris Riley and Doug Niven. Twenty years later they are still labouring to complete the record of depravity, unearthing dusty negatives and yellowing log-books, and interviewing ex-prison guards.

Hell-holes are as distinctive as the revolutions they serve. Although Hitler and Stalin dealt in much larger numbers than Pol Pot, the latter greatly excelled them in puritanical zeal and ethnic thoroughness. 'Smashing' was the favourite Khmer Rouge term, and in fact simple rustic methods – boot, knife, water immersion, a blow to the head to save bullets – realised their purpose better than the high technology of Auschwitz and Sobibor.

Apocalypse Then

In *Peasants*,[9] his classical introduction to peasant anthropology, Eric Wolf observes how rural history has been punctuated by extraordinarily cruel uprisings: *jacqueries*, a fourteenth-century term, where 'the peasant band sweeps across the countryside like an avalanche' and tries literally to drown its oppressors in blood. This 'seems in curious contradiction to the everyday life of the peasant, which appears to be spent in such docile drudgery upon the land', and was often associated with millennialist visions of an imminent new order. Inevitably, such convulsions generated an even more violent reaction, like that called for in Martin Luther's infamous pamphlet of May 1525 – *Against the Robbing and Murdering Hordes of Peasants*. The cure was to be cruder than the ailment: 'Therefore let everyone who can, smite, slay and stab, secretly or openly, remembering that nothing can be more poisonous, hurtful, or Devilish than a rebel.'[10]

In more modern circumstances, Wolf goes on, peasant-based movements occur most readily 'in countries so devastated by war that they experience a breakdown of traditional leadership and social order'. This is the equivalent of the Black Death which preceded the great English Peasant Revolt of 1380. It creates a sense of total, oneiric alteration in which, since the time-honoured no longer functions, almost anything can be attempted. The world can be turned upside down. For Cambodians apocalypse came out of the air, in the shape of the prolonged American bombardment of their country during the last years of the Vietnamese War. 'The most important single factor in Pol Pot's rise', writes Kiernan, 'was the 1969–73 carpet-bombing of Cambodia's countryside by American B-52s.' As the Vietnamese army made increasing use of a supposedly neutral Cambodia, it was pursued and harassed there by the US Air Force. Naturally, most of the resultant carnage was Cambodian.

The beginning of Roland Jaffé's film *Killing Fields* tried to evoke something of the climate fostered by the attacks. One saw the *New York Times* correspondent Sidney Schanberg visiting a border town 'accidentally' flattened by the bombers, and over its ruins the Khmer Rouge rebels advance to the capture of Phnom Penh. The Nixon–Kissinger government had not even the excuse of ignorance. One of the most telling of the declassified CIA documents quoted by Kiernan was already outlining the consequences in 1973:

> The Khmer Rouge are using the damage caused by B-52 strikes as the main theme of their propaganda. The cadres tell the people that the Lon Nol government has requested the airstrikes and is responsible for the 'suffering of innocent villagers'. [Hence] the only way to stop 'the massive destruction of the country' is to defeat Lon Nol and stop the bombing. This approach has resulted in the successful recruitment of a number of young men [and] been effective with refugees and in areas subject to B-52 strikes . . .[11]

– which by that time meant most populated parts of Cambodia. However, this was only the wooden tongue of a disregarded espionage service. Kiernan quotes more tellingly from the eye-witnesses. Near Angkor Wat, the emblem of Cambodia's once glorious nationhood, for example:

> The ordinary people sometimes literally shat in their pants when the big bombs and shells came. Their minds just froze up and they would wander round mute for three or four days. Terrified and half-crazy, the people were ready to believe what they were told, that was what made it so easy for the Khmer Rouge to win people over.

Killing Fields continues with the sufferings of the Phnom Penh press corps and the evacuation of the American and French embassies. It would have been more costly to recreate on film what was happening in the background: the blowing up of the Cambodian Central Bank (after which millions of bank notes were allowed to flutter through the capital's deserted streets) and the stone-by-stone disassembly of the Roman Catholic cathedral. Thus economics as we know it was ended, and no trace of Western religion remained. After apocalypse, the ground-plan of millennium was being laid down: no mere simple-soul vision, but an organised framework to fill the void, egalitarian kibbutzim of peasant-warriors where Adam would delve and Eve spin once more, free for good of cash, gentlemen and, above all, foreigners.

Peasant Chauvinism

Much of Kiernan's study is devoted to the downfall of the Khmer Rouge state. The infernal machine of Party-guided ethnicity had an infernal contradiction built into it. Part III, 'The Slate Crumbles', describes how Pol Pot bit off more than he could chew, and, even before the Vietnamese chased him back into the jungle, had begun to choke to death. The maintenance of mass chauvinist tension inside the country demanded a parallel mobilisation against foreign foes, and particularly against the old national enemy, Vietnam.

Vietnam's population is eight times that of Cambodia, and in the later 1970s it was the only country to have defeated a superpower on the ground. But the Khmer Rouge ideology made light of this. It was possessed by voluntarist delusion: a version of 'triumph of the will', via Mao Tse-tung but ultimately stemming from Schopenhauer and Leni Riefenstahl rather than Lenin. Before they learnt better, British troops in the World Wars used to think each one of them was worth three (or occasionally, stretching it a bit, five) Germans. Pol Pot popularised the demented idea that any true Khmer was the equal of thirty Vietnamese weaklings. Hence Democratic Kampuchea was perfectly capable of invading its neighbour and 'taking back' the lower Mekong River area with its partly Khmer population.

The logic was suicidal. Ethnic cleansing within and irredentism abroad imposed a burden too crushing for any state, let alone one struggling to rebuild the irrigation works of medieval Khmerdom. However loudly the Party rag *Revolutionary Flags* declared the contrary, people in different parts of Cambodia began to realise this. Often they would be shot on the spot, or sent back to Tuol Sleng. But both Angkar and the army were further weakened as a result; hence still more came to feel that something was wrong, panicked and tried to make a break for it. There was no stopping the rot. The border with Thailand became crowded with refugees. Pol Pot had counted on continuing support from China. However, in the dwindling wake of the Cultural Revolution Peking had come to be run by superannuated gangsters rather than madmen. China's own 'peasantism' was moribund, though not yet quite as dead as it has subsequently become. They were quite happy to go on financing a diversionary war on their southern borders, viewing that as a sort of 'influence' over the area. But they never intended to take on the most battle-hardened army in the world on someone else's behalf. In late February of 1978 Hanoi secretly decided that the Pol Pot regime had to go, and one year later it had accomplished the task.

Ben Kiernan appears less secure when it comes to overall diagnosis of the Cambodian storm. This is of course what counts most in any Gellnerian perspective. Was it a peasant revolution? Or was it foisted upon the country by a specially evil combination of intelligentsia and hoodlums? The first view has become particularly associated with Michael Vickery, author of *Kampuchea: Politics, Economics and Society*,[12] who perceives the 1975 takeover as 'a complete peasant revolution, with the victorious revolutionaries doing what peasant rebels have always wanted to do to their urban enemies'. This was the source of the extraordinary violence. Pol Pot's Centre was an elite of deracinated intellectuals like himself, driven partly by anti-colonial Marxism but, more significantly, by 'peasantist romanticism'. Peasantism was their equivalent of Western 'workerism', a creed obliging them to obey what they interpreted as the impulses of the mass.

The opposite standpoint is presented in Kate Frieson's 'The Impact of Revolution on Cambodian Peasants, 1970–1975'.[13] There the rural masses of Cambodia are depicted as essentially innocent: 'unwitting participants' in a movement directed from outside their ken, by idea-led cadres seizing the unique chance provided by the chaos following the bombardments and the fall of Prince Sihanouk's old regime. By and large, mass motivation remained traditional, she argues, if not timeless: the cultivating class kept its head down and did as commanded – 'digging in, bending low, and cursing inwardly'. In time they even put up with the Khmer Rouge's 'high-level cooperatives' where communal eating was enforced and the family was phased out. Private land, the family and religious belief – the staples of peasant existence – disappeared, as they found themselves turned into unpaid indentured labourers.

Drawing on a much wider range of interviews and documents than previous scholars, what Kiernan comes up with is an uneasy compromise between these two interpretations. 'In my view, ideological as well as economic issues were at stake': that is, the peasants at first actively supported the Khmer Rouge takeover and then grew disillusioned, above all when they realised that family life itself was under threat. Pol Pot's rural utopia really aimed at ending rural life as they had known it. Individual land ownership and Buddhist faith were in the end less important to them than 'the devastating blows administered by the ending of home meals and the enforced separation of children from parents'. As for the violence and death, Kiernan judges the peasantry to be guilty but with increasingly extenuating circumstances: initially they must have had it in for city folk, particularly educated ones, but were later forced to repent. His final conclusion (pp. 463–5) adds little to this save a last-minute emphasis upon the significance of racism.

The Brood of Nicolas Chauvin

But what is really emphasised by this final flourish is the oddity of the preceding judgement. *The Pol Pot Regime* is a wonderful if dismaying portrait of ethnic nationalism unleashed. Ernest Gellner explained definitively why nationalism as such is not a malignancy. However, like its Nazi predecessor, the Cambodian version was manifestly a pathological diversion from the mainstream pattern he so often described. Although on the small scale of its nation, the Khmer head count was proportionately the most savage example of genetic pandemonium in history – at least until the Rwandan massacre of 1994, which matched Pol Pot's in numbers but was to outdo even it in intensity. Yet when trying to account for the whole event Kiernan ultimately falls back primarily on social factors. 'Social', that is, in the conventional sense which seeks for explanation in terms of class or individual interests: the peasants, the middle class, intellectuals and so on. A second explanatory motif is provided by political categories like 'central control' and then a more subordinate one by external affairs – the effects of French colonialism and American, Chinese or Vietnamese interference.

In reality, if 'racism' was so vital to the story – as the author asserts from beginning to end – then surely a frankly nationalist explanation grid is more relevant. What bound the revolutionary intelligentsia and the peasant majority together was the historical formation, or malformation, of the Khmer national identity. A combination of marked retardation and uniquely maleficent external blows produced an equally, and fatally, singular reaction. In relation to its size Cambodia probably had the least developed urban middle class and intelligentsia in the world. Yet this had to be the country which was, in one of the century's grimmest phrases, 'bombed back into the Stone Age'. Twentieth-century history exhibits plenty of atrocities; does it show any more extreme example of identity assault and battery? Many forms of nationalism have operated in terms of threats of extinction, often exaggerated or imaginary, and preached a life-or-death struggle 'before it is too late'. But in Phnom Penh in 1975 there was nothing at all exaggerated about fear of extinction, and almost everyone must have thought, or half-thought, that it might already be too late. The French had incorporated the Khmers into 'Indochina', their South-East Asian empire; now, the new convulsions of the post-colonial war had swamped them in another way and put a decimated and almost helpless land at the mercy of the Vietnamese.[14]

By the testimony so massively marshalled in Kiernan's book, Khmer nationalism was a powerful yet very maimed and lopsided sentiment. It was capable of uniting the peasantry with the country's tiny, nascent radical elite – but only through the bias of an exaggerated 'peasantism', as discerned in Vickery's analysis. The feeble native kingdom in whose ruins Pol Pot was raised had disappeared. There was no industry, and the cities were inhabited to a remarkable extent by foreign traders or middlemen. Father François Ponchaud, author of *Cambodia: Year Zero* and one of the last to quit Phnom Penh in the great exodus, wrote later: 'It is little wonder that Cambodian peasants perceived the centres of wealth and power as being dominated disproportionately by foreigners against whom they already held long-standing feelings of racial animosity.'[15] What gave the sense of 'zero' or void was the absence of the articulation nationalist ideas normally undergo amid differing upper- and middle-class strata. In this void it was possible for a *jacquerie* to become the state. By exchanging Marxism for the vilest and most wilful form of chauvinism, that state was then able to remain in power for years though, fortunately, only by the violent erosion of its own foundations. Even so, it took outside intervention to kill it.

These were ideal conditions both for abrupt radical ascendancy and for what is more accurately called 'chauvinism' rather than nationalism. Few terms have been more abused in recent debate. It has become vague enough in denotation to be almost appropriated by gender politics, as a shorthand for 'male chauvinism'. French in origin, like most modern political vocabulary, the idea of 'chauvinism' arose in Paris during the post-

Napoleonic era, and was linked to the popular wartime hero-figure of Nicolas Chauvin: *le soldat–laboureur* or ploughman–soldier. What the diction-aries of every modern tongue define as 'extreme or vulgar nationalism', 'foreigner-hating xenophobia', etc., had its source therefore in a particular person – or at any rate, in the supposed antics of that individual, as depicted on the vaudeville stage from the 1820s to mid-century.[16] But what matters here is that the Gallic original is essentially and incontestably a peasant. He always retires to his smallholding, usually with a wooden leg, where musket and bemedalled uniform are kept ready for action, and the village boys are regaled with lurid tales of the Emperor, Bedouin-bashing and laying the foreigner's women. Blood and soil are evoked in crassly direct fashion: while ploughing, he is forever turning up the ancestral bones of those who died for *la patrie* in times past.

We know from Gérard de Puymège's superb 1993 study of early chauvin-ism that he never actually existed: 'Chauvin' was pure but very significant myth.[17] With roots in Antiquity, what it represented was the profound reverberation of the rural world among those who had left it behind, but only just – the newly urbanised masses painfully adapting themselves to modern conditions, individual opportunity, shops and factories, literacy and the nuclear family. In its infancy, chauvinism was one aspect of how peasants were 'made into Frenchmen'. And what de Puymège reminds us of is that the very same process conserved Frenchmen as – so to speak – ideological peasants. That is, it reconfigured them as the subjects of a national myth system incorporating and forever reproducing the primary ingredients of rurality, blood and soil.

This myth system also instilled elements deriving from the revolutionary state formation of 1789 and later – Frenchmen as citizens, embodiments, like Americans, of the Rights of Man and of a self-consciously liberal and supra-ethnic Enlightenment. There was of course always a clash between these components of Frenchness. It has led to the profound internal warfare of all modern French republics. One of its most striking later episodes, to mention a single important example, was the Dreyfus Affair in the 1890s – a drama which was to define for us the true twentieth-century meaning of the term 'intellectual', and illustrate its determining link to the thematic of nationalism.[18]

However, such a national idea system can perfectly well go on supporting 'contradictions' in a practical sense. All it means is that French men and women have had to learn to move between different personae in different situations, and also to try and compose links between these. If the clash is allowed to become too overt, as at the moment of the Dreyfus trials, then something like civil war threatens. But much effort is normally put into preventing that happening, notably vis-à-vis foreigners. Political and cultural weapons are customarily deployed to maintain in operation an identity structure which, if laid out as doctrine, would be absurd.[19] However, identities are devices for living, not for composing doctorates. Irresolvable contradictions within them must either be concealed, neutralised by some kind of balancing mechanism or – in crises where the devices fail – fought out through open civil war. For the French, this war threatened again at the time of the Popular Front, was precipitated by the 1940 defeat and the formation of Pétain's (literally) 'chauvinist' republic at Vichy, then prosecuted through the Resistance and its immediate post-war aftermath.

The Spell of Rurality

What the true story of 'chauvinism' suggests is that modernisation involves passage through something like a colossal mill-race, in which a multi-generational struggle between the rural past and the urban-industrial future is fought out. 'Progress' occasionally makes it a struggle to the literal death, in particular circumstances. But in any case it is, in an appropriately epochal sense, always a life-and-death contest, where one global mode of existence perishes to make way for a successor. Nationalism is no side-effect of this battle, but its essence: it seems to me that was Ernest Gellner's fundamental intuition of the matter. However, his approach also placed disproportionate emphasis upon the future-oriented factors in the process. He thought modern philosophy was really about industrialisation – the disruptive impact of the future, as it were. 'Modernisation theory' in his original formulation could not help over-stressing the elements of literal modernity themselves – machine industry, the transformation of vernaculars into literacy, the inventive 'rediscovery' of the countryside by the new 'clerks' of national movements and so on. Greater attention is invariably given to these motives and instruments of change than to the 'raw material' itself – that is, the peasant masses who underwent the change and, like 'Nicolas Chauvin', got themselves not only made over into Frenchmen and Czechs but idealised into the very source of nationhood.

In reality, I suspect that the 'raw material' has played a far larger part in the overall genesis of nationalism than Gellnerian theory allows for. Czech nationalism was 'made in Prague', undoubtedly; but its ethnic characteristics came out of Bohemia, Moravia and the Sudetenland, and were not themselves 'made' in the familiar sense of invented, or converted into ideology. Whatever happens to them in the urban vaudeville, or the TV soap opera, 'traditions' are also a real matrix borne forwards from past time by individuals and families. The kind of remaking which features in modern nationalism is not creation *ex nihilo*, but a reformulation constrained by determinate parameters of that past. And the past which has mainly counted here – and gives its 'bite' and sentimental incontrovertibility to all ethno-nationalist belief structure – is that of peasant existence.

The most telling critique of Gellner has been that focusing upon his cheerful over-rationalism. In an essay contrasting Weber and Gellner, Perry Anderson accuses the latter of 'skirting the really spectacular manifestations of 20th century nationalism – not the independence of Czechoslovakia or Morocco, but World War and Nazism'.[20] There is a bias towards economic functionalism in his theory which ends by making nationalism into too much of 'a wholesomely constructive and forward-looking principle' – a series of adjustments demanded by entry into the era of modernity, as it were, rather than a life-or-death trauma. Marxist 'historical materialism' used to be denounced for this style of economism, with its propensity to infer everything from alterations in the mode of production. 'Ironically', Anderson continues,

> there is a sense in which Gellner's theory might be described as immoderately materialist. For what it plainly neglects is the overpowering dimension of collective meaning that modern nationalism has always involved: that is, not its functionality for industry, but its fulfilment of identity. In his tour of reenchantments, Gellner has paradoxically missed far the most important of all in the twentieth century.

Hence he 'theorised nationalism without detecting the spell', in the sense of its binding or passionate attraction, and its capacity to inspire the phenomena of self-sacrifice and genocide.

But where is the 'spell' located? Anderson notes its psychological and emotive nature, but suggests no originating source. I believe that by far the most plausible origin lies in the link between most forms of ethnic nationalism and 'rural' existence as defined earlier. Those 'reenchantments' Gellner faltered over – above all German Aryanism and the Jewish genocide – were examples of unhinged ethnicity which retained a palpable or single-generation connection to peasant existence. The 'fantasies' of Hitler and Himmler envisaged forming another, earlier version of Kiernan's 'indentured agrarian state' – that is, a master race of reconstituted Germanic peasant farmers extending across Central and Eastern Europe, with unfree Slav labourers doing the hard work on their farms. The anti-modern virulence of this vision derived partly from the very closeness of the traditions thus reinvented and turned into philosophy. German industrialisation had been abrupt and traumatic, and it had indeed given rise to nationalism according to the broad prescriptions of modernisation theory. However, the counter-shock against this rise, from the 'raw material' of a society still mainly rural and ethnically homogeneous, proved even more powerful than the originating shock itself. After the experience of national defeat in 1914–18, it was strong enough to overwhelm and carry modernised German society along a different and regressive trajectory: ethnic chauvinism transmuted into a global mission.

One can put what is really the same point in another way. There is a familiar litany of rather abstract terms employed in both the rhetoric of and speculation on nationalism, like 'inheritance', 'community', 'descent' or 'blood', 'common experience' and 'purity' or its many opposites ('pollution', 'the alien' and so on). But since most nations conform rather feebly to these categories in any sociological sense, it is often quite hard to discern just where their emotive authority comes from. A clue may be provided by historical situations where this was relatively easy: that is, situations where peasant rurality has been close, recent, still accessible to the people undergoing 'nationalisation', and, therefore, still capable of infusing violent personal or familial emotions into its language and rhetoric. The resultant mixture is highly infectious: newly eloquent romantic intellectualism combined with the half-healed wounds of actual or recently transmitted recollection – from a rural life in which 'inheritance', 'community', 'roots' and the other standard nostrums all had a perfectly concrete meaning. The colourful mixture is also tailormade for the burgeoning media of early literacy and urbanisation – like the Paris vaudeville, the London nineteenth-century music hall (where 'jingoism' was forged) and the yellow or tabloid press. Gellner's ironic rationality tended always to see traditions being falsified into 'traditions'. But in certain important cases, 'traditions' could actually be infused with the blood – not always figurative – of (real) traditions. A reborn Germany or Cambodia found themselves engorged by the flailing life of a peasant social order which, although 'dying out' in the epochal sense, was still alive enough for a serious effort to 'undo history', as Kiernan puts it. Ideologies of anti-modernism – from Nietzsche to 'Unabomber' Ted Kaszinski, via Martin Heidegger – have occasionally been able to pierce into a vein of 'authentic' rural despair and resentment, and assist the mobilisation of its violence. Not by chance was 'authentic' Heidegger's favourite word.[21]

Both the intense emotionality and the violence of ethnic nationalism acquire much more meaning when traced to this specific root. The sole alternative would seem to be a frankly psychological one: a story of 'human nature', in fact, where feelings of 'belonging' or extended kinship are read as the essential realities offended by the circumstances of modernity. One difficulty with this is of course its sheer familiarity: it is the tale told for the last two centuries by the intellectual protagonists of just what we are discussing here – ethnic nationalism. The theoretical issue which Gellner's modernisation thesis addressed arose only because that explained nothing. Nationalism is only a question because nationality politics and national identities are not all 'ethnic' in the imagined-kinship, fakelore, immemorialist sense. From Hans Kohn's time onwards one of its key dilemmas has always been making sense of these vital differences: whether as 'Western' versus 'Eastern', 'liberal' versus 'closed', or, more recently, 'civic' versus 'ethnic' nationalism.

Beyond the Mill-race

How long did this crucial turmoil endure? Unfortunately, the past tense remains inappropriate. The curse endures to this day. It still exists, notably, within the French state which gave birth to 'Nicolas Chauvin'. That is, in the society also considered by many theorists as archetypally modern, the very hearth of Enlightenment and *égalité* or even, since the 1980s, the crucial site of post-modernity. Not necessarily under his own name, 'Nicolas Chauvin' figures none the less in every Front National speech and pamphlet today. This is not to prophesy his return to earth via a second Pétain.[22] However, one might be a little more sanguine on this count, were not the wider European scene so ambiguous. Its institutional modernity remains deeply weighed down by the ball and chain of the Common Agricultural Policy. Though designed to lever the countries of the European Union out of Chauvin's world for good, by a 'phasing out' of peasant cultivation, it has unfortunately collapsed under political pressure into an instrument for preserving it everywhere from Greece to Ireland. Hence European Union, the principal white hope for 'civic nationalism', remains deeply compromised by a ruralist inheritance which has in the past so often nourished ethnic nationalism.[23]

In a penetrating discussion of violence in nationalist movements, David Laitin has recently underlined this same dimension. 'Why are some nationalist movements peaceful in strategy and outcome while others create carnage?' is his leading question, and he searches for an answer less among 'the great forces of history' than in 'micro-foundations based upon social organisation in rural and small town life', plus contributions from 'fortuitous events' (like assassinations or acts of state terrorism) and what he calls the 'tipping phenomena' of political recruitment (attainment of 'thresholds' beyond which violent tactics seem to be paying off).[24] Thus, the salience of terrorism in the Basque national movement can be contrasted with its remarkably low profile in Catalonia. In the former we find a 'dense rural social structure' where considerations of honour are prominent; the Catalans, however, are more organised into economic-based groups and political parties operating at the national and all-Spanish levels (both city-centred). ETA's long dominance therefore depended upon its links to a specifically rural (or recently rural) society in which 'nationalist leaders could recruit in small villages and towns in which there are many social groups whose members are bound by codes of honour'. But such honourable bonding derives, surely, from a nexus of peasant custom and heritable tradition – that very 'raw material' referred to previously, and infused fairly directly into the idealised nationhood of Euzkadi.

The point is reinforced by the second comparative example Laitin goes on to provide: developments in post-Soviet Georgia and the Ukraine. While in Georgia there have been a series of insurgencies and wars, Ukrainian reconstruction remains remarkably free from armed conflict. In general terms it is certainly not obvious why this contrast should be so great. The Ukraine has a host of important minority problems and, in the Crimea, the site of a major three-way conflict among Russians, Tartars and Ukrainians which has constantly threatened escalation into warfare. Yet the new Ukrainian regime has largely avoided violence, whereas – 'Georgia's rural social structure appears to have maintained the basis for terrorist organisation'. Nearly 70 per cent of Ukrainians will be living in large urban environments by the year 2000, and one result is that 'the populism that was the hallmark of Ukrainian ideologies in the 19th and early 20th centuries has faded. One can even argue that today the concept of the *narod* – in the traditional sense of the poor, oppressed peasant masses – no longer occupies a central place in the political thinking of Ukrainians.'[25]

Post-1989 conditions in many parts of Eastern Europe have made them even more the victim of the inheritance which is fading away in the Ukraine. In a recent study of the underlying causes of the Bosnian war, Sabrina Ramet points out that whereas Titoist Yugoslavia had attempted, however unsuccessfully, to 'impose the values of the city' on South Slav culture, Milosevic's 1987 coup 'represented among other things the triumph of the countryside over the city in Serbia [and hence] the rising tide of Serbian nationalism, closely associated with rural perceptions and rural values, albeit often as synthesised and reflected by urban literary elites'.[26] She outlines the primarily rural character of the new Serb national movement and the extremes it attained in Bosnia, where a campaign for 'traditional values' (meaning in the first place a full-scale assault on any claims by women to equal treatment) – 'represents in the clearest possible way a cultural encroachment of the countryside on the city'. Linking this to the perspective of modernisation theory, she concludes that

> There is a world of difference between a national movement founded on urban mobilisation (even if it manipulates the symbols and mythologies of the countryside, in its own distorted mirror) and a national movement based, to a great extent, on rural mobilisation.

Outside Europe a similar general pattern is identifiable. Laitin distinguishes his analysis from what he feels to be the abstractness of 'the great forces of history'; but the analysis itself conducts one back to one of these forces – the latent power of a mobilised peasantry and its counter-attack upon the spreading tide of 'modernisation', the market economy and the norms of urban liberalism. Although Ben Kiernan's study does not deal with this, we know that the Khmer Rouge by no means lay down and died after the Vietnamese invasion. Presumably because it still enjoys some real support, it is notoriously still around, and a political as well as a military player. Living partly off the timber and drug business in Cambodia's western forests, its guerrilla remnant has survived the Vietnamese occupation and successor regimes. On the day I finished reading Kiernan's book the London *Independent* ran a main news item titled 'Pol Pot's Top Man Quits Khmer Rouge' (13 August) – quits, alas, not to spend more time with his family but to run for office in Phnom Penh. Sentenced to death years ago for his part in the atrocities, Ieng Sary is planning a new party to contest the next elections. He was a member of the founding Paris elite, and one of Pol Pot's closest buddies. Since he has not yet appeared in public no one knows just how the sentence will be avoided. But his chances look pretty good. Joint Prime Minister Hun Sen (himself once a Khmer Rouge combatant) has praised him for 'saving tens of thousands of lives' (by defecting), and the official view seems to be that he should be welcomed back 'if it is the will of the people'.

Nor is this the sole great rebuke to Gellnerian optimism produced by the 1990s. One paragraph in Kiernan's book gave me an almost physical shock the first time I read it. It is in his Introduction (pp. 4–5) and intended as no more than a simple outline of the Cambodian scene for the uninitiated:

At first glance, Cambodia seems a society resistant to transformation. It was geographically compact, demographically dispersed, linguistically unified, ethnically homogeneous, socially undifferentiated, culturally uniform, administratively unitary, politically undeveloped, economically undiversified, and educationally deprived. Cambodia was more isolated and landlocked than any other Southeast Asian country except Laos [and] mummified by ninety years of a colonial protectorate which preserved, even enhanced the traditional monarchy and social structure [and] *80 percent peasant.*

I have added the emphasis. What provokes the shock is the fact that, placenames aside, only one further change ('ethnically homogeneous') is needed to make this a perfect description of another country altogether, located in another continent: Rwanda.[27]

A Counter-example

Near the beginning I mentioned the continuing conflict in Ireland as one of the pointers towards the general significance of rurality for nationalism. But this indicator makes its point still more forcefully when set in a slightly wider context. For Irish nationalism is also the exception within the larger archipelago to which it belongs. In Hans Kohn's old contrast of Western (liberal) versus Eastern (ethnic-authoritarian) nationalisms, Ireland was sometimes grouped with the latter: a violent ethno-religious movement perplexingly located on the farthest geographic fringe of the European West. Physically contiguous and historically intertwined with England – the founding specimen of Kohn's liberal-institutional, state-formed identity – it none the less seemed much closer in both spirit and methods to the characteristic nineteenth-century formations of Central and Eastern Europe. The paradox has been heightened by the remarkable post-independence relationship between old monarchy and new republic. Two generations after secession citizens of the latter are still formally treated (and for the most part, informally regarded) as quasi-subjects of the former when 'on British soil'. Yet simultaneously the IRA's campaign of irredentist violence has led to over three thousand deaths over a period of almost thirty years, and in the 1990s produced episodes of city-centre devastation upon the same soil.

The enigma is intensified again by broad comparison to the fates of other UK nationalities. Both Wales and Scotland have generated twentieth-century national movements aiming at secession on Irish Republican lines, and since the 1950s these have developed significantly over a generation of general British and imperial decline. Such movements have been frustrated by British counter-tactics (notably around the 1979 devolution referenda) and are now also dogged by a more distinct stirring of English resentment focused upon 'preserving the Union', above all against European influence or encroachment. Yet they have also been almost wholly free from violence. The absence of terrorist 'persuasion' is particularly significant among the Scots. As well as representing about 10 per cent of the UK population (easily the largest archipelago minority) their institutions carry forward the traditions of a statehood alive until the eighteenth century, and largely built up in hostility to England. In 1745–46 a Highland-based army made the last attempt to overthrow the post-1688 British state, and the long subsequent experience of empire has generated strong popular traditions of militarism among both Highland and Lowland peoples. However, the fact is that these traditions have, so far at least, had only marginal effect upon a national movement conducted exclusively in political terms – political, and indeed quite self-consciously civic and pacific terms.

But perhaps this puzzling difference between the two main parts of the 'British Isles' yields to analysis along the lines sketched out above.[28] The most striking underlying contrast is the one found between their respective agrarian histories. In England and Lowland Scotland, an early 'agrarian revolution' virtually destroyed peasant society, permanently replacing it with a landscape of large estate-farms, 'county towns' and servant villages. In Ireland it did not. On the contrary, to some extent nineteenth-century land reform reconstructed small-scale agriculture after earlier disaster and depredations, thus laying the foundation for De Valera's rural Catholic state and – ultimately – for the prosecution of Sinn Féin's irredentist campaigns at the end of the twentieth century. It was from such radically divergent social trajectories that equally diverse nationality movements arose: a Hibernian one liberating itself only with great difficulty from 'blood and soil', and British ones mainly configured within the category of an earlier 'civic nationalism', and by the absence, save in romantic fancy, of those elements most propitious for 'chauvinist' or blood-and-soil mobilisation. There is even a partial exception which can serve as confirmation: Wales. In that country, both ethno-linguistic motifs and violence have been somewhat more pronounced in the nationalist movements of the twentieth century; and they are rooted in areas where, in spite of early political and legal incorporation by the Tudor dynasty, the subsequent capitalist transformation of the countryside was much less dramatic.

English national identity itself, the original template of modernisation delineated in Liah Greenfeld's *Nationalism*, finds itself in perhaps the strangest dilemma of any contemporary nationalism.[29] National movements usually arise from what she calls status *ressentiment*, articulated through a deployment of inherited *differentiae* – the 'peculiarities' of people and nation. For the English, however, for over two centuries the most important peculiarity has undoubtedly been 'Britain' – the grander personae of multinational state and empire, worn long enough to feel almost like the 'nature' evoked by nationalists. Redefinition upon much narrower ground needs alternative motifs: the rediscovery of another nature, as it were, whose mobilisation could restore the national fortune. But apart from the despairing one of 'race' (used by all current formations of the extreme Right in England) it has become difficult to see what such motifs could be. What appeared to Hans Kohn as an early and exemplary state-led liberalism now appears in a truer light: a thoroughly archaic version of civic nationalism, 1688's crude, early-modern apparatus of absolute parliamentary sovereignty. Hence the first principles of effective national identity – the 'way we do things', etc. – have themselves become major obstacles to the reform of that identity. But this is an historical context in which *ethnos* can offer no way out or forward. Everywhere in the archipelago it looks as if modern *civis* is the sole solution; but is that attainable only upon the broader terrain of Europe?[30]

By way of over-general conclusion, therefore: the modernisation theory stemming from Gellner's great 1964 essay on 'Nationalism' and more fully elaborated in *Nations and Nationalism*[31] had the effect of foreshortening the future; yet part of its great vigour and explanatory power arose from this very effect – from the way it foreclosed so abruptly on the past. Placing too great an emphasis upon all the cultural factors attendant upon industrialisation, it made theorists too confident that modernity had all but prevailed. In spite of his ironic scepticism and his attraction to social conservatism, Gellner was essentially an Enlightenment optimist. And the obverse of such confidence was a tendency to relegate or discount the enduring pressures of rurality itself – the formative weight of that preceding peasant world which, once the constraints of the Cold War were loosened, has showed itself very rapidly to be anything but mere 'raw material'. Fifteen years ago Arno J. Mayer concluded his masterly synthesis *The Persistence of the Old Regime: Europe to the Great War* with these words:

> The old regime was too vast, resilient, and resistant a target to be felled by a few terrorist bullets in Sarajevo. It would take the two World Wars and the Holocaust, or the Thirty Years War of the twentieth century, to finally dislodge and exorcise the feudal and aristocratic presumption from Europe's civil and political societies.[32]

And even then, we should now add, the social inheritance that underlay such presumption was not really dislodged. It is, alas, still undergoing exorcism to this day, in Western as well as Eastern Europe, and in many other areas of the world. Two generations before 1914 modernisers like Marx and Mill had treated the demise of the old regime as practically a foregone conclusion. Their heir, Ernest Gellner, gave a picture of the modernisation process far deeper and wider than they could. Yet his picture remained in certain respects configured by the inheritance he shared with them – that is, by certain limitations of the original Enlightenment as well as by its intellectual and moral grandeur. Approaching the year 2000, and trying to peer beyond these frontiers, perhaps it should be conceded that we still do so from among the ruins of that ancient rural world which he understood, and yet also under-estimated.

The thunder of its long collapse is still by far the loudest sound in all our ears. From McLuhan to Baudrillard, theorists have sought to discern electronic post-modernity through the clouds of dust. But may not such efforts be only the latest style of rationalist foregone conclusion? Many intellectuals go on believing it is much later than most people and politicians think, and in spite of his sceptical, disbelieving temperament Gellner too inclined in that direction. It is time to doubt it. In any case I believe that an alternative reading which puts nationalism nearer the centre of the theory world will suggest the contrary. The departure of such a great mind is therefore an occasion for reappraising not just 'modernisation' but our own collective and intellectual location within the process. It may be much sooner than most people, politicians and social theorists believed around 1990.[33]

6

Race and Nationalism

Writing in the *London Review of Books* in 1994 I was incautious enough to make some remarks about alternatives to Euro-centrism that history might have generated.[1] For example Progress, like Homo sapiens itself, might have erupted out of Africa rather than from the areas north of it. In which case, instead of indulging in what Edward Said calls Orientalism, there might well be present-day pallid-skin observers 'fulminating over Septentrionalist delusions about colourlessness: the vacant brain-pans supposed natural to the pigmentally-challenged, with their slime-grey eyes, ratty hair and squeaky-voiced irrationality'. Or again, industrialisation might conceivably have emerged in primarily Chinese shape – from the human Middle Kingdom or heartland, rather than the remote archipelago-coast of Europe. Had this happened, there would today be critics on both sides of the 2000 AD development gap, no doubt differently dated, contorted with guilt and indignation over the romantic delusions of Occidentalism.

Having read Marek Kohn's *The Race Gallery* I feel retrospective embarrassment at my own ignorance.[2] It was meant only as counter-factual musing. But some readers must have known about other relevant facts: there already *are* commentators given to fulmination about pigmental challenge and the inherent defects of northernist intelligence, sensibility and general irrationality. They are described at some length in chapter 7 of Marek Kohn's invaluable but sobering new encyclopaedia of racial twaddle and counter-twaddle.

He deals there with Afrocentrism, a strain of devotion which inverts pale-skin racism rather than attacking it. Everything decent is seen as coming out of black Africa, and all non-blacks are held to be genetically handicapped by melanin deficiency. Melanin is 'black peoples' Kryptonite', the general secret of their social and cultural superiority. Northerners by contrast are deemed to have lost important faculties and become squeakily over-aggressive in order to compensate – 'the price Europeans had to pay for the light skins they needed in order to synthesise vitamin D in the gloomy North'. Thus gunpowder, compasses and Newtonian science actually betray an engrained genetic inferiority. The 'electromagnetic pull' of negritude, on the other hand, impels culture towards the great contemporary

113

norms of communal feeling, multi-culturalism, and musical attunement to the ecosphere. These are the views not of some eccentric bookworm but of Richard King, responsible for the Afrocentrist pages on the World Wide Web. Not myself a devotee, I can only quote the electronic address at which surfers should be able to check for themselves:

http://www.melanet.com/melanet/ubus/melib.html

In a sense now discredited by biology and genetics, white racism always claimed to be scientific. The victims of such claims have been in turn always tempted either to construct their own counter-science or else, distinctly easier, to deny special authority to science as such. The 'scientific view' then appears as merely one perspective amongst others. It can be freely disowned in spite of its imperialist pretensions, and treated as no more than a ruling mythology or religion. If most white people regard it as truth that may only be because it suits them. Alternative belief systems have at least an equivalent validity – equal or, from the Negroid, Inuit, East Asian or other point of view, actually superior or more useful.

A striking example is cited by Kohn in the same chapter. As part of their campaign to recover ancestral remains that have been moved or placed in museums, some Native Americans deny the scientific hypothesis of an early migration from Asia into the Americas over the Bering Straits land bridge. The Lakota Indians insist that they were created around the Wind Cave in the Black Hills of South Dakota. Hence their forebears could not have come from anywhere else and if 'science' states that was so, too bad for anthropology and palaeontology. In this way a campaign for ethnic respect and the restoration of dignity seeks help from philosophical relativism. In a general sense, any one tribe's world-view is as good as another's. In the particular or concrete senses more important to particular people – like those mobilised by the campaign – the creation myth must in fact be pragmatically more true than the theory of evolution. It represents our universe as against theirs: a fact not susceptible to disproof by any amount of further evidence on early migratory movements or the DNA of hunter–gatherers.

Actually, such philosophical assistance is fool's gold. If the denunciation of pseudo-science becomes that of science itself, then much more disappears than Aryanist bigotry and pink suprematism. It is the very foundation of non-racial, and anti-racist, development itself which vanishes. After all, if national or civilisational belief systems are really equivalent, and there is in principle no principle for preferring one to another, then on what grounds would the 'Return Our Ancestors' campaign ever be heeded, let alone succeed? The reigning WASP ideology of South Dakota would be 'justified' in disregarding it because white Americanism reigns. As the expression of a *de facto* dominant authority, archaeological and museum culture could then treat the relics of Native America any way it pleases without anxiety about later disproof or historical retribution. Where contrasting cultures no longer inhabit the same universe, what right can there be but transient might?

If, on the other hand, all cultures do share a single universe, then that must have some common rules. The timbers of humanity may all be crooked, as Immanuel Kant thought. But looked at in another way, what matters is surely that all are crooked. If there is at bottom one single story – that of warped human development – then one would expect there at least to be some elements of shared narrative through all the variously deformed chapters. 'Science' is only a way of isolating and explaining these – not perfect, often dim, but the only serious candidate.

What is in any case so terrible about having come originally from somewhere else? The Lakotans feel the admission weakens their old historical case as 'native' or primordial inhabitants whose rights were abused by the later European arrivals. In the short term this attitude is comprehensible: they were around before their persecutors, and there is abuse. But their short story is also part of the longer-term narrative recounting how every existing population must have moved from somewhere else at some time in the usually forgotten or mythologised past. The same scientific tale interprets 'primordial' as ultimately, though still only probably, referring to the area of the Great Rift Valley in Africa, the source of the oldest humanid remains yet uncovered.

Part of this story happens to be that even 'native Americans' once moved there from Asia. Far from undermining contemporary protests against discrimination and unequal treatment, the story provides the sole conceivable foundation for their validity. Had there been a truly separate creation in the Black Hills, assuming the Great Spirit to be in full possession of His/ Her faculties, the result would have been a truly distinct species. Better or, by some awful accident, worse than what we seem to be landed with, deplorable Homo sapiens? Mercifully, this question has been relegated either to the realms of demented and semi-occult speculation explored in *The Race Gallery*, or to science-fiction. But we know from wretched twentieth-century experience that creation parables depict their progeny in a favourable light. They tend to be Aryans rather than half-wits. The wittiest and most pertinent image here remains that of George Steiner, in the conclusion to *The Portage to San Cristobal of A.H.*,[3] his novella about Hitlerism. When the agents of Israeli retribution finally track down the Devil to his Amazonian lair, it is to find the verminous old git cackling hoarsely about the original source of his own ideas – the brilliant Judaic concept of a Chosen Race.

The truth is that the Lakotan campaign of ancestor-redemption appeals to a common human sense of guilt and responsibility whose whole basis denies relativism. Like the Hispanic-speaking Last (so far) Americans, the First Americans are only timbers from elsewhere – bent, but deserving better than the raw deal history has imposed on them in the 1900s. One way of advertising that scandal may be to besmirch the Holy Grail of science, as shock therapy for the slumbering conscience of the majority. But the tactic of provoking an overdue guilty start is one thing; pursuing the literal logic of multi-culturalism is quite another. It is admirable solemnly to exorcise the thoughtless dominance of one culture from the front door; more serious to leave the back door wide open for any post-modern dosser to unroll his deconstruction bag and drug kit.

Deconstruction is mostly reconstruction. What then occupies the basement and hallway could be called post-racism, the astonishing herd of bug-eyed lodgers, pyromanes, scalp-fetishists and intellectual muggers portrayed in Kohn's book. Hell itself is no more, but some neighbours from there are unimpressed by the fact. Their numbers seem to be increasing. Racism may be returning in a lower-key, fragmented and piecemeal form, Kohn argues, but in post Cold War conditions its influence can still be considerable. 'The historical moment of race science as a dominant system of belief has passed', he notes, yet in the new dispensation:

> The prevailing mood is fatalistic. Among the majorities faith has ebbed – in ideologies, in the power of governments to ameliorate social ills, and in the powers of people to change their lives by political action. This loss of faith has been accompanied by a shift towards the belief that human society is preordained to be the way it is; that nature shapes our lives more than nurture.

At the same time, ethno-national distinctions are rapidly mounting. When allied to fatalism and political apathy, thawed-out nationalism too may collude with the drift back to 'nature' as explanation. This will never amount to racism in the Heinrich Himmler sense. Social Darwinism is deader than the skulls in the old race-museums, and science has reached some real comprehension of how genetic inheritance actually works. Nevertheless, sub- or pseudo- or post-science may go on poisoning the social tissues. The new lunatics may be unlikely to take over the mansion, as their forerunners almost did in 1933–42. Yet they can go on making life damned disagreeable, and not just for minorities. Soon no family heirloom may be safe from their slimy attentions. Think of the chronic drain odour rising from the basement, and of small hours rendered permanently sleepless by muffled incantations from *The Bell Curve*.

Kohn draws a parallel here with the reversion to fascism in Italy, France and Austria. This does not require the serious prospect of a Fourth Reich to be a serious influence on mainstream politics:

> by violence, by campaigning on issues such as immigration, and by command-ing small but significant percentages of electoral support [it] may be able to govern as part of a coalition. Such elements have by definition entered the mainstream. Less tangibly, neo-fascist groupings have drawn the mainstream towards them, reshaping political issues in their preferred images.

The author does not mention the UK in this context, but it may be relevant to do so. Even without influence from a neo-fascist grouping, it is possible for the political mainstream itself to tack in the same general direction. Guided by sheer decay, obstinacy and corruption, it can easily default into the decline mode Kohn refers to. A fatalistic apathy then appears to shape its ends, as one pre-ordained disaster follows another and blame gets pinned alternately on the enemy within (immigrants, minorities) or that without (Europe). Himmler's effective legatees are less the tattooed street gangs of the British National Party than a novel strain of noxious, pin-striped populists (also known as 'bastards') given to a tongue-shrivelling mixture of monetarist rigour, Unionist beatitude and anti-Brusselsism. Such is post-Powellism, Great Britain's perfidious footnote to post-racism.

Kohn argues that the resurrection is not entirely down to post Cold War disorientation and ethno-nationalism. It was always implicit in certain traits of what he calls the post-Nazi consensus. The 1950 UNESCO Statement on Race told the globe in no uncertain terms to snap out of it: 'Scientists have reached general agreement that mankind is one: that all men belong to the same species, Homo sapiens.' Races were henceforth to be 'ethnic groups' or 'populations'. Racism had been a plan for new Lords of humankind, under whom the rest would be helots or worse – frankly sub-human, birth-cursed untouchables. Now no one was to be downgraded, especially from a mental angle. IQ tests were frowned on by the Statement since 'Wherever it has been possible to make allowances for differences in environmental opportunities, the tests have shown essential similarity in mental characters among all human groups.'

Evolution had produced the one, culture had produced the bewilderingly many. UNESCO's worthies were unable to ditch broad descriptive classifications altogether, like the 'Mongoloid/Negroid/Caucasian' spectrum still used in American police and identity documents. However, ethnic origins neither implied nor made any genetic difference, and all its groupings had to be considered equally valuable 'human resources' for the world's economy and civilisation. Kohn is worried by all this. The anxiety informs much of the most thoughtful parts of his book, and makes it into far more than a rogue's gallery. 'Many of those concerned with the ethical implications of genetics' – he notes in his concluding chapter – 'are working within a liberal paradigm which holds to an ideal of race-blindness'. This is his main point: anti-racism has to stop entailing race-blindness – or else post-racism (the recessive gene of racism) will continue its poisonous half-life.

Ostentatious indifference towards differences is of course preferable to their abuse and exploitation. But the trouble is that most people will never really believe or accept it. Intellectuals and legislators may cling to the grand ideal; non-egg-heads and the legislated-for tend stubbornly to think otherwise. They are unlikely to return to anything like 'fascism'; but equally unlikely to bend over blackwards, or start affecting liberal indifference towards visibly distinct customs. Popular culture is not so advanced, any-where. Crude suprematism was defeated in 1945; but the vaguer prejudices of ethno-centrism persist and may, as Kohn thinks, actually be gaining ground in the decentred world following the Cold War stasis. Unfortunately, liberation from the latter has also involved a partial freeing of communal dislikes, repressed grudges and resentments about 'them' displacing us, or threatening our dearly purchased and fought-for values, etc.

Since the thaw has coincided with persistent depression, 'readjustment' and welfare shrinkage in the Western power-house economies, phenomena like Le Pen's Front National, Gianfranco Fini's Alleanza Nazionale and what I suppose UK-watchers will learn to call Portillismo are not too surprising. Had it coincided with a second 1960s, another golden age of expansive development, then life might have been easier for the slogan Kohn favours to triumph: 'Variation is our species' wealth.' He is quoting the African-American biologist Fatimah Jackson at that point, but perhaps her assertion can be generalised. The societal equivalent of bio-diversity is culture diversity, a wealth whose effects were in the past menaced by imperialism and which may now be threatened – though in a different way – by globalisation. However, culture diversity is not easily separable from culture trouble. Flourishing variations may imply equally luxuriant dislikes, prejudices and feelings of grateful superiority or resentment. Every wonder of cultural cross-fertilisation may be accompanied by a hundred offences against the Race Relations Act, and there seems to be no arithmetic for weighing one against the other.

Although Kohn does not use the phrase, what he is objecting to in the post World War II liberal consensus should really be called 'all-the-sameism': the rejection of racist hierarchy led by reflex to a fallback posture of unbending uniformity. As physical anthropology became a scientific backwater, he writes, 'External appearances are regarded as an illusion; true wisdom lies in seeing beyond them, and beyond the superficial markers of race, to the genetic essence.'

It was comforting to feel that henceforth nobody would be downgraded. However, the obverse was that nobody could be upgraded either. And who in particular – any real, salty particular – can really be content with a 'genetic essence'? All minorities, oppressed folk, nationalists and, as used to be said in Australia, 'ethnos' want to be something special. Being different means being recognised as different. It means having something to say or contribute, doing certain things differently and possibly better than others. It means not just speech, but having a voice – not the Chomskyan essence of deep grammar alone, but a particular resonance, and possibly a message, previously unheard in the world.

This point has, for example, become sorely familiar to protagonists of the world's largest ethnic minority movement, women's liberation. It is one thing to demand or legislate for strict equality, quite another to think that women's powers would make no difference in any concrete sense. Yet if such a difference is to be made, it can come only from things specific to women: things from their separate nature, beyond the shared genetic essence. Like all nationalists, gender nationalists wish to be loved – not just correctly registered at the Humankind data bank. 'Ethnic' originally had the sense of 'heathen' – 'relating to a people not Christian or Jewish'. In the generalised ethnic or multi-cultural world we have all become equally heathens. But heathenness is difference and, surely, ought to remain so. Only in hopeless dystopias is the world's future imagined as homogeneous. In other words the very rigidity of all-the-sameism preserved a sort of spectre or after-image of imperialism: its etherealised 'one' remained a responsible He, somewhat Judeo-Christian in hue, or at least reflective of high-civilisational aspiration. The Man was never quite so at home, for example, among Australian Aboriginals, the Ba-Twa Pygmies of Rwanda or Tory Conference ladies.

Is relativism the sole answer to all-the-sameism? Now that the centre no longer holds, must heathen ethno-anarchy simply be unleashed upon the world? No: but the intellectual answer has to be relativity, rather than relativism. It should be conceived as the socio-political equivalent of physical relativity theory, not abandonment to the dossing classes. As Kohn shows very well, this would be the equivalent of foundering back into the arbitrary and the non-rational.

There are no longer fixed absolutes in the societal universe, any more than in the physical one. But in the latter case this did not entail the serious rehabilitation of astrology or palmistry. Physics had to change the meaning of Newtonian principles in order to accommodate them within Einstein's revised co-ordinates of space–time. Pursuing the analogy, social science has to alter and encompass the fixities of the Enlightenment credo inside a larger unified story – the equivalent of a 'field theory' which recognises, without surrendering to, the steeply rising input of ethno-national claims and multi-cultural display. I think this is what the famous row over Orientalism between Edward Said and the late Ernest Gellner was really about.

Admittedly, Kohn's survey also shows clearly how far social science is from being able to tell any such story. For example, one fundamental element of it will be the Human Genome project, an attempt to survey everything knowable about humankind's genetic diversity. A 1994 document from this international project stressed its 'enormous potential for illuminating our understanding of human history and identity by investigating the variation occurring in the human genome [from] samples representative of all the world's peoples'. It is also intended to provide information on genetic factors in disease and create 'a unique bridge between science and the humanities':

> Most importantly the results of the Project are expected to undermine the popular belief that there are clearly defined races, to contribute to the elimination of racism and to make a major contribution to the understanding of the nature of differences between individuals and between populations.

Such aims have guaranteed denunciation of the enterprise by nativist romantics and Ku-Klux-Klan nostalgics alike. As Kohn observes acidly in his penultimate chapter, it gets harder to tell them apart. The Central Australian Aboriginal Congress, for example, accused the researchers of being like vampires bent on stealing 'the genetic material that makes us Aboriginal people'. The implication was that the song lines were really blood lines and Aboriginal identity is essentially genetic. But is the same not liable to be true of 'Aryans'? This is just what Klansmen have always been pining for.

Similarly, some gays have been tempted by the notion of the 'homosexual gene' as a natural explanation of their condition: if one can't help it, shouldn't that at least put an end to moral qualms and brimstone sermons? Possibly; at the same time, however – secure in its possession of the normalcy gene – a hetero majority might then see the point of dealing much more strictly with state-registered deviants and 100 per cent incorrigible queers. In this strange zone more than one sort of fool's gold is on sale. Mercifully, apartheid has crumbled away in the land of its conception. This does not mean it could not reappear in other places and forms, if enough bigots are misled by enough techno-mystics, wino-prophets and plastic-bag-ladies. Speaking of whom, *The Race Gallery* is liable to make most readers tire of these monkeys and almost long for the reappearance of the organ-grinder. I doubt if they will have long to wait. According to Kohn's compass, a strong Nietzsche revival is overdue and should soon be with us.

The defence against all this is not refusal of science but advance in real scientific understanding. In other words, understanding nature should not mean resorting to it. Indeed it means grasping, once and for all, why we can never resort to it. Which implies in turn a fuller understanding of how and why culture transcends nature – or, in Ernest Gellner's metaphor, how the inherent variety of ethnicity's wild plants is altered, as it must eventually be, into that of modernity's garden, the cultivated world-terrain where variation must remain the species' wealth – yet under very different rules, and with a more self-conscious guidance. This is surely the true point, and the real difficulty, of 'globalisation': the problem of History, beyond the end of Pre-history.

Kohn repeatedly observes how biological science has always been affected by and occasionally derived from social and political agendas. This is even truer of the social sciences. The emergence of a rational relativity approach is certain to be conditioned by the actual development of ethnic and nationality politics in the post-super-power world. So far that development has South Africa and the peace processes of Ulster and Palestine at one pole, Bosnia-Herzegovina and Rwanda at the other. But Kohn's estimate is based on none of these. The longest study of one particular issue in his book is the treatment of the Rom in post-Communist Central and Eastern Europe. He chose it by guessing that the place to study contemporary racism most effectively would be 'among the politically weakest of peoples', the large Gypsy or Romany population in most of the region's successor states.

'East Central Europe is still a Romantic landscape' is his striking phrase for them – a scene marked by the resurgence of *völkisch* ideas after the crazed environmentalism of the communist years. At that time the Gypsy question was decreed soluble, and indeed solved, by a barrage of briskly integrationist measures including the removal of wheels from Romany trailers and compulsory residence in special apartment blocks: 'Labour will directly change the Gypsies in miraculous ways. They will adopt trades and take part in Socialist competition', etc. One consequence was that by 1991 some 91 per cent of Czechs and 79 per cent of Hungarians confessed in a survey to hearty dislike of the Roma, while about one third of the Czechs thought they ought to be either deported or kept in ghettos. Not surprisingly, right-wing populists like Vladimir Meciar in Slovakia and Istvan Csurka in Hungary have battened eagerly upon this inheritance. They smell like gaseous leakages from the specimen jars of some fusty old *Rassensaal* or Race Gallery, the genotype museums from which Kohn took his title.

This dismal tale has two morals, in Kohn's view. 'Human biological diversity needs to be explored, not denied', he concludes. And then, diversity needs some new political defences in order to survive. The Roma population has become such a renewed scapegoat because it has no such protection, nor any equivalent of the Zionism which served to rally and direct the identity of the other transnational population once so prominent in Central and Eastern Europe. 'The newer era of nationalism and ethnic self-assertiveness has raised new political issues', he notes, which are perfectly incapable of solution either by an abstractly metropolitan liberalism or by a futile fallback on ethnic and racial stereotypes. The justification of nationalism has always been partly as a defence works: the seawalls of diversity, a redemption of particularity within the rising storm of Progress. 'Within' means both for and against. Its accompanying follies have arisen out of the social sources for such constructions – which were inevitably ethno-linguistic or 'racial' in the first instance, or, as anthropologists like to say, the 'primordial'.

What *The Race Gallery* suggests is that this instance has ended. But no other has as yet taken its place. Dead and unable to be born respectively, the contestant worlds at the end of pre-history seem to be those of ethnic nationality politics and a civic or identity politics more worthy of modernity's garden, or – in the other storm metaphor – more suited to the artificial breakwaters of continuing nation-state construction. Unable to embrace the latter, globalisation finds itself sporadically drawn back into the former. A reheated race science revives because no more comprehensive social science is capable of relegating or resituating its claims. Kohn's book is not an easy one. Getting through its digressive and argumentative structure is sometimes more like quarrying than reading. The argument is a crucial one, however, and the material which emerges from it should be invaluable to everyone involved in both the theory and the practical politics of ethnicity today.

7

Cities and Nationalism

If the 1997 New Year was a precedent, there will be serious prophetic constipation till around 2001.[1] Let me remind readers that the *Independent on Sunday* of 22 December last weighed in with a mere forty crystal-gazers, from Ian Angell, 'darling of the doom-and-gloom conference circuit', down to Theodore Zeldin's 'persuasively touchy-feely manifesto' *An Intimate History of Humanity*.[2] Yet quite a few gloomsters were not checked in, notably *éminence noire* Conor Cruise O'Brien. Was the Indie trying to cheer us up?

Or perhaps it was offering a little consolation to those already suffering from the *fin-de-siècle* drowning sensation. More serious victims might also try turning to Martin Thom's careful and deep fathoming of a similar great transition two hundred years ago: the birth of modern nationalism.[3] There is more to be learned on that particular subject here than from most contemporary fulminations, and I'm not excluding my own. Then too, in the decades following 1776 and 1789, the world passed through post-revolutionary rapids which permanently altered the shape and direction of the human river. Then also, society, notably the upper stratum, was suffering from manifestly lost bearings and complaining loudly about it. And then as now pundits of all lands found themselves blessed by the *Zeitgeist*, and redoubled their efforts until no open space was without its fairground tent and its impatient queues eager for lessons in portent-reading. As Martin Thom patiently points out over and over again, the trouble was not that the hucksters were mistaken. They were often quite right about what was going wrong. But that was unimportant, or at least ceasing to matter. As regards what was actually coming into being, on the other hand – the future pressing its way into the present through a myriad of unsuspected channels – they were mistaken or at best accidentally half-right. In one sense that didn't matter: they had spent the money long before anyone could sue them.

In another sense, alas, it mattered a lot. Rune-reading is a ridiculous business. And yet one can also see from Thom's careful account how in those circumstances – just like these now recurring – there was really no alternative to it. The enlivened sensibility of a transition time can never wait stoically upon events. It is compelled to cry out for some notion of whatever

122

lies in store. And the answers to such cries may be terribly influential, as well as wrong. This is the real reason why the curious activity of prophecy counts for so much. The most garbled or even insane forecast can end up moving things in one direction rather than another. Illusions, too, may weigh upon events, sometimes long and grievously. They may not really 'make the future' in the deepest or longest-range sense. But obviously they can powerfully inflect what might be called the middle range of historical development. And then – within that zone – some combination of person-alities and mainly military accidents could always mean there might *be* no other or fall-back prospect.

For example, the belief that an Aryan race was genetically destined to conquer and rule planet earth was a baseless delusion. Around 1940, however, Spielberg fans will be intrigued to know that Heinrich Himmler's Ancestral Heritage organisation *Ahnenerbe* included people convinced that the Aryans were of extra-terrestrial descent, and had been sent to earth equipped with super-human electrical powers. Expeditions went out looking for scientific proof of this hypothesis to the usual location: Tibet. Had the Nazis got away with it, one may be reasonably confident that academic learning of a sort would then have tried to oblige them. Equally, the conviction that 'primitive communism' might be successfully re-created in a supra-national and industrialised form out of the ruins of the Romanov and Habsburg empires was a prophetic mirage. What that involved was the discovery of an entire supra-national social class equipped with equivalent electric powers. Geographical Tibet was not on its menu. However, Lenin did think that a virtual-Tibetan elite of superman-monks was required to galvanise the proletariat. Attempts to realise these prophecies – and the struggle between them – have accounted for much of the past century. Fortunately they ran out of steam before annihilating the species. But does even the most fervent optimist think this *could* not have happened?

Hence it is a mistake to turn one's back on the fairground. Early in the twentieth century it really mattered to oppose Nietzsche and Lenin, and to do so in terms other than those of die-hard conservatism or philistinism. Presumably it will go on mattering in comparable terms as we move into the twenty-first century, accompanied by another bunch of mournful palm-readers and sermonising snake-oil reps. What *Republics, Nations and Tribes* makes very clear is how terribly careful one will have to be. Apocalyptic oratory relies chiefly upon a deft conjury of simplifications: 'globalisation', 'demise of the nation-state', 'Enlightenment', 'global warming' and so forth. The safest assumption is that it may be at least as difficult to define such terms today as it was to define 'nation', *Volk*, revolution and patriotism in the era of the 1790s and early 1800s.

It may, for example, not be quite so simple to record the nation-state's passing. Especially when, as Thom reminds us, practically no one discerned its arrival, or its eventual crystallisation into the general form of nationalism. During epochs of upheaval, educated people naturally look backwards in time for clues and inspiration. Over most of the early-modern globe – in the

Mogul and Chinese empires, in Islamic countries – the literate classes had lived in a retrospect of carefully gilded imperial and religious statehood. They inherited dynasties which were either 'immemorial' or had succeeded other ones with few deeper social changes. Their accompanying faiths were by definition eternal, and delimited only by a shifting frontier against outer 'barbaric' idolatry or unlettered animism. But seventeenth- and eighteenth-century Europe was different. Uniquely, its intelligentsias dwelt in a world which had existed long *before* that of the reigning monarchies and the religions which they increasingly opposed. They lived, that is, in the partly mythic domain of Greco-Roman Antiquity, and enjoyed a common high culture measured primarily in terms of familiarity with Aristotle, Stoicism and the chronicles of Republican Rome.

One crucial element in this extraordinary and remotely transmitted *mentalité* was its configuration not by nations but by the city-state. Hence Thom's title, which denotes an ideological transition from obsession with civic republics to one with tribally configured nations. Pre-transition, the political ideals and heroic figures of the Atlantic intelligentsias remained those of the old urban patriciates: Athens, Sparta and, above all, pre-imperial Rome. 'Patriotism' signified the actual or supposed attitude of ancient aristocratic elites towards their own city-countries, and against malevolent and obscurantist despots – especially Oriental despots like the Persian Darius or, later, the Ottoman sultans, who could be perceived as precursors of the Bourbons, the Stuarts and other early-modern monarchs.

In the semantics of that hindsight 'country' rarely meant 'nation' in anything like the modern sense. Its core significance was always 'city', the civilised nucleus which really counted, with or without what, in Renaissance times, Machiavelli would call its *contado* or *distretto* – an attached countryside that might always be useful but was never essential. It is interesting to note the precise inversion of meaning here, since it lies at the core of Thom's argument. Before long, nineteenth-century Romantic-inclined nationalism would be placing overwhelming emphasis exactly the other way round, upon the virtues of the *contado*. A nation could, it was then felt, do without its cities – dens of decadence, 'cosmopolitan' vice, traitors, etc. – but never without its healthy peasantry, folk-traditions, and a blood stream free from alien admixtures. Thus arose what Thom calls the 'Tribe-nation', a fateful post-Napoleonic idea system which developed unstoppably east of the Rhine, spread to Central and Eastern Europe and then, more patchily and belatedly, to the extra-European and post-colonial world of the twentieth century.

When Napoleon actually took over from the Directory, however, neither the Parisian *têtes pensantes* nor anybody else had much clue about this fantastic Pandora's box. One important point of view – amusingly described by Thom in chapter 6, 'The Cities Eclipsed' – was that the Corsican chap might turn out like Cincinnatus: one more gift from the ever-fertile womb of classicism, arisen providentially to calm the post-revolutionary tumult and thus prevent worse from happening. As no educated European needed reminding in 1796, Lucius Quinctius Cincinnatus was a fifth-century BC Roman patriot who left his estate to become Dictator and save the Republic from the onslaught of a foreign rabble. After a fortnight spent putting the latter in their place he is said to have returned willingly and humbly to man the plough, amid the grateful rejoicing of fellow Romans. It is interesting to remember that quite recently Lucius Quinctius had been popular in America too. True, it had taken George Washington more than two weeks on the job, and he had not exactly returned to the plough. But he did not make himself a bloodthirsty despot, either, or set up in the throne business against George III. Hence Classical retrospect had emerged fortified by the American Revolution. The weakness of native American and imported Afro-American nationalism meant that it would take them over a century to effectively challenge its regular porticos and grand Roman avenues.

Alas, France, and Europe, and the rest of the globe, were not America. In them the mirage of classical republicanism was soon exposed as worse than useless. Enlightenment pundits were convinced that modern liberties could be based on the template of Ancient Liberty, as divulged in semi-sacred scrolls handed down across a time of darkness, and then given a new and glorious articulation through the Renaissance. In reality, the old model was reaching its limit of usefulness even as they meditated so stubbornly upon such timeworn themes. Romanticism was already through the hallway and halfway up the stairs. The new template was upon them: terrible, wildly destructive and creative, and, above all, *popular* in a sense undreamt of by Antiquity. Though the label was not invented until much later, 'nationalism' had been unleashed by Napoleon's armies. Intuited and half-described by the great woman whose name recurs more frequently in Thom's pages than any other, Germaine de Staël, its angel-demons were soon to bury classical civism deeper than Atlantis.

Half a century later it was Karl Marx who pronounced the finest and most quoted elegy of the classicist delusion, at the start of *The Eighteenth Brumaire of Louis Bonaparte*. The nightmare of dead generations weighed upon living brains, he pointed out, and ensured that those 'creating something that has never existed' would most likely perceive it as something that had always existed. One result was the 'world-historical necromancy' through which

> Danton, Robespierre, Saint-Just, Napoleon, the heroes as well as the parties of the old French Revolution, performed the task of their time in Roman costume and with Roman phrases ... In the classically austere traditions of the Roman Republic its gladiators found the ideals and the art-forms, the self-deceptions that they needed in order to conceal from themselves the bourgeois limitations of the content of their struggles ...

But the 'bourgeois' limits were also *national*. Elites might imaginatively reconfigure themselves along transnational guidelines; *peoples* could not. Least of all those increasing masses of people now drawn, forcibly and relatively quickly, away from their countrysides and into workshops, offices, stores and conscript armies. Speaking Greek, Latin or French, the elites might believe they ultimately had more in common with one another than their respective *canailles*; the *canailles* themselves never could. For the latter, civic 'patriotism' was never a direct option; but nationalism was – modern, majoritarian, populist, vulgar, battling, emotive, the tabloid successor to the bewigged austerity of Greece and Rome.

Republics, Nations and Tribes tries to follow this transition in extraordinary detail, through the texts, memoirs, letters and other records of many participants. It is, so to speak, a capillary view of how one world gestated and inched forward in consciousness until at last it began to burst out from the womb. At one end of the process we find polite effigies of Cincinnatus and Solon; from the other emerges the scarred, maudlin and yet irrepressibly alive, and comical, figure of 'Nicolas Chauvin', the Parisian vaudeville hero of the 1840s. Patriotism had turned into Chauvinism – originally a crazy concoction of Napoleonism, blood-worship, seven-year military conscription, Bedouin-bashing and sex. It soon caught on everywhere else. Sociologists like to tidy all this up under deceptively calm headings like 'urbanisation' or 'modernisation'. It was what Marx, with an awful sense of vertigo, felt rurally descended France lurching into as he sat composing his *Eighteenth Brumaire*. The people were misbehaving themselves; if they turned into Frenchmen in *this* way, even a third-rate bum like Louis Napoleon would get his chance.

The detailed retrospect Thom conjures up also helps answer one obvious question about the transition. The *philosophes* were brighter than the nationalist intelligentsias who followed them; so how could they have been fooled for so long by the legend of Antiquity? The whole Enlightenment depended upon this narrow, rickety and backward-gazing cultural structure, on which the *social* modernity envisaged in the *Encyclopédie* could never conceivably have been built. However, one reason they remained unaware of the contradiction was that an important dimension of Antiquity not only lived on but structured the daily life of most eighteenth-century intellectuals. Indeed it influenced particularly strongly those who became revolutionary leaders in America, France and Britain. This was Roman law. It was conceived as anything but limited or outmoded. Indeed its resurrected forms were to be the mainframe of the civilisation articulated by the politician–lawyers behind all the great declarations and constitutional pronouncements of the time.

Then, secondly, as Thom emphasises (also in chapter 6):

> it is worth dwelling upon the survival, up until the very end of the eighteenth century, of small European states ... Notwithstanding the repeated attempts of the absolutist monarchies to destroy them, their position was, by 1748, more or less secure. At times they served as laboratories, with rival *philosophes* squabbling over their respective merits or shortcomings, as was the case, to a pronounced degree, with Geneva, in whose political affairs D'Alembert and Voltaire both meddled.

Geneva was also the inspiration of the most radical of these thinkers, Rousseau. In 1746 the Republic of Genoa had regained its independence and the astonishing deeds of its People's Assembly were the talk of polite Europe. Thus, not long before the great revolutions which led to nation-building, it was by no means obvious that city-states were finished and small or micro-states obsolete. Nationalism was to be more successful than absolutist monarchy in suppressing or sidelining them. But this came later, and its long-term costs were frightful. The broad band of small states which until the nineteenth century stretched across Europe from the Baltic to the Mediterranean were indeed 'absorbed' into the would-be tribe-nations of Germany and Italy. This process has traditionally been noted with a curious kind of bluff satisfaction by 'internationalists' and big-state wallahs of both Left and Right: the overcoming of feudal anachronisms, etc. They have usually ignored its most distinctive by-product: fascism. If the Germans and Italians then succumbed to ethnic-electrical supermania (as one might say) this was partly in response to the digestion pains attending suppression of so much recalcitrant tradition and localism.

The now forgotten persistence of smaller-scale civic identities, Thom goes on, meant that the idea of federations or confederations of these entities also endured as a competitor to nationhood. The revolt of the United Provinces in the Netherlands had updated this conception, and after 1776 the American upheaval was at first interpreted in a similar way. All these tendencies served both to forestall and conceal the deeper current gathering momentum underneath them:

> Tenacious traditions of city-state liberty and the wider arcs of Enlightenment conviction together inhibited for several decades the formation of the fully-fledged doctrine of the tribe-nation ... thereby providing breathing room for the otherwise endangered notions of city-nation and the general city of mankind (p. 172).

Yet that breathing-room could not long endure. The rising *canailles* were stifled in it; Clausewitz's total war flattened it; then industrialisation shattered its stilted partitions more irreparably, and delivered the remains over to the new national Leviathans.

Admirable as Thom's account is, no one should think *Republics, Nations and Tribes* is an easy intellectual stroll. Dominated recently by the writings of Professor J.G.A. Pocock, the history of early-modern ideas is notoriously a zone of intricate and ambiguous exploration: the borderland of the modern age, a shadow time *entre loup et chien* where nothing was in its own estimation the way it now appears to us. This book raises the shadows to a level of almost divinely mad scholarship, in which no byway goes unexplored, including the dead ends, and each route diversion leads inexorably to seventeen others. Take Chapter 8, for example, on 'Nations and Tribes': an introduction on 'The Mores of the Germans' (as seen in Tacitus, Aeneas Silvius Piccolomini, Houston Stewart Chamberlain and Eduard Norden) leads one on to the Asiatic Society of Calcutta, Friedrich Schlegel, Indo-European linguistics and Ernest Gellner's essay on Bronislaw Malinowski; then back to John Anderson – the 1938 editor of Tacitus – as a prelude to the vital, yet *en passant*, observation that 'the history of modern ethnology is inseparable from that of nationalism'; and so to Franz Boas, antiquarianism, assorted reflections on *L'Esprit des lois* and Rousseau, the method of voting in the pre-1789 *parlements*, and the numinous properties of many ancient Breton monuments. Certainly, all this 'alerts us to that great hall of mirrors in which tribes and nations meet', and it also brings a superb conclusion:

> Whereas tribal liberty had been a dying song in a mountain fastness, it was now construed as immanent, ubiquitous and eternal, inhering in lichen-encrusted stones, or in 'monuments' carried in speech across countless generations.

So a century and a half after Chateaubriand's *Mémoires d'outre-tombe* we still hear echoes of that dying song. Countless generations are still whispering a monumental message onwards to their even more numerous successors in an unimaginable future time. Thom tries to trace just how this *mentalité* was formed, and each step in the itinerary is itself fascinating. Yet it is only fair to observe that most trail-followers are likely to expire somewhere along his convoluted way, and even the survivors will feel like breaking a few mirrors themselves before they reach the end.

These features of the book are all the more maddening because of the importance of the wider vistas it opens up. Romanticism and its political analogue, nationalism, were the greatest expansion of human sensibility and vision which history records. Whatever other ingredients flowed into modernity, these were surely among its necessary conditions. Had neo-classicism endured much longer, even for the proverbial one thousand years, it could never have become the vehicle of *mass* democracy and culture. On the other hand, the actual vehicle which took over from it has now accomplished a good deal of its work: over a quickly expanding area of the world, 'modernity' has happened. During the same time nationalism saved the world from imperialism, at appalling cost. And yet these costs of what Thom calls 'tribe-nationism' remain far lower than the alternatives presented by successive waves of conquest and colonisation, or by the mutually assured destruction super-power confrontation of the 1960s and 1970s.

If this is the case, then a successor transition must be under construction. Something profound did end around 1989, even if it wasn't History; hence another world should be gestating in ways broadly analogous to those described by Thom, but probably much more rapidly, leading us into a futurity as surprising and unforeseen as that of first-round industrialisation and nation-statehood.

The author's own prophetic stance is conveyed most clearly in the 'Introduction':

I write from the conviction that before the age of nations there was an age of cities, and that after the age of nations there could be, if there is not a pandaemonium of 'ethnic cleansing' instead, a new age of cities, in which regional assemblies, freed of the terminal claims of providence, could answer in all clarity to the rightful demands of cosmopolis.

What this stalwart reasoning seems to suggest is that the demise of the 'tribe-nation' and ethnic nationalism may lead onwards to a revival of what the book correctly identifies as the much longer tradition of civic or city-focused nationalism. It is true that civic nationalism, or as the elitist intonation of the Enlightenment put it, 'patriotism', lasted for over two thousand years, while its tribal cousin and successor has been around for less than two centuries. Ethnic nationalism proved a different ball game, and in some ways a far more important one. *Republics, Nations and Tribes* is an admirable study of how different its rules were, and of how practically nobody understood them until they were actually in operation. Through their play the majority came into history. Nor was there any other way in which that decisive entry could have been made. Once it has occurred, however, further and different rules are bound to impose themselves. 'Internationalist' ideology itself provides no clues about what these will be: it was essentially a mental *cul-de-sac* reacting against, but also tied to, the tide of ascendant ethnicity.

Surely some different mode of differentiation is now more likely – a different vestment of nationalism, as it were, drawing elements from both ethnicity and the far longer *durée* of the civic-territorial past? If I interpret Martin Thom's insight rightly, he suggests that the latter ought to become more significant than the former. Whatever the 'rightful demands' of world order turn out to be, they will make space for hundreds or even thousands more independent states, but not – certainly not so easily – for thousands of ethnically configured nations. This is an attractive argument, but with a central weakness. It remains hard to see how any contemporary and future statehood can remain other than a by-product of nationalism's moment in history: that is, 'all-embracing', numinous, cultural, democratic and deeply personal in meaning. A world where all individuals *belong* can never return to being like the countries of Antiquity or early-modern Europe. There must be no return to ethnic-tribal cleansing; yet there can be no return to pre-pandemonium conditions either – that is, to the custodial governance of liberal elites acting out a civic spirit deemed forever inaccessible to the mob. Doom-mongering like O'Brien's *On the Eve of the Millennium* pleads precisely for this impossible reverse motion, the salvation of an Enlightenment which began to be transcended in the period of Martin Thom's book. No, another salvation than this is due, and the implication is that we need to be both wary and sanguine about its coming.

Part III
The Small Battalions

The Question of Scale

France was the most important political model for modern and contemporary statehood. Although other formative revolutions preceded that of 1789, none established such a general template. For around two centuries after that date, most actual and all would-be nation-states could not help aspiring to be 'something like France', in fact where they could and in fantasy where they couldn't. There were also imitation Westminsters, repeat Hollands, Belgiums or Portugals, petty Russias and Americas. But even these have often been influenced by the mainstream blueprint which dominated Central and Eastern Europe, Latin America and of course all the territories of French colonisation.

One vital feature of that blueprint was its scale: the medium-to-large nation-state, capable of constructing a distinguishable political economy of its own, the range of cultural and administrative institutions needed for managing this, and an army capable of defending it. Although not created by central force alone, France was undeniably articulated by and dependent upon such a power: the Leviathans of modern times were armoured from the outset, and much of their inner being was configured by and for survival. That configuration acquired a name: 'viability'. Being like France meant being viable, or self-managing and self-moving to a degree considered sufficient – possessing the autonomy required for independent action in the arena of states and nations. Hence 'independence' was no mere legal status. It registered not just formal rights, a proclaimed and accepted recognition, but 'real' or effective powers of assertion (most authentically felt when some other country's toes are trodden upon, and retribution is called for). 'Independence' is being able to make a nuisance of one's collective self. The most *real* independence therefore lies in being able to do this – in the entirely French phrase – *dans tous les azimuts*, all out and in any chosen direction, and preferably with a nuclear *force de dissuasion*. By contrast, phoney and unreal statehood is identified with 'dependence': being a 'puppet' country which either cannot or dares not step out of line.

Fortunately, nationalism has never accepted 'realism' (the appropriately dismal title bestowed upon this theory of international relations). Its own relationship to the universal cannot help being essentially different.

Historically, too much of it sprang out of opposition to the French
Revolutionary attack on the rest of the world, and then from rejection of all
the successor attempts at colonisation and the imposition of blueprinted
hierarchies for the Greater Good. Realists perceive anarchy as a deplorable
state of nature, to be contained and if necessary repressed; nationalists see
it as the only genuine kind of internationalism – the equality of corporate
being, as it were, and the sole foundation for a tolerable universal order.
An authentic *Internationale* can only be based upon the liberation of human
nature; which means (in the first instance) nationalities, the precondition
for democracy and individual emancipation; which means (given the
difficulties in defining 'nation', and the inevitable plethora of candidates)
an equally inevitable bias towards permission rather than restraint; in this
game all credentials are forged, and notably those of the prime movers
themselves, the French and the Anglo-British.

But if this is so, then scale and 'viability' are certain to lose their once
semi-sacred meaning. They were actually part of the armoured Great Power
world of (approximately) 1750 to 1950, which was less that of nations than
of a sustained and destructive contest between nationality and empire. The
scale of nationhood was imposed primarily by those ambient conditions.
The conditions finally disappeared in the later 1980s. Both independence
and dependence are altering in significance. It is argued here that this deep
shift is bound to be favourable to smaller-scale polities which increasingly
diverge from the French and similar models of nation-state propriety,
metropolitan rectitude and armoured potency. The augmented mutual
dependence of 'globalisation' entails a mutual enhancement of nuisance
value, and of the real significance of recognition, juridical status and treaty
rights. Being independent once meant the power to blast an enemy capital
out of existence (and to carry on testing the relevant devices in 'remote' –
i.e. helpless – zones of the globe). Although it is still not clear just what
independence will mean in a small-state world, it will surely be nothing like
that.

8

Andorra

For three years the media have been filled with news about the reborn nations of the East and their sometimes bloody conflicts.[1] In the West things are supposed to be different. Here integration rolls calmly ahead, apart from a few minor problems: Italy, Ireland, Belgium, German reunification, French chauvinism, Ukanian Alzheimer's, Maastrichtitis, and the monetary system's fatal heart attack.

Last month, however, I visited a newly born nation-state of Western Europe. In March this year it got its constitution approved by referendum, with a 75 per cent majority. The remaining powers of the former monarchical regime have been removed (though some of its forms are retained) and the new state has been accepted as a full member of the United Nations. Though a quarter of the electorate voted against the changes most people seem now to have accepted them. Rapid if belated conversions to the independence cause have been common, notably in the business community. Nobody was fleeing the country. A provisional government is in place, and the first fully independent elections have been set for 12 December.

One reason no one has heard about these surprising events is the size of the country in question: Andorra, smaller than Fife and with a population of only 54,500, slightly larger than Kirkcaldy's. Most of them live in or around its capital town, Andorra la Vella. The Scottish political debate is often couched in terms of 'small countries', meaning places like Luxemburg, Denmark or Wales, but this is a different league altogether. The European Community already has five such micro-nations within its boundaries (San Marino, Monaco, the Channel Islands, the Isle of Man, Andorra) and will probably soon have a sixth – the Gibraltar peninsula.

There are those (even in Scotland) who think them too small to matter. The British Empire got us all used to thinking big, and in some ways Europe has prolonged this affliction.

Let anyone still troubled by it reflect on the following fact. I was talking to ministers in Andorra la Vella on 9 September, which happened to be the date of a recent cross-party delegation to Brussels. Led by the Scottish TUC's Campbell Christie, it represented approximately 75 per cent of the

135

Scottish population and was there to complain formally to the European Community about having no collective voice at all. They are not represented in their own capital, never mind in Brussels or at the General Assembly of the United Nations.

As we talked, through the windows of the new government building a much older one could be seen perched on a rocky outcrop overlooking the high street – Avinguda de Meritxell – and a bit of the old town. A cluster of bright red, yellow and blue tricolours flew in front of it to mark the first National Day celebrated in independence. It was the Casa de la Vall or Andorran parliament house, where representatives of these valley communities have met uninterruptedly for over seven centuries. There was (I had to confess) a scenically comparable edifice in Edinburgh. But it had a Democracy Picket permanently stationed in front of it, and it now seemed unlikely that a parliament would ever reassemble there since Her Majesty's representative in Scotland had decided to sell the place off.

After the first mild incredulity they were of course terribly nice about it, with perhaps just a touch of complacency (which I readily forgave). 'Well', said the Minister of Culture, 'don't forget the constitutional process here took over twenty years, and we sometimes thought there would be no end to it . . . But when democracy is on your side, the important thing is never to stop talking.'

A history as long as Scotland's lies behind the recent changes. But theirs has been like one long, delicate balancing act between Spain and France. It began in 1278, when the first *Pareatge* or joint sovereignty agreement was signed, and concluded with a formal UN reception in New York this year. Although keen to remain on good terms with the elephants on either side, for the first time they no longer depend upon them. Does it really matter, this kind of 'independence' in an interdependent world ruled by great corporations and global markets? The question may seem over-familiar since it has been so endlessly debated. But there is no staleness about the answer you get in Andorra – a matter-of-fact 'yes'.

Situated in an almost inaccessible no-man's-land between two great kingdoms, the Andorran valleys were always disputed and yet not important enough to go to war over. Early on the neighbours realised it would be simpler to agree on a form of joint rule, under which both sides would leave the area alone and demilitarised. So the small mountain community was in effect omitted from the long Pyrenean frontier – and from the wars which surged to and fro across it.

Another side-effect of this strange interstitial existence was home rule. The co-sovereigns of Andorra were formerly the French Count of Foix and the Bishop of Urgell, the nearest big town in Catalonia on the Spanish side. They appointed regents who occasionally intervened in valley affairs but rarely concerned themselves with everyday life. The latter was managed by a cantonal democracy very like the Swiss one: representatives of seven valley communes meeting in the Casa de la Vall as the General Council of the Valleys (the body which has evolved into today's state).

Later, dynastic complications transferred the French Count's rights to the Kings of France and then, after the Revolution, to successive presidents of the French Republic. Thus it was President François Mitterrand who signed France's agreement to Andorra's separation. When push might have come to shove – after the April referendum – there was simply nothing else for the representative of the most centralised *étatisme* to do. The alternative would have been to flout a clearly democratic will equipped with national credentials. Did the scale of that will matter, or the supposed 'unviability' of such a minuscule society? Not in the slightest.

Once France gave in, Spain had to follow. After a tenacious, ten-year-long rearguard action against every constitutional move from the Casa de la Vall, Joan Martí Alanís, Bishop of Urgell, was to be heard giving a warm welcome to the new constitution at the Andorra National Day festivities on 8 September. I was there, but my Catalan was not up to so many sonorous hypocrisies. Later on people were only too happy to translate and savour them, recalling past episcopal predictions of the doom to come. Thus (I could not help thinking) might Douglas Hurd or any voice of Britannic order endorse a Scottish constitution on some future St Andrew's day, hoping against hope that past intransigence might be half-forgotten in the new day's euphoria.

A glorified duty-free emporium at the bottom of a ski slope: Andorra's reputation is not high in today's Europe. But surely Scots have suffered enough from stereotyping to distrust such images. A few miles above Andorra la Vella's hectic high street stands the sanctuary of Our Lady of Meritxell, where the Andorrans traditionally gather on 8 September. Coaches and cars from the remotest slopes disgorge a constant stream of families into what is really a large, untidily extended family reunion. Everyone half knows everyone else, and most of the time goes in embraces, recollections and the showing off of children. There are almost no outsiders. In the chapel one thanksgiving mass merges into another, with no particular relationship to the officially printed timetable.

This year a new European government was attending the ceremony. 'That's the Prime Minister over there', said the friend I was with, '. . . the one with the pipe and specs, would you like to say hello?' Oscar Ribas Reig is a severe-looking banker known for dry Alpine humour. He gravely inclined the head and apologised for having so little time to talk properly just then. But Bishop Alanís was only a few yards away, enthusiastically pressing flesh prior to his surrender speech. 'Yes, God is undoubtedly with us on this lovely day . . .', the Premier went on a little louder than necessary, gazing outwards to the Pyrenean heaven all around, 'I hope you enjoy your stay in our country.'

Nowhere could be more appropriate to the new Andorran identity. A fire destroyed everything at Meritxell in 1972, including the tiny old wooden effigy of Our Lady. But an exact replica of the statue was made, and housed in a great theatrical structure commissioned from Barcelona architect Ricard Bofill. He built huge windows opening out on to a black and white cloister itself open to the sky. At the foot of his rectangular bell tower, on either side of Our Lady, are seven niches representing the communes – the antique social structure of the land, honoured but also transformed by soaring modernist arches which now reach (in a sense) as far as New York.

Later an irredeemably Spanish band erupted in the cloister for the *Sardana*, the long, grave, complicated dance which Andorrans share with their Catalan neighbours. Its circle of linked hands does assert communal feeling and a sort of enclosure. But the circle can be of any size, and its sense seems to be that of reproducing the world in miniature rather than simply shutting it out. On that day at least, in the glory of an Indian summer, there didn't seem to be chauvinism or exclusivity about it. The message felt more like: here also – even on this scale – the world translates into the joined hands of community rather than individuals alone. And no scale is much smaller than Andorra's.

Yet Andorra does exclude the world – beginning with the European Community. Odd as it must seem, one thing the new-born state will never be is 'independent in Europe'. Membership of the Maastricht Union would remove all the economic differentials upon which its commerce depends. Just as important, the free movement of individuals entailed by Euro-citizenship would rapidly destroy all the communal values celebrated by the *Sardana*. Neither individuals nor companies pay any direct taxes in Andorra, and the value-added tax is blessedly unknown. Were unrestricted entry to this fiscal paradise possible, its population could quadruple in a matter of weeks.

So in another sense scale does matter. If you are small enough, 'swamping' is a real possibility and there have to be mechanisms of exclusion. Certain big countries of Europe despair about having a 5 per cent immigrant population. In Andorra the majority of inhabitants are already foreign – 42,000 'recognised residents' as against only 10,500 born in the country. The former are increasing at a far more rapid rate than the native-born, though that may change in the coming decade. During the boom years of 1960–88 a young working class moved into the valleys from Portugal and Andalusia, and their larger families are being born into Andorran citizenship. But other newcomers still have to wait twenty years for passport and vote.

The 'free movement of capital' is as restricted as that of people. Companies have been kept out of paradise by the draconian requirement of 66 per cent Andorran ownership. Ministers talk of using independence to relax both rules, but such changes are not likely to alter the basic configuration of the economy – an ultra-free market confined (and kept going) by a state perimeter of cast iron. Far from dissolving itself into Europe, the new country seeks to eternalise these boundaries. Independence is another and better way of maintaining the differentials upon which this Lilliputian society depends.

Even more surprising, Europe has consented to the deal. Andorra's new trade agreement with the Community makes it, in effect, into a duty-free ship permanently moored in the middle of the Pyrenees. Yet what else could those much maligned bureaucrats in Brussels do? Build up their own customs perimeter around it, thereby converting reasonably free commerce into crime? Smuggling is an old way of life in the Pyrenean borderland, and there was no realistic way of forbidding it. Also, they were not dealing with a province or a colony but an independent land which cared less than tuppence about getting its feet under 'the top table'. It must have seemed best to leave such a trifling anomaly alone and hope it wouldn't prove contagious.

Yet it is worth thinking for a moment on what contagion might mean. In all civil and cultural senses the Andorrans are of course as 'European' as anyone else. A democratic political confederation would not in itself dismay them. What they find impossible is an economic federation based on a single huge and homogeneous free-trade bloc – a nation-state structure without many of the cultural advantages and compensations which European nationhood traditionally brought. Such mega-order may once have appeared inevitable, when the whole world looked like congealing forever into blocs. But now the conviction seems to be draining out of it, fast. If Maastricht is merely a postscript to that past, then even tiny anomalies may prove more significant than one could have imagined. The Treaty of Rome was constructed for elephants. If Maastricht is leading us to an elephant graveyard, may not the hour of the flea have come?

For what it's worth, the Ribas Reig government must think something along these lines. One plank of its foreign policy is a proposal that Europe's micro-polities combine to seek a new style of Community membership. This would presumably be a collective deal like the EC–Andorra one, yet its sense would inevitably be quite different. Tiny as these places are, the threshold of mere anomaly would be crossed by any accord of that kind. The 'exceptions' would acquire general rights. Europe would become an arena within which such 'oddities' possessed their own charter for (frankly) a degree of anarchy and privilege.

Those still plugged into Bigthink may feel the United Kingdom to be far above the dilemma. In point of fact, the curious anachronisms of the Unwritten Constitution will directly expose her to it. Should Gibraltar be added to Jersey and the Isle of Man, then in terms of population and territory (though not of wealth) Britain will account for most of next century's micro-states.

Not that such thoughts will make any difference. Even in small countries it is astonishing how many people hate tiny countries. The engineered free trade or fiscal incentives which the latter rely on are almost always subjects of fulmination: 'parasitism', 'havens' of a privilege denied to ordinary mortals used to being scalped by the exciseman at every cash till. How dare they get away with it! Like Switzerland, their very existence can appear sinful, a standing reproach to nation-state normalcy.

However, that kind of outrage conveys little real conviction. The fact is that 'havens' exert a near-irresistible appeal to which, given the slightest opportunity, most of the fulminators would eagerly respond. There may be a few professionals of expostulation (MPs and so on) of whom this is not true. But most normally constituted beings would join a low-tax, VAT-free, banking-secretive, canton-sized heaven tomorrow if only *they* could get away with it. Regrettably they can't: the havens are booked out, most with interminable queues of applicants. So what good (if envious) democrats feel is really that no one should be allowed to enjoy such luck.

In the Andorran case disapproval is aggravated by anti-commercial snobbism. No one can deny that in that sense Andorra la Vella may be a culture shock – a teeming, termite-like confusion of blaring publicity, hard-sell pushers and dazed consumers deadlocked into the notion of something for (almost) nothing.A few minutes of drift in the crowd and anyone can be overcome by a strange consumerist frenzy – a compulsion to shop at all costs and bend the plastic till it snaps. Much of what people purchase is cheaper than outside, of course. But not always that much cheaper, and the cost and time of getting somewhere so inaccessible must be added. It cannot be cost-consciousness alone which brings in the vast crowds from both Spain and France.

I suspect it may be the teeming frenzy itself. In Andorra high street it always feels like the day before Christmas, and the giddy atmosphere turns ordinary shopping into an event. The main tourist guide has its own version of this:

> Throughout the length and breadth of the lively, cheerful Andorran streets, shops, department stores and *boutiques* tempt visitors with their enticing windows. Resistance is useless ... Everyone buys something in Andorra, and shopping becomes almost a sport in which everybody takes part.

Most shopping malls are located in flat suburbs or just off motorways. By contrast the Andorran equivalent feels like fairyland – especially approached from the French side, through endless hairpins and the bizarre half-built ski station at Pas de la Casa. 'Everyone expects some kind of fabulous bargain here', said a local high-street hotelier I went to see, '. . . something to boast about or show off at home.'

Raymond Canut was showing me his own latest investment at Les Escaldes (named after its hot springs). This turned out to be the Andorran version of the humble high-street sauna: the *Caldea*, an aluminium and glass atrium slightly smaller than Sydney Opera House, capped by a space-needle taller than the Scott Monument. 'Our new multi-purpose Health and Fitness Centre', he explained, '. . . which will appeal to the ecologically minded.' It pipes the thermal water to industry-sized jacuzzis (hot, tepid or cool, perfumed or plain) in great solariums where the environmentally conscious will be encouraged to recover from shopping frenzy or skiing accident.

But he was also a parliamentarian, and keener to discuss the political breakthrough. 'What you must clearly understand is that most people thought we were daft', he began, 'in fact that's what we were called – *les quatre fous*, that handful of loonies.' A small group of them had been to French universities in the later 1960s and got all the wrong ideas. Then they returned to make their piles out of the great shopping boom, still dreaming of democracy. And eventually things began to move in their direction. The Andorran co-princely regime was so absurd that everyone came to be in at least verbal agreement: it just had to be 'modernised'.

But what was that to mean? Andorran communalism resembles the Swiss model also in its social conservatism. Women only got the vote in 1971. What the loonies had to confront was a two-part bloc: Catholic conservatives headed by the Bishop, and the businessmen, who felt that any constitutional move at all might be bad for their admittedly handsome profits. The former gradually mellowed after democracy came back to Catalonia and the great changes there proved fairly harmless to the faith – 'they inched their way out of the bunker' is how he put it. The latter proved more recalcitrant.

Yet this recalcitrance was also shallow. Since the new government of Andorra consists entirely of successful businessmen like Canut I assumed they knew what they were talking about. Although their merchant and shopkeeping colleagues had gone to the last ditch in defence of the old ways, there was little true conviction among them. Hence – once Catholic opinion had taken even a mildly democratic turning – it was only a matter of time. Meanwhile the madmen were worming their way into the General Council, and labouring patiently towards a new constitution. At last they won a tiny majority, and proposed a test of opinion on it. When that was accepted by the co-princes – as it had to be – the game was up.

My parliamentarian recalled their very quiet revolution with malicious pleasure, leaning over the table and stabbing his finger up and down: 'The Business Community, huh, big deal! *From one day to the next . . . yes really, overnight*, the blighters all changed their minds! They knew there was only one likely result to a referendum. Now every shopkeeper up and down this street is a democrat, warning us about sticking to our own constitution.'

The equivalent of the British monarchy remains. Andorra is still a principality, not a republic. To ease the transition for the 25 per cent who still voted for the status quo, Mitterrand and Alanís have been redefined rather than got rid of. And their sole remaining function will be precisely that – to safeguard the new, written constitution of the Andorran people. 'Can't you do the same with the Windsors?' he asked. 'I mean, neutralise them and let them fade away?' Andorra could become a republic tomorrow if the co-princes misbehaved; but until then – he smiled sarcastically – '. . . there's more than one way to make a Revolution'. These days the spirit of 1968 often seems extinct in France. It was (I realised) not only alive and well in Andorra, but actually running the place.

I left heaven for Spain on a sunny Saturday morning, hitting the traffic almost at once. It was solid all 10 kilometres to the frontier post and beyond, thousand upon thousand of *peseta*-laden purchasers aiming to live it up on

Avinguda de Meritxell. 'Nothing like what it was', people had told me, 'you should have seen the crowds in the old days', when General Franco's corporatist economy held back consumer capitalism.

But the numbers were still impressive and (with European complicity) likely to continue. People won't stop adoring mountains, snow and shopping (above all for a bargain). This is just as well for the Andorran economy, whose income derives mainly from a small import tax on all goods sold there. At the moment it amounts to about half current public expenditure – which is certain to increase markedly with independence. But no one appeared much bothered about that. They are counting on markedly increasing the through-put of both goods and visitors, by astounding visitor-traps like the *Caldea*, Pas de la Casa and the brand new Meritxell Clinic in the capital.

It is not a formula applicable everywhere, I agree. On the other hand, in tomorrow's more untidy and loose-end Europe it may be applied a lot more widely than many people think. I doubt if it belongs only to miniature and interstitial formations like Andorra. Some parts of the recipe may be taken up by small (as distinct from micro-) countries, and even regions (as the Swiss have done for centuries). Democracy is the key. In the new order of things politics will become more important, not less. So in certain respects the Andorran model may prefigure what the British would no doubt be tempted to call 'Thatcherite Europe'. This may be as different from that lady's ideas as 'Thatcherite Britain' has turned out to be: a chancer's jungle, a liberated cacophony, a coat of contrary colours far distant from the monochrome classicism so dear to Europe's founders and ideologues.

9

Micro-states

Along with boundaries and identities, we need to consider scale.[1] What I would like to suggest is that the factors of 'scale' (size, population, relative economic, social and cultural weighting) have usually not been adequately taken into account in reflections on the significance of frontiers and the identities which these delimit.

Most theorising about nationalism has gone on since World War II, and most of that has tended to assume a typical or average scale applying to the units or entities it is concerned with. Though endlessly debated, this ideal-typical 'nation-state' – the theorist's 'building-block' – can be defined for the purposes of the succinct statement in order here, as: 'something like France'.

The model was of course a composite of different assumptions about physical size, likely population, economic resources or development, culture and so on. It is (incidentally) perfectly well understood today by most observers that France was actually never very like the model type which both patriots and theorists made of it – i.e. the 'hexagone' was and is a 'multi-national' agglomeration rather than a semi-miraculous gift of nature. But this counted for little on the plane of generalisation and international-relations theory. There, France – the France of absolute kingship, 1789 and Jacobinism – was the forge, the original template of modern state-formation, and this is why it remains the most convenient way of summing up these assumptions.

They could also be summarised in a single conceptual term, however – in the word 'viability' (*viabilité, chances de succès*). The implication was always that this bundle or package of assumptions represented the minimal necessary conditions for modern statehood. Unless certain general conditions were met, a population or territory had no chance of being a nation-state, or a proper and effective nation-state – a respectable or non-joke building-block of the modern international order. Without the minimal equipment, forget it.

On the level of high theory the point was put across most famously, and influentially, by the late Ernest Gellner. It was a key feature of the 'modernisation theory' of nationalism first expounded in *Thought and*

Change (1964) and elaborated in *Nations and Nationalism* (1983). There he maintained that post-eighteenth-century political nationalism was in essence a world-wide forced response to the rapid or shock impact of West European led (or later, Atlantic-led) modernisation. I don't need to recapitulate this famous theory here and now.[2]

It was that theory which first made overall sense of the nationalist phenomenon, and the assumptions about scale and 'viability' I mentioned before were written into it. Nation-statehood in the new mode was configured by the pressures and constraints of development, in other words, and these ensured that only entities above a certain threshold of scale had any chance of surviving, or of attaining independence – or indeed, any right to do so.

Lilliput and Brobdingnag

This was never just a theoretical assumption. It was, for example, the practical rule of thumb employed by the League of Nations in the 1920s and 1930s. Monaco and Liechtenstein existed then as today, exasperating small pebbles in the otherwise perfectly fitting shoe of viability's conventional wisdom. But the League viewed them as unworthy nuisances, feudal vestiges capable only of provoking conflicts among serious nation-states.

The same standard was of course never applied to entities betraying the norm in the other direction – by being too big. The Wilsonian norm was in practice asymmetrical: it had to be lived up to at one end but could be exceeded with impunity at the other. The British, French and other empires, the Soviet Union and other multi-national amalgams had to be tolerated because of their power, and also because – then as today – many people thought that the national state was obviously declining, indeed doomed, and (equally obviously) could only be replaced by something bigger, not something smaller. Lilliput, therefore, would soon be forgotten on the world's inevitable route to one Brobdingnag or another.

From the vantage point of the 1990s, how is this world altered! Changed utterly, and in a sense heartening to any protagonist of smaller-scale sovereignty. This is not – incidentally – a question of small being necessarily beautiful, any more than gigantic was before it. I believe that scale is a question of structure and functionality, and not of either ethics or aesthetics. Since the 1970s, in the twenty years which culminated with the end of the Cold War and the dissolution of the Soviet imperium, conditions changed in ways highly favourable to the existence, the prosperity and the proliferation of tiny states.

What were the shifts which brought about this transformation? A wry summary of some of them can be found in Eric Hobsbawm's recent history of the twentieth century, *The Age of Extremes*.[3] He points out there that though, on the whole, the world economy of the post-war boom period (1950–75) remained an 'international' or home-centred one in the old pre-war sense, there were significant signs of change in the later 1960s. It was at this time that a 'transnational' economic system began to emerge – 'a system of economic activities for which state territories and state frontiers are not the basic framework but merely complicating factors'. This new system was characterised by transnational firms ('multi-nationals'), an accompanying international division of labour, and the rapid rise of offshore finance.[4] He goes on to single out the last factor, offshore money and financial movements, as perhaps the most important novelty of the era – the thing which provided the vital leverage for transnationalism to emerge and begin to seriously affect the world. But it was also the thing which most directly transformed the possibilities for very small states.

The huge Cold War expenditure abroad of the US government and the expansion of US-based companies into multi-nationals created the Eurodollar, a new de facto world currency replacing the pound sterling. There was of course no state authority regulating Eurodollar transactions, the consequence being (in Hobsbawm's words) 'a vast, multiplying flood of unattached capital that washed round the globe from currency to currency looking for quick profits'. By the 1980s a forced freedom from exchange controls had become general, assisted by the ideological wave of anti-state liberalisation and privatisation which marked the whole decade. Existing nation-state economies initially tried to protect themselves against its effects, but were forced to give up. The micro-economies of places like Monaco, Liechtenstein and Jersey, on the other hand, experienced prodigious and sustained development.

> Such units had been regarded as economic jokes, and indeed not real states at all but in the Golden Age it became evident that they could flourish as well as, and sometimes better than, large national economies by providing services directly to the global economy. Hence the rise of new city states (Hong Kong, Singapore) a form of polity last seen to flourish in the Middle Ages.

He focuses upon Asian examples here, but the same observation could be made over the same period about older units like the European micro-states (Andorra, Monaco, San Marino, Liechtenstein) as well as the greater number of new, mainly island states now scattered around the globe in the wake of decolonisation.

Defining the Micro

Who are they? One recent survey took as its criterion having a land area of less than 1,000 square kilometres and a population of less than 500,000.[5] There is no obvious distinction between the micro and the very small, but if one follows this criterion then there are twenty-two in the ranks of today's United Nations. The majority of these are small islands in the Pacific and Indian Oceans or in the Caribbean, with one in the Mediterranean (Malta). Most of these were former British colonies. Unquestionably it has been the collapse of British Empire which has bequeathed most micro-states to the New International Order or Disorder. French decolonisation followed a different strategy of political incorporation, making similar tiny territories into *départements* of the homeland. The British followed the contrary strategy of disincorporation: getting rid of them by making them independent, with or without bribes. The one case where that policy was not pursued, the Falkland Islands or Malvinas in the South Atlantic, brought unfortunate consequences in 1982.[6]

They are extremely tiny. In Europe, for example, the total population of all five micro-countries amounts to only 136,000 souls (the population of Bournemouth) occupying an area of 687 square kilometres (most of this being the uninhabited higher mountains of Andorra). These are figures too small to count as a percentage of the European Union's present total of 326 million inhabitants spread over two-and-a-quarter million square kilometres. It should be noted right away, though, that a figure like 22 is no reliable indicator of micro-state reality, since a considerably larger number of small territories are 'self-governing' (notably self-governing in an economic and fiscal sense) without being members of the UN. The United Kingdom itself comprises a number of these, for example, like Jersey, Guernsey, Gibraltar and the Isle of Man – territories which so far have not sought the status of formal independence or sovereignty.[7] If these are taken into account then there are over sixty such miniscule countries in today's political world.

Tiny states are jokes, rarely referred to in the metropolitan media except in terms of quaint happenings and uniforms – the equivalent of the 'feudal vestiges' or 'left-overs' theory mentioned earlier. The sole alternative to this seems to be the reprobates theory, which views them essentially as disgraceful and probably germ-laden fleas of the world order, about which (unless one has an awful lot of money) the less said the better: tax-havens, unseemly focuses of conspicuous or super-rich consumption (Monaco), or vulgar pustules of duty-free commerce (Andorra).

However deplorable many of them may be, the persistence and virulence of such prejudices about microstates should sound a warning bell. Hobsbawm's point about their place in the new economic system is in no way invalidated. Indeed the contrary point can all too easily be made. Singapore did not cause the failure of Barings Bank; it was the operations of Barings (and a hundred other banks like it) which made Singapore what it has become in the multi-national economic order of today. Liechtenstein's sleaze and secrecy stand as nothing set against the corruption of, for example, the Italian Republic since the 1950s or the Spanish Socialist regime of Felipe Gonzalez in the early 1990s. In a period when sleaze has become universal and public perception of large-scale political life and motivation has sunk to the low common denominator displayed on every Western newspaper front page, practically every day, there is surely something absurd about outrage over Robert Maxwell's dealings in Liechtenstein, Cayman Island accounts, or money-laundering in Curaçao or Jersey.

Anarchy and Scale

The fact is that people dislike and despise tiny states. They do so out of a mixture of motives including loss of conviction about their own great state-nations and envy of places where, in a congenial climate, others either pay no VAT and income tax at all, or far less than what we are used to. Although perfectly understandable, such resentment should not be allowed to obscure a search for understanding of the anomaly. Hobsbawm's history is sub-titled 'The Short 20th Century', but there is now another analysis which, I believe, carries understanding of the same point further: Giovanni Arrighi's *The Long 20th Century: Money, Power, and the Origins of Our Times.*[8]

In his Introduction Arrighi refers back to what he calls 'the conventional view' of statehood and inter-state power 'consisting primarily of relative size, self-sufficiency, and military forces' – the same original, developmental model we see reflected in Gellner's theory. But, he underlines at once, this model has never been essential to capitalist economic development as such. Nor is it only since the 1970s that the two have diverged. It may be true that for a particular epoch that development favoured the formation of larger competitive entities, the nation-state units of (approximately) 1750 to 1950. First-wave industrialisation had to emancipate itself both from the confines of the city-state (where capitalism had always been at home) and from the bureaucratic hierarchies of the ancient empire-state. This is why everywhere had, for a time, little option but to be, or try to be, 'something like France'.

But that time is over. If one over-identifies its political template with economic and social necessity, then one ends up misunderstanding the very large and the very small alike:

> The capabilities of some Italian city-states over several centuries to keep at bay the great territorial powers of early-modern Europe would be as incomprehensible as the sudden collapse and disintegration in the late 1980s and early 1990s of the largest, most self-sufficient, and second-greatest military power of our times: the USSR.[9]

After 1989 first-wave capitalist development reached an important boundary. The disintegration of the USSR was also the attainment of that limit, in the world-wide formation not of a traditional military-political empire but of something better described in Justin Rosenberg's recent phrase – 'the empire of civil society'.[10] This can in his view equally and more tellingly be called the final generalisation of anarchy – not in a loose rhetorical or philosophical sense, but denoting the new circumstances of a global marketplace and political liberalisation or democracy.

World-wide or 'globalised' anarchy in that sense denotes a system in principle unified along certain structural lines – unified and (for the first time) liberated from any prospect of 'empire' in the old political and colonial or territorial sense. Unified, in other words, but not of course united politically or territorially. On the contrary, tendentially more disunited than at any time since early-modern Europe set up the provisional political template of modernity with the Treaty of Westphalia in 1648. Among the symptoms of the anarchy are that disconcerting reappearance of city- and micro-states Hobsbawm notices, and their troubling tendency to become more numerous, more economically important and to get themselves permanently established and recognised in the UN.[11] Picturesque theories like Alain Minc's *Le Nouveau Moyen Age*[12] have envisaged this as a sort of regression, or relapse into quasi-medieval conditions, but I suspect these lay too much stress on superficial similarities. They may also be influenced by the broader millennial and multi-national industry of doom-prediction.

Implications of Lilliput

Soothsaying apart, what are likely to be the implications of Lilliputian revival and statehood for post-1989 boundaries and identities? 'What benefits, or what misfortunes to mankind may hereafter result from these events, no human wisdom can foresee', wrote Adam Smith in *The Wealth of Nations*, in 1776. He was discussing the tendency of capitalism to 'unite, in some measure, the most distant parts of the world, by enabling them to relieve one another's wants, to increase one another's enjoyments, and to encourage one another's industry', a tendency beneficial on the whole although qualified by appalling misfortunes and oppressions. He was discussing, well, 'globalisation' (proof, were any needed, that familiarity with *Star Trek* and world-system theory is not required for this task). The trouble, he thought, was 'the superiority of force' which then happened to be on the side of the Europeans, and which made development not just Euro-centric but consistently brutal and antagonistic. Only once greater equality was established and guaranteed everywhere could that be righted. That – a post-imperial climate of international affairs, as it were – 'can alone overawe the injustice of independent nations into some sort of respect for the rights of one another'.

Some doom-predictors believe it will never happen. Irrepressible optimists like me think it may be happening already, and one of the arguments for this sanguine view must be the phenomenon of the thriving and proliferating micro-state. One thing which goes on irritating theorists, especially grand-metropolitan theorists, is that fleas are not mammals. They are not real nations. They are indeed pretend-nations, miniature simulacra of true nation-statehood, that noble condition for which masses have struggled, armies have fought, and mighty empires have crashed to the ground. Not being real countries, they cannot be really independent; nor do they seriously pretend to be other than dependent, itself an almost sinful form of *lèse-majesté*. Hobsbawm is particularly irked by it, and argues that no one should be taken in: 'The most convenient world for multi-national giants is one populated by dwarf states or no states at all', he snarls in conclusion. Such independence cannot therefore be worth having, and all that Singapore or Andorra are doing is providing a kind of political alibi for the new ogres of economic imperialism.

I suggested earlier that moral thunderings about micro-state sleaze are themselves suspect, and in a sleazily liberated world can be easily stood on their head. Is not the same true here? Of course today's tiny and city-states are not 'real' in the sense most characteristic of the Age of Nationalism. They never corresponded to being anything like France, or to the theoretical model promulgated in theories of modernising nationalism like Gellner's. In one sense banal, the accusation is also misleading in that (like the tax-haven sermons) it ignores the now quite general circumstances of dependence, vulnerability and objectively diminishing sovereignty. If these are pretend-polities, so increasingly are we all. In 1992 the UK was forced to devalue its currency by an international speculative movement orchestrated by the financier George Soros, through his Quantum Fund. Though managed from New York, this is an offshore fund which happens to be headquartered in the Caribbean micro-state of Curaçao.

Micro-statehood is 'synthetic', runs the complaint: since they have no armies or missiles, tiny states rely upon artificial conventions of sovereignty maintained by international law and treaties, upon (in Smith's words) 'some sort of respect for the rights of one another' prevailing over the 'injustice of independent nations' larger than themselves. The five original European examples all count upon special treaties with the European Union, by which, without being members, they retain certain privileges and are (in effect) granted absolution for their various fiscal or commercial sins and permitted to carry on business. So do the UK's semi-states of Jersey, Guernsey and Man. Their frontier with Europe is in this sense essentially an odd set of legal provisions which includes them out, as it were – the very opposite of that tradition of superiority of force which Smith denounced.

What I do not see is what is in any way deplorable about artifice of this kind. The 'independence' which it recognises and fosters is not, of course, in the traditional style hallowed by ethno-nationalist ritual, romantic culture, the cult of war memorials and *le sol sacré*. However, it is both a theoretical and (more seriously) a political mistake to think these things are inseparable from national identity or character, nationality politics or the general – and probably growing – need for self-government. The more inter-dependent countries become socio-economically, the more 'independence' is likely to be needed.

10

A Civic–Nationalist Divorce:
Czechs and Slovaks

Held just over a year after the decease of Czechoslovakia, this conference can't help being like a coroner's court.[1] What has the court concluded so far? Exact cause of death still uncertain. The Czechoslovak (or as they preferred in Slovakia) Czecho-Slovak state might have survived, had different individuals been round the table, had negotiations been longer pursued, had referenda been held – and so on. But what such ingenious counter-factual arguments avoid is the larger question which has also hung over the proceedings. Had Czechoslovakia been saved in 1992, would it have made any difference in the longer run?

In the same hypothetical mode, I'm bound to say: I doubt it. However, my reasons for this derive from theoretical considerations as well as from the rather little I know about the events of 1989–92. The Czech–Slovak split is a very interesting example from a theoretical angle, because two general modes of explanation can be used to analyse it. The question is: which works best and explains most?

'Primordial' Slovakia

The deeper debate about nationalism has always been between the 'primordials' and the 'moderns'. The former think that there just are nations in Homo sapiens, which assert and (since 1989) reassert themselves through, across or against other trends like empire, and cosmopolitan or multinational culture. The modernist faction (to which I adhere) thinks on the other hand that the study of nationalism is primarily about the '-ism'. It is this '-ism' of nationhood, its systemic political edge, which has caused both the forward movement (modernity) and the trouble. But that arose only recently, and is inseparable from other closely related modern phenomena like industrial development and democracy.

As regards the Czechoslovak breakdown it is quite easy to present both cases rather strongly. Slovakia is a *locus classicus* for ethnic primordialists. At different times during the conference I could not help thinking repeatedly of one famous illustration of this, sometimes quoted during the break-up rows. In 1969 a Bratislava weekly paper called *Nové Slovo* published a document which had been kept hidden in Communist Party archives for twenty-five years. It was a report from the Slovak Communist Central Committee about conditions in the then independent Slovakia set up (with German support) after the Third Reich had taken over the Czech lands of Bohemia and Moravia in 1938. Originally sent to Moscow, where Clement Gottwald led the Czechoslovak communists in exile, the document must have found its way almost instantly to archival oblivion.

One can see why. In 1944 Allied and Soviet official opinion needed to believe that Nazi 'puppet states' like Slovakia were unrelieved hell-holes awaiting liberation. Yet here were Slovak communists reporting that –

> Generally speaking after the experience of six years, Slovakia is capable of an independent economic and financial existence. It is in a position to stand on its own feet and has sufficient resources (even technical ones) and production potential to face international competition.

The political implications were also disconcerting. Far from being 'swept away' (the one prospect permitted in Allied speeches) most Slovaks wished much of their recently established independence to remain. The report pointed out how differently the war had affected Czechs and Slovaks:

> After the war only those prepared to adopt a firm position (on the national question) can hope to receive support from the population . . . In this respect there is a difference between us and the Czech lands. The Czechs have lost not only political freedom but their national freedom as well. The Slovaks are politically worse off than during the Czechoslovak Republic, but from the national point of view Slovakia has gained.

Anti-Nazism obliged them to forget about such ill-gotten gains. But nationalism would not really let them do so. The fact is that some serious and long-held national aims were realised during the 1938–44 era. And all the native communists were saying is that it might be a mistake to throw these out along with fascism's filthy bath-water:

> If this state had a different political structure . . . there would be no objections to independence from a Slovak point of view. Not surprisingly, many honest people are seriously considering and participating in movements whose aim is to change the regime, to give the state a different substance, but to keep its independence.

In 1969 the biggest surprise was the authorship of the long-buried document. One of its three authors was none other than Gustav Husak, Dubcek's successor as Premier of Czechoslovakia. It was known that he had been imprisoned in the 1950s for 'bourgeois nationalism', but few realised how grave these sins had actually been.[2]

Federal Correctness

But at least Husak's rehabilitation and post-1968 elevation were also accompanied by the fulfilment of some Slovakian national goals. 'Normalisation'. comprised a few satisfactions for its honest people. An elaborately federal system was set up and proclaimed (at Husak's insistence) from the old Pressburg Castle in Bratislava on 28 October 1968 – the fiftieth anniversary of the foundation of Masaryk's First Republic in 1918. It came into operation on 1 January 1969 – twenty-four years before the final political separation of the two federated entities.

The longer the perspective, the stronger the ethnic argument seems. Dorothea El Mallakh's admirable monograph *The Slovak Autonomy Movement, 1935–1939*[3] traces the fortunes of autonomism through the closing years of the First Czechoslovak Republic. She points out how Slovak separatism 'has been viewed overwhelmingly ... as a factor in Nazi Germany's expansion of power', issuing in the 1939–45 protectorate status of Slovakia:

> But also without doubt, although less clearly presented in the historical literature, is that Hitler did not manufacture the Slovak autonomy movement, rather that its existence was of long standing and could be exploited at a critical juncture. The multi-party, democratic experiment of interwar Czechoslovakia failed to control, direct, or effectively respond to the Slovak autonomy movement.

Scots often compliment themselves on how well Scottish autonomy has survived nearly three centuries of political integration. The 'long standing' mentioned here extended back over nearly one thousand years, and ended in a half-century of aggressive assimilationism by the post-1867 Hungarian state. But as Jan Carnogursky relates in his speech, the result was merely to drive this archetypally 'historyless people' into an alliance with the Czechs. Czecho-Slovakia was the temporary result.

Ms El Mallakh's subtitle is 'A Study in Unrelenting Nationalism'. The constancy of Slovak demands is indeed remarkable: from the 'Petitions of the Slovak Nation' of 1848 up to Vladimir Meciar's post-1989 ascendancy, they demanded much the same things over and over again, and in much the same style. It was not the call for statehood which was unrelenting. Independence figured only now and then in the list: but 'autonomy', linguistic and cultural rights, recognition and equality of status were never absent. These ethno-religious pressures were unremitting, and simply re-presented themselves in successive generations.

When Dubcek's 'Czechoslovakian Spring' arrived in 1968 it too had to sort out the issue. As El Mallakh writes – 'By mentally eliminating certain catch phrases ... [the Dubcek Action Programme] could stand as the product of the Slovak autonomy party of some thirty to forty years earlier.'

It cannot be denied that even in Socialist Czechoslovakia, in spite of outstanding progress in solving the problem of nationalities, there are serious faults and fundamental deformations in the relations between Czechs and Slovaks.

The famous programme then went on to demand a 'final federative arrangement' in a new constitution 'which in a new way, on the basis of full equality, will solve the status of Slovak national bodies' once and for all. With the advantage of hindsight we know that this is what Husak's post-1968 regime did (formally speaking). A further dose of hindsight reveals what was to become of the once-and-for-all definitive constitutional formula: the 1992 once-and-for-all break-up. What actually proved definitive was the introduction of democracy. Far from validating these laborious and complex federal recipes, this sent them very quickly to the scrapheap.

Peter Pithart underlines one reason for their futility in his contribution. This was a federal polity with but two units in an awkward 2:1 ratio, where no vote was possible on matters of joint concern (for fear that one or the other might be seen as 'dominating'), and no breathing-space was left uncircumscribed by stipulations of angelic symmetry. It proved beyond merely human powers to operate. Long before that phrase arose in the West, in fact, the Czech-Slovak Federation was a monster of well-intentioned Political Correctness, which substituted phraseology for unavoidably asymmetrical fact and hoped that the former would somehow mould the latter.

Under Communism it could be pretended that this worked. In her comprehensive study of the system Carol Skalnik Leff has described in detail how the pretence was maintained. Her conclusion, written well before 1989, was that 'Czechs and Slovaks expecting the birth of a joint society have at least another generation to wait'. The regime still faced 'the same two choices with which earlier leaders have wrestled':

> The acceptance of political arrangements that honour the assumptions of bipolar politics will only serve to institutionalise and reinforce the national distinctiveness of each region still further, perhaps irreversibly. Integrationist policies, on the other hand, given the current social structure and national sensitivities, are out of step with the character of the binational society and will thus breed conflict . . . It is not an enviable choice for a regime to make.[4]

It was able to go on pretending to make it for so long, because Czechoslovakia was in effect governed from 'outside': by a one-party order which managed the constitution, and was in turn propped up by the Soviet imperium. When that ceased to be the case, the pretence quickly foundered. So, as any 'primordialist' would declare, ethnic verity reasserted itself, and two natural nations shook themselves free of the previous multi-national wreckage. Factors 'beyond reason', in Walker Connor's phrase, resurfaced to put merely civic and constitutional nationalism in its place. In an LSE lecture two years ago Connor argued that the 'nature of the ethnonational bond' has been the key to the post-1989 disorder:

> The fault lines that separate nations are deeper and broader than those separating non-kindred groups, and the tremors that follow those fault lines more potentially cataclysmic. What underlies ... 'man's inhumanity to man' is all too often 'nation's inhumanity unto nation'.[5]

Hence the past explains the present – in this case, the 1992 split. A general crisis allowed ethno-national bonds to reaffirm their force, since they represent a communitarian inheritance upon which people can fall back – what seemed an abiding reality after the failure of complex multi-national formulae.

Czech Unevenness

The only flaw in this theory is that it fails to explain the break-up of Czechoslovakia. The explanation may appear to work if one considers Slovakia alone, or primarily, and leaps rapidly over the actual politics and negotiations of 1991–92. But any more cautious approach discovers a quite different story. Slovak ethno-religious bonds were of course a necessary condition of what happened. But the sufficient condition emerged from a different direction altogether – it came from the Czech side, and took the form of a new intolerance of unevenness.

One recent economic account of the Czech 1990s puts it this way:

> The Slovaks pushing for separation were motivated more by questions of identity and pride than by worries about the economy. Czech politicians (such as Klaus) who pressed for a clean break were largely motivated by economic considerations ... Klaus's pragmatism is rooted in a commonsensical view that markets work better than central planning, that a stable currency is better than hyperinflation, and that the Czechs' future lies in rapid integration with Western Europe.

Such attitudes are often attributed to the influence of Friedmannites and Western advisers. But Peter Rutland points out how well these accorded with quite traditional Czech attitudes. They are 'views ... which have more to do with Czech history and traditions than with off-the-shelf reform programs'.[6] Hence the desire for ultra-rapid Europeanisation was not mere rhetoric: it became identified with an impatient national will to get out of past entanglements, including the weird cobwebs of post-1968 federalism, and forwards into a more viable modernity.

But that will was clearly going to be slowed down by the inherited joint arrangements with Slovakia. Carnogursky's categories of 'Central European' and 'East European' assumed their full meaning here. The Prague city-state desired the shortest possible route to capitalist integration, while Slovaks

argued for a more phased approach allowing time for a cushioned readjustment of what Carnogursky calls their 'artificial' heavy economy. On paper
it looked like an argument over timing. For a nation-state it would have
been an argument over timing. But for the strange dual entity of Czecho-
Slovakia it inevitably assumed two contrasting forms, implying differing
choices.

The Slovaks alone did not make that choice, even after Meciar became
Prime Minister. Jan Carnugorsky, for example, relates here how he strove
to hold some sort of federal deal together until both countries could be in
Europe. Such a policy of 'Independence ... but not yet' was the clearest
Slovak national interest in 1990–92. It was Klaus's new Czech government
that drew the line: 'Independence ... now'. That line was equally plainly
in the interests of Czech Sinn Féin – the expression of what Rutland
describes as 'a nationalism ... alive and well, in spite of a self-effacing
nature which testifies to its inner self-confidence'. Peter Pithart has sometimes called this 'regional egotism': a more outward-looking identity which,
as it were, eschews ethno-national drag because it feels essentially
'developed'.

Confronted with such logic, Meciar's brand of ethno-nationalism had of
course to react in its own terms. It had to make the most of it. We now know
what a colourful and disastrous result this was to be during the first year of
Slovak separate existence. Western comment over the whole period overlooked the nature of Czech nationalism and unduly emphasised the sins
and antics of Bratislava. But in reality the latter had derived partly from the
former – from a coherent developmental will rooted in the history of the
Czech lands as, by far, the most industrialised area of the former Habsburg
Empire. Bohemia–Moravia was the repository of a unique inheritance only
partly describable in ethnic terms: Protestantism, early industrial development and the preponderance of one great urban culture also contributed
to its ascendancy.

To this was added unusual ethnic homogeneity after the post World-War
II mass expulsion of the German population: one of the largest examples in
European history of what is now routinely referred to as 'ethnic cleansing'.
However, the equally unusual circumstances of the change – a practically
unopposed act of revenge, supported by the international opinion of the
time – meant that it deposited remarkably little ethno-national content in
Walker Connor's sense. Mono-ethnic and mono-lingual, the Czech Republic
was to inherit the social reality of an almost completely successful nationality
struggle with comparatively little of the standard ideological tension and
culturalist flourishes.

The very dourness of Klaus fits into this perspective. As Rutland observes:

Paradoxically, Klaus's relative obscurity might have worked in his favour.
More well-known dissidents, such as Petr Pithart and Jiri Dienstbier, were
associated with the tribulations of the past, while Klaus was a new face who
talked only of the future.

Slovak-style ethno-nationalism calls on its past in order to face the future; in contrast – having fully achieved its nationalist aims – Czech-style 'regional egotism' could afford to feel the past consisted mainly of 'tribulations', and turn in a far more determined and aggressive way towards the European future. If it has become the 'success story' of post-1989 Central and Eastern Europe, this may be because it was really the sole area where, for deep historical reasons, most of the population could be counted on to go on supporting such abrupt development policies.

Models of Disorder

So there were two 'fault-lines' at work in the split. One was Connor's ethno-national bond. The other was a developmental gap between the two parts of Czechoslovakia. Some analyses have underlined how this socio-economic gap was far less than it had once been, and argued that, therefore, the federation might have been saved with some good will on both sides. 'Leadership failure' is blamed, and emphasis is given to the primacy of politics. The conflict can then be retrospectively renegotiated to make it come out differently.

But what this account overlooks is the developmental storm of post-1989.[7] Although its effects had been anticipated to some degree here and there in Eastern Europe, the full force of capitalist transformation and conversion could not burst across it until the final dissolution of the old state. When it did so, the effect was like a hastened recapitulation of the century preceding the advent of communism. During that time the primal nationalism of the region was formed by resentful mobilisation both for and against the Western and Great Power example: the will to emulate or catch up, and the determination that this be accomplished 'on our own terms' – the terms furnished in most places by pre-existing ethno-linguistic or ethno-religious identity.

Ulster

On a golden autumn day
All my dreams came true in Orangefield
On a Throne of Ulster day
You came my way in Orangefield.
(Van Morrison, 'Avalon Sunset', 1989)

In last year's Channel 4 week of Ulster programmes Mary Holland inter-
viewed Jack Redpath, a Belfast Protestant intellectual.[1] He painted a
depressing picture of Protestant retreat and fearfulness. But what about the
city's most famous contemporary cultural phenomenon, she persisted:
singer-composer George Ivan Morrison (b. 31 August 1945)? Couldn't
Loyalists take some heart from that inimitable voice – 'one of the few artists
of the rock era to whom critics can accurately ascribe genius', according to
Donald Clarke's *Encyclopaedia of Popular Music?* The location of Van the
Man's own heart has always been unmistakable. Though sometimes dis-
guised as Avalon or other kingdoms of the soul, its truth lies somewhere:

On Hyndford Street and up Cherry Valley
from North Road bridge railway line
On sunny summer afternoons
Picking apples from the side of the tracks.
Playing round Mrs Kelly's lamp
Going out to Holywood on the bus.
(Hymns to the Silence)

Hyndford Street is an ordinary brick-built, working-class row looking like
hundreds of others. Yet it is to this terrain that the almost unbearable
nostalgia of his music always returns. The outside world now mainly sees
Protestant Belfast in terms of Ian Paisley Snr, a man who believes that
bridges are built primarily to let the Devil in. But the bridges of Morrison's
music have connected Hyndford Street outwards to a strange semi-mystical
realm of angels, children and (ultimately) the Calvinist Nirvana of clear
water and silence – *Hymns to the Silence* was his last double album:

I wanna go out in the countryside
Oh, sit by the clear cool crystal water,
Get my spirit way back to the feeling
Deep in my soul, I wanna feel
Oh so close to the One, close to the One,
Close to the One, close to the One
And that's why I keep on singin' baby
My hymns to the silence.

Anyone who knows the poems of Hugh Macdiarmid will not miss the connection, a contemplative mystique of the absolute. However, Macdiarmid also tried to make himself the voice of a nation. In the same interview Redpath went on to admit that Morrison is nothing like that for Protestant Ulster people. He is just someone who lives in the USA, occasionally comes home to sell-out concerts, makes remarks about peace and brotherhood, and then goes away again. Some critics say what he is really harping back to is always that brief era just before the post-1968 troubles, when youngsters on both sides of Ulster's religious divide discovered a musical liberation culture which could take them away from all that – from the old parochial grouses of their respective extended families.

Unlike most of them Morrison had the power to keep on flying. Yet in a sense Hyndford Street has haunted every second of his transcontinental parabola: small terraced houses still awaiting their impossible redemption, an Orangefield of all the epiphanies, beaches somewhere in County Down on which an ocean of transcendence beats:

> Too long in exile
> You can never go home again
> Too long in exile
> Too long not singing my song
> Too long in exile
> Too long like a rolling stone.

In Juris Podnieks' great film *Homeland* we see a one-armed man returning from forty-seven years of American exile to a dark, ruined house in a field overgrown with weeds. He rests in it, overcome with recollections and gazing up through its shattered roof to the sky. 'I still feel the light', he says. Against all the odds his Latvia is still in existence, and still able to sing as he remembers in his childhood: a choir in the Baltic forest, a sort of heaven. So you can go home again – home to an imagined community with real foundations which have re-emerged from the wreckage of an empire. A few years ago he would have been forced (like many others) to ask for his ashes to be scattered with flowers somewhere in the sea outside the territorial limit. That was as near the ruined house as exiles were then allowed to go. Special Baltic cruises used to be organised for them. Mocked as nostalgic reactionaries from both sides of the great imperial divide, they crowded together and gazed over the rails at all they would ever see of their countries, a single black line on the horizon.

It is over against this scale and pace of change that the Northern Ireland peace process should be set. The whole world has changed its skin, not just Ulster. But as the world changes, so does nationalism. Too much emphasis has been placed on the latter as a phenomenon of blood and belonging. Nationalism is also a by-product of the world order itself, the system and general assumptions of the states congregated (rather than ordered) together in the United Nations. The Baltic émigrés pined for homelands of ancestral song. However, what brought the latter back to life again was not their commemorations but an international earthquake, the collapse of the tectonic plates upon which 'international relations' had been based for half a century. When the Wall was demolished no other frontier would ever be the same. Five years later the internal borders of Ireland have been drawn into the same mutation – a 'peace process' reflecting the true end of Cold War stability and empire.

Some verdicts upon the process so far still reflect that stability, which was also stagnation. Conor Cruise O'Brien's recent postscript to *Ancestral Voices*[2] is a good example. He foresees disaster for peace because no real movement in Ireland is possible at all:

> The peace dreamed of, both by Church and State, is as always the peace of nationalist assumptions: the peace that is invariably ultimately identical with the triumph of nationalism and the coming of a united Ireland. The only road to that kind of peace in our time is through civil war. Things are not better than they were before the cease-fire. They are worse.

Roddy Doyle's Ireland may (he admits) look different to outsiders, and be notable for an absence of 'wild Serbs or furious Croats'. Be not deceived. Just beneath this secular and European veneer dwells the ancestral dark: 'God Land is in there, deep down. It whispers to us in the watches of the night. Our ancestors, faithful to God and Mary, once held this whole island before the foreign heretic took it from us.'

And they will have it back again come what may. The long-awaited framework document for a new Northern Ireland states that the Republic intends renouncing its constitutional claim on the whole island, in order to encourage a settlement.[3] Don't believe it, especially if you are a Unionist. Blood will out, in this case with the vestment of faith. Hence the Protestants must not lower their guard for a second. The only reply to nationalist assumptions is anti-nationalism, Britishness. But what appears as 'anti-' on the local scale is of course itself a grander version of nationalism: the culture and assumptions of 'the Brits'. What about their ancestral voices? O'Brien never says much about that, as if on his terrain only the ethnic and the sacral deserve to be taken seriously. The world stands both judged and condemned with reference to a changeless Irishness.

Thus the only road 'in our time' leads through civil war. But whose time?

Verdicts like this have not been lacking since the calamities of Bosnia-Herzegovina and Rwanda, as well as of pre-1994 Ulster. Is there really no other nationalism than the ancestral-voice, blood-sacrifice sort? That philosophy perceives nothing but abscesses beneath the old skin, hopeless and incorrigible instincts which left to themselves will foster a world of predators and carrion. Such a world can never heal itself. Hence hope lies solely with larger-scale civilisation, whatever metropolitan tolerance is still available in North America, the United Kingdom or the new Europe. Humankind's inherent variety – its eight thousand languages and hundreds of ethnies – is the equivalent of original sin, good for play but not politics, indulged where absolutely necessary but otherwise repressed for the spirit's sake.

> Oh we gonna go back, back to our favourite place,
> Oh look at it again
> See it all through different eyes,
> When we get the healing done
> Oh when we get the healing done.[4]

Like South Africa and Palestine, Northern Ireland may be turning into a testbed for these broad assumptions. Will ancestral voices never learn a different song? Are favourite places like Protestant Hyndford Street fated never to be seen through different eyes, or to attain to their own healing and permanence? Are they incapable of taking over the universal and, in time, lending it their own imprint?

How these questions are answered depends partly upon how the causes of the post-1989 great change are understood. Was it descent into atavism, or ascent to democracy? The easiest reply is 'both', and in many cases both did obviously apply. Over most of Central and Eastern Europe peoples did recover their nations and discover democracy simultaneously. However, it does not follow that both were equally important. Still less that both will be of equivalent weight in (say) ten or twenty years time. The decisive issue is where the emphasis is put. In the short run nationality politics may be more salient; but over a longer period either democracy or its failure will fix its shape and meaning. One must distinguish between initial shock waves and the longer-term pressures for change which are inherent in the move towards a more global and single-system society. When an old order dismantles itself (Ernest Gellner has written of Eastern Europe) 'nationalism emerges with all its vigour, but with few of its rivals'. The rival forces of civil association, representative politics and local government were more severely repressed and take far more time to build up. In spite of which (he continues) – 'it remains to be seen whether irredentist nationalism, or massacres and population movements, or a diminution of ethnic conflict in the interest of a federal-cantonal co-operation, will predominate. Each of these elements is present, and no one knows which one will prevail.'[5]

The same can be said of Ulster. In a recent study of the Protestant community Steve Bruce concludes that 'it seems clear that Ulster Protestants

form an ethnic group and that the Northern Ireland conflict is an ethnic
conflict. The depth of the ethnic divisions in Northern Ireland is such that
it is almost impossible to think, and harder to act, in any other terms.'[6]
Since the 1960s the depth has become an abyss. Twenty-five years of warfare
have brought about a situation where 3 out of 5 Catholics but only 1 in 50
Protestants call themselves 'Irish'. More astonishingly the ideological vari-
ance is now reproduced in terms of social geography: 'The 1991 census
revealed a degree of residential segregation that surprised even many
people in Northern Ireland. Half the population now lives in areas that are
more than 90% Protestant or 95% Catholic.'

Ethnic self-cleansing: a war to unite the Irish nation has generated this
cantonal reality of physical separation. The maintenance of central authority
prevented large-scale 'massacres and population movements' like those of
Bosnia, but could not stop a capillary movement in the same direction.
These are communities which have decided to live apart. The major surgery
of redrawn frontiers and expulsions was averted, but nothing could arrest a
micro-surgery of mutual aversion, 'peace walls' and patchwork division.

The consequences have been outlined and commented in another
admirable analysis which appeared just before the framework document,
Kevin Boyle and Tom Hadden's *Northern Ireland: The Choice*.[7] The authors
point out that any new agreement on governing Northern Ireland hinges
on a choice between fully acknowledging this existing separation or trying
to wish it away through administrative magic. Either the communities can
be treated as two ethno-religious cantons sharing some common services, or
an over-arching 'community' can be imposed where inevitably the ideas of
one or other actual community will end up prevailing. For the second
category traditional ethnic criteria offer only two candidates: O'Brien's Irish
ghost-voice nationalism, bent on imposing a unification within which
Protestants who resisted exile would end up as a dubious minority; or a
smaller Protestant-dominated northern state where the Catholics would end
up similarly reviled, probably in the aftermath of a Bosnia-style war. In his
States of Ireland (1972), published twenty-five years ago, O'Brien provided a
famous complete scenario for both ugly solutions. These are requoted
almost in their entirety in the conclusion of *Ancestral Voices*.

But Boyle and Hadden argue that the first choice is preferable, and might
now be realisable. The Downing Street declaration and the stalemate of the
peace process could bring about a novel sort of civic-national administration: a 'Swiss' governance of what would (in relation to the traditional
ethno-national alternatives) effectively become a no-man's-land. Unthinkable? A few years ago, were Mandela's South Africa or the Israeli-PLO
accord any more thinkable? The fact is that they were as conceivable as an
independent Latvia anguishing over what to do about its huge Russian
minority.

The clear choice is between 'policies based on the acceptance of
separation and policies based on the objective of sharing'. Both ethno-
nationalism and official government policy stand 'committed to the objec-

tive of greater integration and sharing between members of the two communities', goals endorsed by a thousand sermons, humane exhortations and committee reports. But, these authors ask, 'Would it not be more realistic to accept that the forces of communal separation are irresistible and that official policy should be altered accordingly to provide for a deliberate move towards developing structures for separation?'

Cantonal arrangements are still not literally possible everywhere in Ulster, they concede, but could be complemented by functional co-operation over the provision of services like education, health and welfare. Belgium and Switzerland both provide models of how communal separation can be combined with a broadly confederal authority over such shared concerns. A 'power-sharing' centre regulates common affairs which cannot be left to the separate localities, guarantees community and individual rights, and represents the state in most external relations. The result would of course be a state-nation, a country defined by its institutions and laws rather than by its ethnos or imagined kinship. The only nationalism it can lay claim to will have a civic character, and political history must take the place of common descent or language. One corollary is that time alone will turn such history into something like instinct, the mutuality of an inherited common culture. For Belgium the time has been short, only since 1830; for the Swiss, it has been long enough to create a powerful political entity out of four nationalities and languages and twenty-eight cantons.

> I'm a dweller on the threshold
> And I'm waiting at the door
> And I'm standing in the darkness
> I don't want to wait no more.
> ('Beautiful Vision', 1982)

The incomparable voice of Ulster Protestantism has no political significance for it, because no nationalist culture of the usual sort lends him that sort of meaning. Protestant Unionism traditionally clung to Britain, and being British in that sense was like a cargo cult. Among the treasures guaranteed was the common culture of the first Elizabeth and all her successors. If Shakespeare is yours by right, what use is Van Morrison? The national question has already been answered by incomparable endowment – the culture-laden Crown of a pre-eminently civilised state whose riches eclipse all meaner forms of ideological cement. Only lesser breeds need incantations of a community to come. It is the protagonists of a confined and ethnic cause who require idioms and songs to keep their collective spirits up, or the antics of the Gaelic Athletic Association. Those born to the Law can do without such heroes, and indeed often despise them.

Unionism's version of national self-determination was not a form of nationalism. The principles of the old international order acknowledged it none the less, as equivalent to a claim for independence or self-government. But such equivalence depended entirely upon one thing: the willingness of the host-nation to reciprocate. Already low in a psychological sense, that willingness was formally withdrawn with the Downing Street declaration, and the decisive phrase has reappeared in the framework document:

> The British government reaffirm that they will uphold the democratic wish of a greater number of the people of Northern Ireland on the issue of whether they prefer to support the Union or a sovereign united Ireland. On this basis, they reiterate that they have no selfish strategic or economic interest in Northern Ireland.

Selfish strategic and economic interests define nations. In this instance, for example, they obviously separate Ulster from Scotland and Wales. The British government appears to retain a strong ego-investment in the latter two and (as John Major and Douglas Hurd have repeatedly said) would feel 'diminished' if they turned away from England. Ulster Unionists are right to stress the importance of such feelings. They register what is really happening – a psychological withdrawal from Ireland prefiguring political and military disengagement. The framework document's committee-speak envisages an alternative of extraordinary and convoluted length: a proportionally elected Belfast parliament to take over the functions of the Northern Ireland Office, and an array of 'cross-border' initiatives and bodies to be sponsored equally (in a formal sense) by Dublin and Belfast. Its emphasis is significant too – much more on the cross-border authorities than on the new government in Belfast. Unionists have not misread this and are right to object (at the time of writing, by threatening to bring down the Major government at Westminster).

On the other hand, only they can do anything about it. It is they who have (as the same song says) 'crossed the burning ground and watched the great illusion drown'. Here, one side's 'betrayal' is the other's rational interest in limiting its Irish commitment. An O'Brienite perspective sees genuine (in the sense of ethnic) Ulster nationalism as following the burning ground. The view suggested by *Northern Ireland: The Choice* is that only an unusual form of civic nationalism can possibly be appropriate in Ulster. The Protestants are an unusual kind of nation. Their historical formation has turned them away from the standard version of nationality politics found in Sinn Féin and the SDLP; but it may have equipped them quite well for post-standard nationality politics – that is, for a more civic and institutional nationalism of the sort which the post-1989 *longue durée* will surely favour. In their actual evolution all countries have to make strengths out of weaknesses, or convert retardation into unexpected ways forward. It is true that in the past Catholicism, Greek Orthodoxy and Islam have often provided a more cohesive foundation for ethno-linguistic nationalism than Protestantism did; but the latter's hour may still come in an age of generalised civic nationalism.

Sometimes the post-1989 transition has been read as implying the decline or moderation of nationalism as such. The normal implication is that the term really denotes wild Serbs and furious Croats, who may get meeker and milder as things improve. The heroic world of the ancestral dark will give way to 40-watt uniformity (out in the sticks, that is: the metropolitan standard remains at 100 watts throughout). However, this interpretation rests upon an over-narrow understanding of the subject. Nationalism has always been about modernity as well as about *ethnos* and inheritance. It has fallen back in order to fall forwards, or modernise. Accidents in which the ancestral dark is eternalised are failures, not successes (and the longer duration deals with thousand-year eternities). *Ethnos* was what happened to be around when modernity struck, a once-off inheritance; but 'modernisation' itself is only another word for forever – the ongoing processes of industrialisation, through which in time far greater human and cultural variety will certainly be produced.

> Feel the angel of the present
> In the mighty crystal fire
> Lift me up and soothe my darkness
> Let me travel even higher.

The 'angel of the present' also tends to be short-sighted. She sees mainly encroaching uniformity, Fords and Burger Kings everywhere, a Bali only climatically different from Ballymurphy. In his essay on Fukuyama's *The End of History* Perry Anderson has analysed the twentieth-century genealogy of 'this collective vision of a stalled, exhausted world, dominated by recursive mechanisms of bureaucracy and ubiquitous circuits of commodities, relieved only by the extravagances of a phantasmic imaginary without limit, because without power'.[8] Phenomena of transition, the 'catching up' inseparable from the formation of new plateaux of development, are projected endlessly forwards into a vision of brain-dead sameness.

Were such sameness a real threat, I suppose wild Serbs and furious Croats might be preferable. Fortunately it is not, and 'recursive mechanisms of bureaucracy' or a democracy boringly identical in all climes offer few clues to the present, let alone to a futureworld of reborn city-states, regions restored to life and imploded metropolitan fragments – post-ethnic communities with limits and powers. Some perceive only the accidents attending this process, like spectators at the French *ancien régime*'s prodigious firework displays who complained of their train of deaths and injuries. But even the accidents are not always unfortunate. The opportunity given by the Downing Street declaration and the new framework is indeed partly accidental: military stalemate, coinciding with a conjuncture of interests between a failing metropolis and its former colony, now enjoying a European florescence. Major's shrivelled UK and Mary Robinson's Ireland are unlikely progenitors of a new Ulster state, but I think Boyle and Hadden may be right: this accident could have come at the right time, and may predispose the Protestant community towards a successful European formula of their own.

A few weeks ago new leaders of Ulster Unionism like David Ervine, Chris McGimpsey and Ian Paisley Jnr. attended a Glasgow conference sponsored by *Scotland on Sunday* newspaper. Articulate, aggressive, yet in search of compromise, their collective voice sounded to me like that of a new civic nationalism which could in time easily be ranged beside those already functioning in Scotland and Wales. None wanted the old Stormont parliament back. More surprisingly, none wanted the old Unionism either: ideas of an impossible integration – the equivalent of *Algérie française* – had vanished along with the dependency cargo cult. Instead, the British Union was depicted variously as an umbrella or an external guarantor of Northern Ireland's autonomy: roles in the long run probably better played by Europe than by Britain. In sharp contrast, the Sinn Féin oratory on display at the same event did appear as unchanging in more or less O'Brien's sense, its peace policy simply another version of assimilative nationalism.

Arriving at a better answer than that could be long and difficult. But even this may have some advantages. It has taken two years to get this far, and another two could elapse before anything like the framework's proposals is in place. But by then it could also be very difficult for the paramilitary forces to resume their activities on the scale of 1994. The wave of popular revulsion against atrocity politics shows no sign of slackening on either side. There should also be a rising level of commitment to the new institutions. Among the Protestants, obviously, but possibly also in that substantial part of the Catholic population which has always hedged its bets about staying within the UK.[9] It wanted to combine being Irish with the advantages in certain areas of being British, and the framework plans allow for this going on provided the new institutions are given a chance.

In two years time there could also be a very different government in London, more pro-European and more interested in serious constitutional reform. Both these factors will count in Ulster. The SDLP has consistently pleaded for a direct European part in the changes, but there can be no hope of that as long as the Conservative regime persists in its current creeping anti-Europeanism. On the wider constitutional front the Tories have succumbed to an obdurate negativism: intensified centralism everywhere but in Ulster, withering scorn for the tentative stirrings of English political regionalism. They perceive Ulster as unique, and justify the framework ideas entirely in terms of provincial exceptionalism. The Labour Party has changed its attitude towards the Province in any case, but its evolution on these two grander issues might be even more important in supporting whatever formula finally emerges. A context would be provided in which the novel formula would appear more possible, or even normal. Together, European regionalism and a long overdue political restructuring of the UK's periphery could then support the consolidation of the new Ulster sub-state.

> I'll be waiting there, waiting on that shore
> To hear the cry for home

You won't have to worry any more
When you hear the cry for home

Inarticulate Speech of the Heart (1983) contains one of Morrison's daftest and most sixtiesish lyrics, 'Rave on John Donne'. It rambles pretentiously over theosophy and the Golden Dawn with occasional compliments to past ravers like Walt Whitman, Omar Khayyam and W.B. Yeats. Mercifully the words give way at last to music of the heart, the nostalgic splendour which has made Morrison into a *sui generis* world figure. 'Hyndford Street, Abetta Parade, Orangefield, St Donard's Church': this is the nation from before the world was made, all countries apprehended as emanations of the one from which the singer came. Nostalgia is not only for the past, it looks for horizons yet to see, for revelations in the order of the world. Such parochial universalism does far more credit to the spirit of Orangefield than 'The Sash my Father Wore'. I like to think that a great non-ancestral voice may yet bury all those curses in the watches of the night. Who would have thought it – that in the revolution of the times, it may yet come to mean more than they do on the actual terrain of Hyndford Street?

Palestine

The politics of dispossession is nationalism – an over-generalisation which at once calls for precise qualification.[1] It is quite true that all nationalists are not dispossessed: possessors have their own (often strident) variations on the theme. It is also true that nationality politics did not originate among the crushed and uprooted: indeed its primary source was the *nouveaux riches* or upwardly mobile of early-modern times, in Holland, England and France.

However, their national-state politics only became national-ism later on, when such entrepreneurial societies inflicted their success upon the rest of the world in the nineteenth century. This infliction was Progress, which caused the un-progressed to feel for the first time dispossessed in the general and inescapable sense which amounts to an '-ism'. And it was out of that sense that the storm of modernisation emerged (since the first innocence, Progress has been constantly relabelled). The rest of humanity's patchwork-quilt (most of it, mostly due for dispossession) could neither evade industrialisation nor put up with it on the imperial terms initially offered. The result was a counter-blast aiming at modernity 'on our own terms' – the terms (inevitably) of what existed before the newly rich (and armed) nations emerged to rewrite the entire script.

That script – the 'history' which some imagined terminating around the year 1990 – was mined by the very reality which it sought to recompose. In the dominant storm centre itself a certain calmness could prevail: a false calm, as Edward Said constantly repeats in these books, founded upon arrogance, ignorance and superior military force.[2] The metropolitan view was that Progress was greater than its bearers and destined to triumph, regardless of the particular language it spoke. The Russo-Soviet or Anglo-British empires (e.g.) were simply vehicles for its dissemination. But outside the centre, wherever the contemporary frontiers of 'development' happened to be, metropolitanism was perceived the other way round. The driving-cabin view was different from that beneath the wheels. For the latter, these 'vehicles' were exploiting Progress in order to eternalise a particular national hegemony. *Their* civilisation will end by dispossessing *us*.

For collectivities, dispossession brings decease. The same is not of course true for individuals. All individual Palestinians could (theoretically) have opted to become (or at least try to become) Israeli, Jordanian, Syrian or (one of Said's own identity dilemmas) American. This option has always been warmly viewed in imperial or sub-imperial capitals (like Tel Aviv). But in practice it applies only to the educated. The unvoiced logic beneath it goes like this: if only the 'intellectuals' (trouble-makers) would mind their own (individual) businesses and honestly assimilate, then the non-intellectual majority would, after a certain lapse of time – well, disappear. Before nationalism arrived to change things, most ethno-linguistic communities we know about did disappear – or more accurately, were 'disappeared' in the Argentinian sense, like the Picts of north-eastern Scotland. There was a time not long ago when the Palestinians looked like ideal candidates for disappearance. They could see the last sky coming, and after it nothing. Right up until the peace agreement last year there was no certainty of reprieve.

Another way of reading nationalism is just that: no more disappearance. For the majority of the collectivity, the collectivity itself remains the sole redemptive possibility. Hence its 'death', though metaphorical, is all too easily translatable into individual or familial terms. On the West Bank and Gaza, even though many Palestinians became successful exiles and émigrés like Said, there could never have been two million individual escape routes of that kind. If 'Palestine' doesn't make it, few living Palestinians will. The point is not quite that nationalism is a matter of life or death – like the more raw nature which once prevailed – but that 'nationalism' has altered the nature of the species to make it such a matter.

The Politics of Dispossession and *Representations of the Intellectual* can be read like a single meditation on this theme. An intellectual earmarked for escape and successful metropolitan assimilation has turned back, and tried to assume the burden of those left behind. The burden is a crushing one. In a sense frankly admitted in these pages, it is too much for him or for any other individual. He has become the best-known intellectual spokesman of the Palestinian cause, yet was always far too honest and too honourable to be merely its loudspeaker. As the gross contradictions and failings of the cause have accumulated over thirty years, he has been unable to avoid registering and criticising them. So more is collected in *Politics of Dispossession* than scattered essays and reviews. It reads like a memoir of the Stations of the Cross, one single journey or travail through the agonies and humiliations which have broken him apart – above all when inflicted, as so often, by those 'on his own side'. The critique of Arab nationalism and Palestinian parochialism in these pages is more devastating than anything put out by Zionists or the US Israeli lobby.

Said suffers from acute identity problems. So do all nationalist intellectuals. But since he is a famously fashion-conscious individual, critics have rarely resisted the temptation cheaply to assault his identity pangs along those lines. Paul Johnson, for example, wrote of him recently in the *Sunday Times* as 'a fashionable figure [with] modish problems of identity. It is not clear to me who, or what, the real Edward Said is.' The implication is that 'identity' in the political or nationalist sense is something like posturing in front of a mirror. It is not: Johnson is the poseur here, not Said.

My father as a boy sold crowns of thorns to tourists near the Sepulchre. Yet a few yards away, underneath a declivity in the city wall, we stumbled on Zalatimo, the renowned pastry shop whose speciality *mtaqaba* was a great family favourite. A wizened old baker was in there stoking the oven, but his ancient form suggested something only barely surviving.

Astonishingly, Said Snr the Jerusalem relic-vendor turned into an ace moderniser: he was the man who, via his Egyptian business, introduced filing and the typewriter into Arabic culture. He saw identity as principally a question of backbone, and was chronically upset by his son's inability to stand up straight, in the ramrod style approved by the Boy Scouts and Victoria College, Cairo. The family were Greek-Orthodox Christians, converted to Anglicanism in the late nineteenth century. When young Edward's vertebral slackness got too pronounced for them he was packed off to America, aged fifteen. He had never seen snow, and was compelled to invent a new personality at a puritanical New England boarding-school. A few years later he escaped to Princeton, and then in 1963 to New York's Columbia University as a teacher, where he has remained for thirty years.

This background provided a very unusual identity humus. What he likes most about New York is its anonymity. Paradoxically, self-consciously nationalist intellectuals are often very susceptible to cosmopolitanism: secretly (or in Said's case openly) they feel most at home on the neutral terrain of exile and alienation. This is because the very mechanism of identification – 'standing up for' a people and a cause – can unfold only out of a certain distance, an implicit separation of the self from background and community. A nation can only realise itself – register its patent rights, so to speak – via another community of voice. But that voice is also for others: it would fail unless the rights acquired an outside or international resonance. So those articulating the message, the intellectuals, necessarily risk standing in an ambiguous position, one exposed to accusations of betrayal from both sides. Said has had more than his fill of these.

Conservative metropolitans like Johnson like to portray nationalism as an invention of intellectuals. There is some trite truth in this: all ideologies, including fogeyism, must initially be synthesised by the educated, a process which may then be misrepresented as wilful 'forging', 'dreaming up', etc. However, an ideology which has convulsed the world must be more than wilful. At this deeper level it is nationalism which has invented modern intellectuals, rather than vice versa. Their pre-history lay in the European Renaissance and Enlightenment; but those only prepared the ground for the increasingly extra-European modernity of which nationalism is an inescapable part.

The development of industrial modernity could not avoid gross unevenness; the antagonisms created from such disparity were bound to be registered; those observing and reacting to them sought another language for the new facts; that language had to be at once vernacular (accessible to the less educated) and universal (translatable into rights and principles). The parochial and ethnic had to be transcended (rather than disappeared). It had to establish a new connection with the universal and only the paradox of 'nation-ism' (as it might also have been called) could do this. Its machinery for doing so was distinct nationalist intelligentsias: egg-heads of *ethnos*, laying (as Said does) an increasing emphasis upon the choice of what once lay far beneath any conscious choice: 'identity'.

'Nationalism' is in one sense no more than a general title for this language – the evolving tongue of modernity. Said began to speak it in earnest in 1967, after the Arab-Israeli Six-Day War: 'That awful week in June', he calls it, when he grasped more fully that 'I was an Arab, and we – "you" to most of my embarrassed friends – were being whipped.' From this cat-o'-nine-tails initiation was born *Orientalism*, his most celebrated work. Imperialism had fostered a self-interested mythology of the Arab Orient, he argued, in which academics and poets had colluded with missionaries, statesmen and entrepreneurial desperadoes. The result was a romantic conception frequently exalted by love. But (alas) this was love for the noble natives as they were, or rather as they were imagined to have been – infants of an Edenic Islam untarnished by Atlantic pollution (including filing cabinets and typewriters). The converse of such affection was of course contempt, mutating into hatred whenever the natives went 'beyond themselves'. Orientalist duty demanded they stick to their true, veiled selves. Failure to do so merely revealed (as in the 1967 war) their congenital inadaptation to modern ways: as useless with tanks as with democracy and women.

Arabism and anti-Arabism have something in common: the belief in a pan-Arab *Geist* capable of effective, nationalist-style unity. Although he started off wanting to subscribe to this, an irreverent observer like Said could not long put up with it. He soon realised that it was no better than Pan-Hellenism and Pan-Slavism: conservative ideological trances employing a rhetoric of racial solidarity to stifle popular and national trouble-makers – notably trouble-makers like him. In the 'Introduction' to *Politics of Dispossession* (one of the best parts) he recounts how an earlier study of Palestine failed to find an Arab publisher:

> It's an interesting footnote to all this that when *The Question of Palestine* came out a Beirut publishing house approached me about an Arabic translation. When I agreed, I was stunned to learn a moment later that I would be expected to remove from the text any criticism I had made of Syria, Saudi Arabia, and the rest. I refused, and to this day none of my books on Palestine has been translated into Arabic.

His new one stands even less chance, unless West Bank self-rule makes unexpectedly quick progress.

To get anywhere Palestinian nationalism had to distinguish itself from this miasma. The author's quaint way of putting it is as 'a reductive process', or 'an attempt to decompose Arab nationalism into discrete units finely sensitive to the true cost of real independence'. It took the Palestinians twenty-five years, through a series of fearful defeats – the worst of them at Arab hands, in Jordan, Lebanon and Kuwait. 'The countries that make the loudest noise in support of Palestine treat Palestinians the worst', he remarks angrily. On the other hand, when the *intifada* mobilised the population of the occupied territories directly against Israeli control from 1987 onwards, it met with at least limited success quite rapidly. 'Recognition' is no gratuitous extra benefit for a nationalist movement: in a sense it is the whole point (even if elaborate negotiations are needed subsequently to establish a polity). By March 1988, Said recalls, this was in effect won and symbolised in the meeting between himself, another Palestinian professor, and Secretary of State George Schulz: the world now had to confront the reality of a limited but indefeasible national demand, one which would not be disappeared. Even so the effects of the confrontation were further postponed by the Gulf War, and the PLO's reckless support for Saddam Hussein.

Said sometimes wobbles badly on the latter topic. 'Both wrong and embarrassingly silly', he concedes; but at the same time he denounces Israeli peaceniks for using such support as an excuse to break off relations – 'as if the Palestinian situation under Israeli military occupation had been just wonderful before the Gulf War'. This is feeble rhetoric. I shouldn't imagine the Israelis thought that for a second; but the Iraqi government had just been raining missiles down on them (as well as preparing a new big-gun variant of the Final Solution).

Orientalism was a scathing analysis of metropolitan-racialist nonsense. But nationalist counterblast always carries its own danger: an obsessive sensibility over-attuned to its object of denunciation. The cat-o'-nine-tails never ceases its work (one feels in these pages), the skin will never grow back over the tortured nerve endings. In part this has been due to Said's particular circumstances. In New York he has had to endure daily combat with another kind of exile intelligentsia, the formidably organised Israeli-American lobby. Not all European readers may be aware of just how aggressive and unscrupulous that mode of nationalism can be, and if so they will find *The Politics of Dispossession* enlightening. It must have been like fighting the Six-Day War over and over again.

The obsessive undertow accompanying *Orientalism* brought the author into conflict with Ernest Gellner. Reviewing a successor volume, *Culture and Imperialism*, in the *Times Literary Supplement*[3] Gellner accused him frankly of 'inventing a bogy called Orientalism' and attributing far too much to its pervasive cultural influence:

> Truth is not linked to political virtue (either directly or inversely). To insinuate the opposite is to be guilty of that very sin which Said wishes to denounce. Like the rain, truth falls on both the just and the unjust. The

problem of power and culture, and their turbulent relations during the great metamorphosis of our social world, is too important to be left to lit crit.

This must have been like having a cheese-grater applied to the raw nerve endings. The resultant row has become famous. Famous but (it seems to me) mistakenly blown up into a supposed clash of *Weltanschauungen*. In fact, asperity on one side was matched by an exaggerated touchiness on the other.

There were two sides to Gellner's attack. He was accusing Said of not locating his chosen cultural polemic accurately enough within a grander or epochal framework of development – the 'transition from agrarian to industrial society' which has long been Gellner's own preferred theme. Lacking this degree of theoretical articulation, the anti-Orientalist crusade had too often sunk into a banal vindication of its victims. If most Western scholarship and writing about the East is Orientalist conspiracy, then hope must lie solely on the other side: in the camp of those put down, crassly categorised, or adored for the wrong reasons. But the trouble with this anti-imperialist 'camp' is the hopelessness of so much of it: vile dictators, censorship, clerical mania, and traditionalism incompatible with any sort of modernisation (Western-led or not).

On the first count I feel Gellner is quite right. Said is no theorist, and rarely situates his cultural forays within a wider historical perspective. It is quite true that Progress was bound to take off in one region of the world rather than another. Unevenness could only have been avoided by guidance from outer space by something like the miracle-stones in Arthur C. Clarke's *2001*. It might, for example, have erupted out of China, in which case some Atlantic equivalent of Edward Said might by now be denouncing Occidentalism and the near-universal contempt for the bulbous-nosed and straight-eyed displayed by the academic lackeys of Peking. Or it might (like Homo sapiens itself) have come out of Africa. In that case both Said and Gellner would today be fulminating over Septentrionalist delusions about colourlessness: the vacant brain-pans supposed natural to the pigmentally challenged, in spite of their charming irrationality. In fact, for reasons still imperfectly understood, it originated in Atlantic seaboard societies and gave initial leverage to a congerie of pinkoid clans.

On the second count, I am not so sure. Out of unevenness came nationalism, including the sort Edward Said defends, and I would have thought that in the long run the victims would be likely to tell a better and more accurate story about what happened to them, and about their own social and cultural histories before the big developmental change. The truth-rain has never fallen evenly. After the change, as during it, it will have a differential distribution, and probably one closer to the kind of justice dreamt of by anti-Orientalists.

The trouble is, we live in the short run. And within this they will go on finding it extremely difficult to do anything like that – except in terms of rhetorical aspiration (which is what Gellner was denouncing). The reasons for this are not (as the victim ideology tends to assume) subjective and moral ones – betrayal, bad faith and so on. They are institutional. Colonised and less-developed societies lack the means to evolve an adequate cultural riposte to the 'advanced' offensive. By contrast the imperialists are over-endowed with professorships, research institutes, well-heeled anthropologists and literary periodicals (as well as with missiles and aircraft-carriers). Most serious inquiry can only be done from their point of view, even if the risks of Orientalist astigmatism remain inherent in it. To get a sense of the opposite and what it means one need not turn to Gellner: Edward Said's *Politics of Dispossession* will do.

'There isn't a single decent library in the entire Arab world', he complains. 'To do research on our own past, our culture, our literature, we still have to come to the West, to study at the feet of Orientalists, many of whom have openly declared themselves enemies to Islam and the Arabs ... [but neither has there been] any effort to pour money into Western universities to promote the study of Arab and Islamic civilisation, to promote that study in our interests. On all sides it is evident that as Arabs we are the world's intellectual and moral lumpenproletariat.'

So what 'the long run' entails is long indeed: a more integral process of modernisation, within which 'lumpenproletarian' status can be left behind, and both state and civil institutions built up. That is what nations are for. Or at least, no better way of doing it has yet been lastingly demonstrated. 'The Arab world', he goes on, 'is undergoing a premature technocratisation' on the lines laid down by his own father: typewriters before democracy, as it were, leading to the ascendancy of the right-wing brutalism typified by Saddam Hussein and President Assad.

However, 'the Arab world' is a large part of this problem, not a solution. It denotes not a nation but something more like a 'people', in that purplish after-dinner sense so dear to Winston Churchill: 'the English-speaking Peoples' who have spread themselves round a bit, acquired a sense of destiny, retained certain elements of common culture – and never quite got over it. Under Thatcher some of us thought the bloody thing would never go away. Feeling that 'a world' is on one's side is a serious malfunction, something like the nationalist equivalent of muscular dystrophy. Yet victim status makes it more tempting to indulge such feelings, since 'worlds' may always be imagined as possessing a redemptive secret denied to mere nationalities. If the secular version lets down the dispossessed, then an even headier possibility can step in: the 'other world' of a common faith, in this case Islam.

Not that Said can be accused of wobbling in that direction. He remains aggressively secular: 'We must see the issues concretely, not in terms of the happy and airy abstractions that tend to dominate our discussions. What distinguishes the truly struggling intellectual is, first, his or her effort to grasp things as they are in the proper methodological and political perspective, and, second, the conception of his or her work as activity, not as passive contemplation.' This is the struggle recipe which is also outlined

in *Representations of the Intellectual*. Said has nobly lived up to its criteria
during his long activity as champion of the Palestinian national cause.
Among nationalist intellectuals I know or have read about, I cannot think
of anyone less like the 'Professor of Terrorism' so often invoked by the US-
Israeli lobby.

The accusation has been revived none the less, in connection with his
denunciation of last year's agreement between Arafat and Rabin. The story
here is mainly in the Introduction and the Epilogue to *The Politics of
Dispossession*. The former recounts his mounting disillusionment with the
PLO leadership long before the Historic Accord. The most surprising aspect
of this to many readers will be the practically bottomless and mulish
parochialism of that leadership. In Said's account it had no idea at all of
how American politics and public opinion functioned. 'All through this
period' (the 1980s),

> Arafat was neither fighting to expand solidarity for Palestinians in the West
> nor nurturing the logical Palestinian constituency of liberals, dissenters, the
> women's movement, and so on. Instead he and his associates seemed to be
> looking for patrons in the West who would get them a solution of some sort.
> This quixotic fantasy originated in the notion that the United States worked
> like, say, Syria or Iraq: get close to someone close to the Maximum leader
> and all doors will open.

When the door did inch open at last, Arafat rushed to get his foot in. In
1985 he had told Said that he had no intention of ending up as the Mufti of
Jerusalem had done at an earlier stage of Palestine's Calvary, and 'ending
up with nothing to show for his decades of effort against the Zionist
movement'. Said now accuses the PLO of accepting something uncomfortably close to nothing: the tiny roof of Gaza and Jericho against the last sky,
the most cramped space for manoeuvre one can imagine as qualifying for
'self-government'.

But it is also characteristic of Said that his denunciation of this climb-
down is at once accompanied by modest, practical proposals for making the
most of it – for enlarging the space and turning his country, Palestine, into
a genuine nation. He contrasts the old nation-building slogan of Zionism –
'another acre, another goat' – to the apocalyptic assertiveness which has
dogged both Arab and PLO rhetoric. In the new situation, he suggests, a
version of the former must now be worked out for Palestinians. 'An idea
like "limited autonomy"', he goes on,

> might lead to independence or it might equally well lead to further
> domination. In either case the main task for Palestinians is to know and
> understand the overall map of the territories that the Israelis have been
> creating, and then devise concrete tactics of resistance. In the history of
> colonial invasion, maps are always first drawn by the victors, since maps are

always instruments of conquest [but] Geography can also be the art of resistance if there is a counter-map and a counter-strategy.

This counter-strategy has nothing to do with what the Professor of Terrorism was once regularly convicted for. It is a nation-building prospectus founded upon maximisation of the very few assets the Palestinians possess. This almost uniquely dispossessed people, he argues, has one hugely under-exploited advantage: perhaps the largest, most able and most dispersed intelligentsia any national movement has ever been able to claim. Zionism is the obvious historical precedent; but it should also be remembered how divided Jewish intellectuals were, and how strong anti-Zionism remained among them until World War II. By contrast, Said observes how

> Throughout the Arab world, Europe, and the United States there are extraordinarily large numbers of gifted and successful Palestinians who have made a mark in medicine, law, banking, planning, architecture, journalism, industry, education, contracting. Most of these people have contributed only a tiny fraction of what they could to the Palestinian national effort.

Thus the new national effort called for is different in quality from both the old one of the PLO and the *intifada*. It should be an international effort at nation-state building, an invention of 'ways of countering the facts with our own facts and institutions, and finally of asserting our national presence, democratically and with mass participation'. Small-country, secular, democratic, institutional, acre-and-goat nationalism, in other words. It resembles Jewish nationalism minus the Zionist component. Also, it is virtually the opposite of what Saddam Hussein, King Hussein, President Assad and (intermittently) the PLO have stood for: the 'Arab world' of dictatorial cliques, violent paranoia, mass oppression and (potentially) theocratic convulsions. No wonder they hate Palestinians so much: both in spite of and because of its extraordinary dispossession, its diaspora and prolonged sufferings, 'Palestinism' (if one can call it that) should be the one sign of political hope within that world.

'Happy the nation without heroes' is often quoted these days as self-evident truth. I'm not so sure. I feel more confidence saying 'Happy the nation – or the nationalism – with intellectuals like this to speak of and for it'.

Part IV
Scotland

The Question of Scotland

For reasons restated in different parts of this book, everybody concerned with the theory of nationalism has some special stake in it. Being a theorist or historian depends upon being a certain sort of individual; but in modern times all kinds of individuals cannot help being 'nationalists'. This is not a matter of moral stance or aspiration. Anti-nationalists, 'internationalists', cosmopolitans and self-consciously post-nationalists cannot avoid defining their respective attitudes in relationship to the mainstream of national identities. The mêlée of modern times affords no real respite at that level, permitting nobody to be *au-dessus*. Nor is this because of any mystic power attaching to the nation as distinct from identification-competitors like locality, religion or romantic love. It arises, rather, from the contingent authority acquired by a certain level of communal consciousness under the pressures of accelerating (and disturbing) societal change.

Being an 'individual' is possible only because of non-individual traits and reflexes that account for most of any given individual's personality: whether defined as 'instinct' or as 'the unconscious', these are either inherited, or impressed upon personal character through familial upbringing and social experience (including education). Individuals do make themselves, but mainly by the internalisation of things held in common with others. They are forged by families; however, 'families' are themselves notoriously elastic and extensible – from the nuclear to the extended, to speech communities and the metaphorical or 'imagined' communities of co-religionists, compatriots or fellow denizens of the World Wide Web. Modernisation made one of these reservoirs particularly important, or even decisive: that linked to nationality. The weakness of psychology among the social sciences means the machinery of this reconfiguration is ill-understood, but its consequences are not: the salience and inescapability of 'national character' in the discourse of modernity. I argue above that this is what informs most modern philosophy at a deeper level, but its joke visibility is famous too: the undilutedly French internationalist, the unspeakably British representative of common sense, the helplessly American one-worldist – all are figures of legitimate everyday fun (especially among their smaller neighbours). In other words, this is a theoretical area which ought to command more caution than it usually does about any theorist's own motives and back-ground. The only exculpation I can offer in this regard is that I have never hidden the fact that my own dilemmas and oddities emanate from those of my country, Scotland. These undoubtedly explain a good deal of my intellectual passions and concerns. It is easier for others to sense, interpret and make fun of this, but I have not tried to evade it. There is no point, and dubious auras like pride and shame have nothing to do with this.

This section of the book looks from different angles at the question of Scottishness and its repoliticisation. Scottish twentieth-century intellectuals are an ambiguous mixture of Pict and metropolitan, of ancient peripherality and recent centrality. They used to be on the edge of everything, like the Pictish mythical leader Calgacus: 'There are no lands behind us . . . we are the most distant dwellers upon earth, shielded till today by our very remoteness and the obscurity in which it has shrouded our name.' Refor-mation and Enlightenment diminished that obscurity, but a subsequent British Empire propelled them too far into metropolitan limelight. Picts became Brits (so to speak) and have had some difficulty in returning to being Scots (or, as some of them still can't help feeling, mere Scots) again. A previous history of independence made assimilation impossible; and yet the imperial alignment with England and an habitual posture of universal-ism made ethno-national liberation difficult too. The result was a slow, staged return marked by many setbacks and detours, partly synchronised by an equally gradual imperial run-down whose last dramatic moment, the return of Hong Kong to China, took place only two months before the 1997 referendum on a new Scottish Parliament. 'Return' here means (as with all forms of nationalism) reinvention and discovery, sometimes of nature, more often of novelties reclothed in vernacular.

The predominantly civic and constitutional mode of twentieth-century nationalism in Scotland was partly an accident: the fate of a population which had conserved institutional nationality without statehood, and there-fore never *had* to have a state for its national identity to survive. None the less, the accident may have some redeeming features. It has delayed statehood into the post-1989 world, which looks likely to be a far better general *Heimat* for smaller polities who want the benefits of self-rule with-out an armed chauvinism, a blood-and-soil ideology – without hating (or at least hating less) their neighbours, one-time metropolitan oppressors, colonisers, 'big brothers' and so on. The Scots, the Welsh and the popula-tion of Northern Ireland may have the opportunity of exploring and developing nationhood within the new circumstances of 'globalisation', rather than the ancient, wretched ones of imperial contestation, warfare and racial dementia. They also share a common way into that future, via the evolution of a European Union. All too little is said here about *la Grande République* to come, and I must apologise for it. I did think and write about this greater theme before the period reflected in most sections of *Faces of Nationalism*, from 1979 to 1997 – the era during which the Scots tried to re-enter the political game of modernity, failed, fell in a heap, slowly picked themselves up and tried again with more success – and look forward to doing so again.

A fear of philosophical relativism often attaches to any admission of just how biased speculation normally is by a theorist's or historian's national background. In my view, this is wholly unfounded. It nearly always emanates from some metropolitan thought-world within which the thinker assumes his or her privileged and instinctive access to the universal. Its standard accompaniment is cant about the Enlightenment (menaced, sinking, to be saved from the masses without delay, etc.). It so happens that Scotland was a significant site of the actual Enlightenment, and later a museum site in which far too many of its cranky, cramped, elitist, authoritarian, stuffed-shirt and anachronistic relics were preserved. No doubt this is why I feel a particular impatience with what Christopher Hitchens has labelled as today's 'Windbags of the West'. They accuse nationalists of dreaming up unreal communities, on the basis of a dreamt-up past community of Reason whose virtues were genuine, but not universal or deserving of uncritical veneration, let alone of fanatical defence and preservation. No doubt it also explains why I have always been an anarchistic optimist, and felt instinctively that enlightenment (without a capital letter) must lie somewhere pretty far ahead and away from 'all this': through the community of national identity from which we were preserved, rather than abstractly against it.

Identities in Scotland

L'Ecosse a été redoutable tant qu'elle n'a pas été incorporée avec l'Angleterre; mais, comme dit M. Voltaire, un état pauvre, voisin d'un riche, devient vénal à la longue: et c'est aussi le malheur que l'Ecosse éprouve.

Encyclopédie (1765), art. 'Ecosse'.

Auld Claes

'Identity' is a very contemporary term.[1] Contemporary, that is, in the sense of being at once newly puzzling and politically significant. Older meanings like 'being the same', 'personal identity', a classical philosophical problem or the humble bureaucratic insignia of 'identity cards' seem to have given way to something else.

It might be described as a terrain of uneasy collectivity. Upon it whole nations or peoples can now be described as looking for, and perhaps less often as finding, 'their own identity', the things that make them different and worthwhile, or, at least, peculiar. In one sense this usage may look like new clothes for the distinctly old-fashioned beasts of 'national character' and 'destiny'. Yet it is not really so. On such ultra-sensitive ground, alterations are never 'merely verbal', matters of stylistic whim.

The word use is new because there is something new. 'Identity' has emerged from neutrality and become a positive term because new claims are instinctively attached to it. Nationalities have always had identity. But now it seems they must have it. No longer taken for granted, identity has to measure up to certain standards. The comfortable old clothes won't do: identity must toe a line of uniformed respectability. If defective, its shames call out for remedy, or at least a cover-up; if 'rediscovered', it must then be 'preserved' from further violation; and above all it has to be asserted ('proudly') and so get itself recognised by outsiders. Yes, it's time the world stopped smirking about *our* identity.

It is no coincidence that the most critical investigation of this theme is by a Scotsman, W.J.M. Mackenzie. Though often jocular in approach ('Murder of a Word', 'Life Story of the Victim', etc.), his *Political Identity*[2] is a serious work consciously reflecting the Scottish confusion of the 1970s. 'A discussion of political identity', he concluded, 'is primarily a discussion of the conditions in which it is possible to realise "common purpose"'. Conscious, collective 'identity' in other senses – cultural, linguistic, religious – may figure among these pre-conditions; but only when common purpose and action emerge can their significance be complete.

New Clothes from Nowhere

The new self-consciousness, as Mackenzie realised, would bring particular vexation to the Scots. At a recent Glasgow dinner party I found all the wounds and grudges on open display. Its presiding spirit was a prickly yet strangely helpless nationalism: a passionate will to look forward driven – by what weird machinery of self-contradiction? – into fits of backward-looking self-laceration.

An animated political debate about the state of the British Union led, as intended, to speculation on our own future in the crumbling *palazzo*. But the very use of 'our' in the heavyweight sense reminded everyone present that when Scottish politics and nationality meet, nothing can ever be taken for granted. Modern patriotism has no natural persona in Scotland. Our old clothes are romantic rags, yet – embarrassingly, inexplicably – none of the new uniforms seems to fit either. Hence the whole company – conservatives, Labourites, nationalists, anti-politicals – found itself pitched onwards into the morass of 'Who are we?' Or, more portentously, 'What is Scottishness?'

But the forward motion is often in a backward direction. An exit is hard to find from this bog, and soon the point was proved once more. The familiar spectres broke surface and sank again, one by one – that somehow pre-destined succession of abandoned hopes and touchy debating points which reduce most dialogues about Scottishness to furious silence, or alcoholic despair. 'How the Scots love a good argument!' a French friend once observed. He was right, but failed to notice how what they love most of all is a fiery debate edging on violence, yet leading safely nowhere. 'Nowhere' is in this sense a distinctive Scottish place. What it means is the reassuring void we ken, rather than unfamiliar gestures of political agreement or compromise: the limbo in which our nation happens to have settled down, as distinct from the common ground of modernity.

Most of our rhetorical ghosts were summoned to this particular feast. There was the deliberate tunnel vision of Scottish Toryism, bluntly happy with the *auld-claes* identity and obdurately convinced that adding politics would bring Cambodian disaster: 'Independent Scotland? Fine – just as long as my seat's booked on the last train out!' Snowflake cultural nationalism featured prominently on the other side, an ancestral soul too precious for rough political beasts to trample on: 'What we really need is a new Enlightenment, Scotland's direct line to the Absolute – why ruin the great gift with shoddy politics?' In this way, bluff conservatism and a craintive intellectual purism have met and reinforced one another over the generations: united in dread of native narrowness.

Topography of Nowhere

The fatal terrain was further delineated by what one might call 'fragmentosis Caledoniensis'. From their earliest bookish encounters Scottish intellectuals imbibe a form of national nihilism, the sense of a *Heimat* lovable yet incurably divorced from the modern. The road is short to belief that the charm must depend upon the backwardness. So the divorce becomes permanent; and one consequence is a disarmed love, constantly beset by fear. But there is a way of countering this dread – by the wilful dissolution of 'Scotland' into just so many competing parishes and social classes. The crucial weakness of Scottish identity – political nervelessness, absence of common purpose – ends wrapped up in assertions that after all there's ('really') no such thing as Scottish identity.

These claims are invariably pursued with a suspect intensity, which derives from the nature of what is being asserted: a paradox so absurd that passion alone can enunciate it without shame. 'Scotland?: which Scotland? – Highland or Lowland, Hugh Macdiarmid or the *Sunday Post?*'; 'Scotland': *if* that word means anything – which I doubt – then surely it means utterly different things in Grampian and in Clydebank?' Scotland's internal contrasts (actually no greater than in most other nations) are thus weirdly elevated into mountain ranges of peculiarity – barriers exclusive of all possible consensus and common interest.

Exclusive, therefore, of both the ambitions and the risks of a national politics. Haven't other peoples acted to overcome or balance their variegated inheritance, and not invariably by suppression? Yes: but such calm comparisons slither around the main point at issue – the fact that the Scottish middle class wants to feel paralysed in advance by this problem. Self-inflicted stalemate gives them two things at once: a dramatic, if somewhat doleful, sense of uniqueness, and continued absolution from political sin.

Elective Idiocy

No doubt because we were in Glasgow, Edinburgh New Town was the parish pump provoking most spleen among the participants. What few national vitals may be left us, it was implied, are now being devoured in a feeding-trough of Anglicised depravity. The task of resurrecting Scots identity, superhuman in any case, will before long be unthinkable amid Edinburgh's sell-outs and south-eastern incomers: the 'fragmentosis' will soon be terminal, thanks to this *quartier maudit* devoted to the trashing of all native virtues and institutions.

That stance too is laughable to outsiders. They know that only an hour away the roles are always comically reversed. In the capital 'Scotland' is perceived as menaced primarily by the other city's 'Miles Better' capitulation to everything most frenzied and flatulent about Mrs Thatcher's enterprise culture. Socialism has had its problems; but why this wilful infatuation with a capitalism run to seed? In a recent show Victor and Barry described themselves as 'quite the funniest duo in Scotland . . . or even Gle-e-esgow!' And the great city-state does believe its identity to be, in some inscrutably bloated sense, larger than that of the nation as a whole. European Culture Year is bound to do further damage here.

What has this delusion ever shown, but that our largest village has its normal share of idiots? *Invisible Country: A Journey Through Scotland*,[3] Glaswegian James Campbell's nicely titled voyage of discovery around the *Heimat*, contains some relevant remarks on the too famous contrast. He points out that his own city has been stamped mainly by all 'the metropolitan influences of industrialism' – non-native forces like Empire, immigration, an outward-looking socialism and, we can now add, post-modern capitalism. In contrast – and however many sleekit demons patrol her streets – Edinburgh has resisted these influences to remain a place where 'the past is imperative . . . and strengthens the feeling of belonging to a distinct tribe with its own myths and traditions'. In other words a Scottish society may exist, and, arithmetically speaking, has to exist, around Glasgow; but the Scottish nation will always be unimaginable without Edinburgh. So, therefore, will any identity in that newly crucial sense I began by mentioning.

Politics: The Scottish Knot

It often happens at such discussions that foreigners strike a lonely note of sanity, and in this case an Irishman obliged, periodically intervening to chide the brawling factions. He seemed particularly moved by the sight of one journalist – a saintly man renowned for personal forbearance and Olympian judgement – who snapped suddenly under the strain, thumped the table, and declared that he had positively nothing whatever further to say on the subject. There were a few seconds of silence. During them the black hole behind 'Scottishness' was visible to everybody. Then we all fell back into it again.

Observers find these situations of divisive self-flagellation absurd, even demeaning. A *nation sans état* like Scotland has many faults; but not enough, surely, to justify intellectual suicide? What they sense is the lurking self-indulgence – a contradiction still more enjoyed than resented, the posture of an elite suffering from mounting exasperation and fear, yet unwilling, so far, to shake itself free from the customs of a once remunerative impotence.

That is exactly the knot of attitudes which paralyses the formation of 'identity' I mentioned earlier. New identities have to be made. Nationalists like to imagine them as pre-existing – Sleeping Beauty awaiting her Prince's speech – but they are not in fact a ready-made inheritance. Politics alone brings them into effective being: Mackenzie's 'common purpose', struggles or movements bestowing a sense of possibility and of a strategy pursuable against obstacles and over time. These alone create a practical standpoint in the present from which an 'inheritance' can be estimated, or rendered less ambiguous. Great risks and defeats are the usual accompaniment of such struggles.

What is most worth underlining here is that while this 'making' may be of a nation, it is also of a class – those social groups and alliances with enough passion for the novelty to run its risks, and face the initial defeats. Though in the name of an indeterminate 'people', national-liberation struggle can only be led by certain people with more determinate and vested interests in the process; nor could it conceivably be otherwise.

But in that case a less comfortable converse must also be true. The familiar argument has a shadow implication, falling heavily upon us in Scotland. Because national movements require such a motive force, they may be stymied by the lack of one. Nationalism may find itself paralysed and indefinitely held back where the class in question remains unable to seize the initiative. If the most likely identity-forming and identity-bearing groups remain stuck in the Gordian knot of their own past, then even favourable objective circumstances may permit astonishingly little forward motion – a movement always too little and too late to grasp its chance.

The point can be put another way. Social forces bent upon national self-assertion are unlikely to avoid excess and rashness: with nationalism, overdoing it tends to be the only way of doing it. But by the same token, can one not also imagine a class so afraid of rashness that challenge makes it retreat into compromise and prevarication – into a craintive moderation whose very 'reasonableness' is a kind of alibi for failure and retreat?

Institutional Identity

Well, of course there is such a class. I am a member of it. I happen to be a recalcitrant offshoot who stopped paying his dues years ago, and as a result gets labelled 'intellectual' (though the tedious thing about renegades is the way they always bear their class – and their nation – with them). This class runs Scotland. No collective presumption is involved here, for the important term is 'runs': the Scottish institutional middle class has never ruled this country, it merely manages it.

Its dilemma of the present day – under the Thatcherite onslaught – is one of both conscience and consciousness. Round dinner tables and elsewhere we find it fretting characteristically about whether or not the moment has come for it to rule, rather than merely administer. But that needs a new common purpose, a determination fed by a new consciousness – by, precisely, a renovated sense of 'identity'. And the awful, paralytic truth is that an upper-servant class may find it far harder to take such a decision than those who are genuinely below stairs – the outcast or dispossessed whose life chances have, suavely or brutally, been defined for them. The latter may quite easily tell itself there is nothing to lose. The Scots managing class is not brought up to think that way at all; and it has permeated the nation with its caution.

After all, its main articles of faith derive from the history of a not-so-petty bourgeoisie. Until very recently, post-1707 experience seemed to be showing it that a country – and for a time an empire – comfortably in the hand was worth any number of other possible ones, out there in history's dark bush. Even when the country then rots in the hand – some parts of it surviving on sufferance, others snatched away by assimilation – such a stratum finds it congenitally difficult to let go. To risk letting go, that is, and reach out more determinedly for a visionary one, the one which measures up, in the new clothes, etc. The old 1707 gene structure goes on regulating its primary reflexes: 'canniness', the crippling sense of how much there is to lose.

Other segments of the Scottish 'people above', like the landowners and the industrialists, may have had different attitudes; so may the working class at times. But neither have had the importance for 'identity' which these organised middle ranks have so consistently borne since the eighteenth century. In this sense the institutional cadre has been like a continuing armature of the wider Scottish bourgeoisie – had it been annulled by the Union, then both capitalism and class relations would have assumed quite different forms here, and Thatcherite Conservatism would not be facing the problems it does. All comparative studies of nationality have underlined the crucial place of such professional strata in generating the identity shifts behind nationalism: it is teachers, clerics, lawyers, journalists and loose screws who cause the trouble, far more than landlords, bankers, manufacturers or trade-unionists.

A Too Civil Society

But by the very same token, may not the same people be able to stop and contain 'the trouble' – to *prevent* identity from getting political and stirring up a common purpose? The Scots middle-class complex is of course rooted in the autonomous 'civil society' bequeathed us by 1707. In this descriptive, and quite uncomplimentary, sense, we are too civil to be nationalistic. The old trinity of Kirk, Law and Education still accounts for most of it. But in recent times it has been heavily reinforced by a devolved bureaucracy; and then, after the reforms of the early 1970s, by a formidable new apparatus of local government as well. It is during this era that the Labour Party has become the stratum's dominant political expression: terminal-condition socialism in the service of major-domo politics.

The result is a uniquely castrate formation, devoted to low but uncomfortable with high politics. It 'represents' Scotland's working class in much the same mythic fashion as the nomenklatura once did in Eastern Europe, but with a lot less power over it. Since 1979 it has also found itself somewhat furtively half standing in for the nation, like a butler unexpectedly offered the keys of the mansion. In that situation, what would Gordon Jackson/ 'Hudson' of *Upstairs, Downstairs* have done but muddle through meantime, hoping desperately that he could follow the Admirable Crichton's example and hand them back again as soon as possible? With, maybe, just a bit more self-management downstairs?

It's quite true that nowadays Hudson/Crichton has a disreputable younger brother who has left service and taken to tearaway rhetoric and fulmination. Every now and then he breaks out and dispenses enough ideological firewater to assemble a crowd. For a time this glowers threateningly at the old mansion (seen as peopled by 'traitors', 'hirelings', etc.), and chants 'Independence now!' When nothing happens it gets depressed and goes home again. No windows are smashed, and the hirelings of the too civil society (now including poll-tax registrars and a swelling number of sheriff-officers) continue responsibly about their business. 'Something-must-be-done' editorials make their seasonal appearances in *Scotsman* and *Herald*. There is some tut-tutting down south (less and less with the passage of time, and the regular postponement of 'doomsday').

If such 'SNP revivals' have become Heritage-events it is for a good reason which Scotland's main *mittelstands* myth quite easily explains: firewater-Hyde is of course none other than feartie-Jekyll in altered guise – blowing off his repressions with another bout of noisy inaction.

Common in all pre-political societies, millenarist movements have often preceded the growth of statehood, fostering a dream-like identity which may or may not, eventually, flow into the aggressive 'common purpose' of nationalism. However, such versions of identity tend to be based upon utopian purism, religious in form (if not always in content) and can never themselves be that purpose. Rightly scorning the marsh politics of self-colonisation, they count on quasi-divine mass conversion to put things right. This is of course the pure nationalism so dear to SNP fundamentalists, and manifestly in the ascendant since January 1989. However, pure nationalism remains inseparable from pure fantasy: 'one bound, and we shall be free', on that day when the pure Scot in all of us sees the light.

Circles of Identity

So the SNP is 'bourgeois' all right; a fact which, unfortunately, has nothing to do with tartan, the Tories or CBI (Scotland). It is much more like the alter ego of the institutional bourgeoisie: a Doppelgänger which, though intuited in the past by Stevenson and others, has only grown up and become really important during the era of the larger state's decline. Paradoxically, an institutional elite deprived of an elite's most important characteristic – command power – is far more comfortable with a rhetorical than with a practical nationalism. The verbal apocalypse of anti-English raving suits it fine. Through this a sense of 'national character' is preserved without the vulgarity of actual rebellion or practical over-assertiveness. Since the magic bound will never be made, we see a 'nationalism' which, disconcertingly, has become another way of going round in circles, rather than of escaping from them. Doomsday would mean getting *them* off our backs now. But an apocalypse always postponable to next time keeps dependence in business: in actual, historical time all those 'next times' will inexorably become never, as actual people just give in, give up or emigrate.

These perennial circles of 'Scottishness' – our identity complexes – all derive from a compensated impotence: 'venality' as the *Encyclopédie* authors diagnosed it. But this is a chronic condition with a definite class backbone, not a question of individual hand-outs or petty corruption. It is structure, not an endless series of individual 'sell-outs'. And the basis for it is inscribed into the circumstances of an early-modern nation-state decapitated and then offered – instead of the usual oblivion – very substantial and long-lasting advantages. Though enjoyed by all classes, some have got a lot more out of it than others.

I believe that the one I'm focusing on here derived the most enduring benefits: that petty and middling bourgeoisie involved in what George Davie once euphemistically called 'the balanced harmony of our institutions . . . the steady rhythm of independent institutional life'. This was the class most devoted to what he described as 'the formula of unification in politics, separation in ethics', a mode of existence 'still national, though no longer nationalist'. The Democratic Intellect, and its many imitators, have often praised the marvels inherent in such separation, and then gone on to mourn their attrition and eclipse: a national distinctness mercifully free from political evil, and maybe best uncorrupted by it.

In reality that 'formula' was a pre-modern one, increasingly useless in a reformed state – in the modernity where, as Gramsci put it, 'politics is everything'. After 1832 'harmony' became the entrenched routines of a provincial sub-Establishment, ever more stupefied by its steady rhythms of 'responsible', and unchallengeable, dependency. National-legal dignity collapsed into a prostrate legalism. The broad-based educational system mutated into a sickly hermaphrodite: the British worst of both worlds, Knox below and Oxbridge on top. Only the Kirk rebelled, in the 1843 Disruption: but, inevitably, to produce something worse, 'free' clerics determined to guarantee their purity by withdrawing from political modernity altogether.

Without political democracy, the important democratic strain in Presbyterianism was bound to be drowned by the authoritarian. I once tried resentfully to sum all that up in a phrase which caught on, about Scotland's rebirth depending on the strangling of the last Minister with the last copy of the *Sunday Post*. With hindsight, I can see that what the gibe really aimed at wasn't just dog-collars and D.C. Thomson. It was the whole self-strangulating class presence of which these have become symptoms: the unique Scots phenomenon of a national sub-mandarin class cringeingly proud of its 'responsible' addiction to political *coitus interruptus*.

Modernity summons us to show our identity passes. But all the Scots have to pull from their pocket is a set of identity malfunctions rooted in this decrepit corporate persona. Unable to escape from nationality, the latter has devoted itself to containing the beast and evading its political consequences, including democracy. Hence its innumerable and complex alibis for the avoidance of common purpose and action, its prolix labyrinths of subterfuge and bombast, its deft and wordy combinations of the parochial and the evasively 'outward-looking' (often ennobled as philosophy, a talent for abstraction), and its penchant for self-dramatisation. In a structuralist perspective, 'Scottishness' appears as a deliberately exit-less maze. Its whole point is permanent circular wandering, punctuated by ritual offerings at one sacred lamp-post after another: nostalgia, the divided soul, 'equality', moderation, *esprit de clocher*, 'use of England where the UK's meant' and a prescribed daily prayer for Gaeldom.

What the Jekyll-&-Hyde mythology actually expresses is an unnaturally united stratum glumly yoked to higher British servitude. Inevitably, its principal political task has been to reproduce self-colonisation – a process which, against mounting odds, demands both a constitutional cringe and the retention of some national dignity and substance. And, as with the 'fragmentosis' malady mentioned before, one way of accomplishing that is via a collective fantasy of really being unspeakably different. The dourly apparent persona hides a 'real' one. In Macdiarmid's phrase, 'an upswelling of the incalculable' must always be just round the corner. Impotence flows not from what we are, but from a more distinguished sort of soul malady. We are being sent down the plug-hole not by abject mediocrity but by fated contradictoriness: being forever in two minds and out of our heads, the 'tragedy' of instinct versus intellect and so on. Macdiarmid's 'Antizyzygy' symbolises the condition of being politically nobody; but also colours and disguises it, in a way palatable to the sufferers themselves.

The Castration Metaphor

So, it is hardly surprising that the new identity garments won't fit the Scots. They have been manufactured for more recurrent and standard situations where factors like language, ethnic culture, religion and the memory of forced integration prevail. In this mainstream of modern nationalism, institutionally forged identity has almost by definition been unimportant: national movements normally have to demand 'their own' civil institutions on the basis of other identity signposts. Hence politics is an ethnic-cultural, sometimes a religious, mobilisation foregrounding such signs – a process in which intellectuals naturally take a high profile.

In our odd historical sidestream, however, things are the wrong way round. Certain bequeathed institutions are the real if unpicturesque sign-posts. Among such fossils of statehood, the more usual form of nationalist militancy – mobilisation via language or culture – is something of a dead end. Sometimes effective against colonialism, it is relatively useless against our kind of institutional self-colonisation. Our *auld claes*, Walter Scott's tartanic romanticism, have been an all too effective spiritual antidote against the least romantic, the most boring of bourgeois societies. This has been very upsetting for intellectuals like Hugh Macdiarmid. But it also explains why he and others have gained so little influence on nationalist politics, or – reversing the argument – why Scottish nationalism, alone among European nationalist movements, has proved so remorselessly philistine. Since 1979 things have felt different. Until then grumblingly at home within a patriarchal *ancien régime*, the civil corporatism of the Scots instantly detected and bristled against the new metropolitan challenges. Such a second-in-command class knew instinctively that it could never survive a drastic overhaul of the UK command structure. What counts here is that 'Thatcherism' is an alteration of the state, as well as a range of economic reforms. It set out to destroy not just public-sector economics but the old tradition of patrician liberality within which these had grown up. Quickly discovering that this tradition already had one foot in the grave, Thatcher's new court understood it could soon be toppled over for good.

But as it did so the south-eastern government was unwittingly demolishing the external buttress upon which the old balancing-act identity of the Scottish middle class had so long depended. The term 'castrate' I used earlier may have seemed merely a literary insult. But there is a serious point to the metaphor, the one Ernest Gellner describes in his *Nations and Nationalism*. He points out there how techniques of 'gelding' were often employed by antique empires to sustain their power: actual eunuchs, but also 'priests . . . foreigners whose kin links could be assumed to be safely distant; or members of otherwise disfranchised or excluded groups who would be helpless if separated from the employing State'.

For such subordinate strata, everything depended upon the absolute stability of the 'unwritten' elite structures of central power: the dispensation of privileges and rewards by, in the old UK sense, 'decent chaps' who could be counted on to see a eunuch's point of view. If some crazed sultan or warlord got rid of these intermediary cadres, however, eunuchdom was obviously in deep trouble: although either physically or culturally conditioned against initiative and command, it could not tolerate the sacrifice of all separate status and dignity. Self-subordination is one thing; the dissolution of its whole social universe is quite another.

Planks of Identity

So it was from 1979 onwards that suddenly we began hearing so much about 'community', and the humane anti-materialism of the Scots – 'our way of doing things', so distinct from the vile egotism of the south-east. After 1987's doomsday debate these seeds of identity started sprouting everywhere – far more widely than in the SNP's ideological greenhouse. The most unlikely voices could be heard saying that we, responsible folk, had not abandoned responsibility for 'the philosophy of greed', or the vulgar individualism later extolled in Mrs Thatcher's Edinburgh speech to the Kirk. Suddenly, reminders of Scotland's many past tributes to greed and the capitalist road fell on deaf ears.

This is because they had, in a new sense, become irrelevant. A new, more broadly based identity is in formation: the middle classes are being compelled to defend their old civil corporatism by new and more aggressive ideological means. Ideology apart, they are doing so with the canniness and circumspection one would expect: 'responsibly' and in thought-out, collaborative stages. The political form this process has assumed is the Scottish Constitutional Convention: the high point so far of a resumption of real, rather than rhetorical, common purpose. In this way the Campaign for a Scottish Assembly has come to reflect the middle class's still very sideways and hesitant motion towards political nationalism, rather than the SNP. Not surprisingly, the latter greatly resents this fact.

A German journalist I met after the Convention's inaugural session in Edinburgh commented on the sight, remarkable in today's Europe, of representatives from so many institutions and walks of life actively talking and trying to accommodate to one another – a living and civil corporatism. 'But, my God', he concluded, 'it was all so boring, too!'

A good sign, I replied, and deeply reassuring. True, nationalism can't be made from boredom alone; but the point is that our upper-serving or 'eunuch' classes are at last trying to educate themselves out of their inheritance, and can't help being rather boring about it. They gave up independence in an odd, one-off fashion and are only likely to resume it in some similar, sidelong, untypical way: nerving themselves for the break through lengthy corporate rituals, elaborate charters and stuffy proclamations redolent of both court- and class-room.

In this sense, perhaps, the SNP version of national identity has never been half 'bourgeois' enough – it was a twopenny populism aimed at a bit of everyone and no one in particular. Hence the boredom-producing classes never took it seriously. But now at last, under the lash of Thatcherism, they have started to take identity seriously. The identity alibis have begun to acquire a political edge. Our own 'common purpose' is in a sort of formation – probably the only sort really possible. It's still far from the fully upright posture, I know.

14

Empire and Union

Next time it will be different.[1] Or so almost everyone in Scotland now believes, as they look forward to another election and back over the long trail of wreckage from 1979 to the present. The Conservative regime began by aborting constitutional change and has ended in a state of constitutional *rigor mortis*. John Major's government contemplates no political evolution whatever on the mainland, as distinct from Ireland, and advertises this rigidity as 'defence of the Union'. When it founders, however, such intransigence will be overtaken by long-overdue movement which can hardly fail to include parliaments in Wales and Scotland, as well as more European integration.

Just what is it that the Tories are defending? In Scotland they can be seen as trying to preserve what that sound Tory Sir Walter Scott called 'the silent way'. After the Union he thought that 'under the guardianship of her own institutions, Scotland was left to win her silent way to national wealth and consequence'. The source is his *Thoughts on the Proposed Change of Currency*, written in 1826 to defend the right of the Scottish banks to continue issuing their own banknotes and coins. But the context is more specific than most quotations of this celebrated remark allow. The Treaty of Union by itself had not brought wealth and consequence. It was 'from the year 1750' that these changes had at last begun to emerge – the epoch when Scotland was 'no longer the object of terror, or at least great uneasiness'. When, indeed, she had more or less sunk out of London's view altogether. Contempt had replaced fear, and Scott thought this was just as well. It was, he reckoned, 'because she was neglected that her prosperity has increased in a ratio more than five times greater than that of her more fortunate and richer sister'.

Lack of a distinct political voice was not necessarily an impediment to such distinctive prosperity. Certainly, the state is generally considered to be the key modern institution. But only under extreme totalitarianism is it all-important. Other less important national institutions can, as in the Scottish case, furnish a separate national configuration of society and culture – an 'identity' in the contemporary jargon – quite capable of sustaining nationality, a degree of patriotism and even varieties of chauvinism.

So the way is 'silent' only in the sense of its wider international resonance.

On the native terrain it has been associated with an uninterrupted cacophony of noisy complaints, grudges and chip-on-the-shoulder moaning over
non-recognition. In his *Thoughts* Sir Walter himself was contributing powerfully to the latter: 'whingeing' would be the contemporary description. Alas,
dignified mutism among the nations is compatible with (and may even
entail) constant pandemonium at home. On that sounding board of the
national soul, the *Edinburgh Scotsman*'s letter page, I doubt if a week has
passed since Scott's time without its quota of resentful jibes about non-
equality and southern arrogance. Back in 1925 we find Macdiarmid scorning
them for it in 'A Drunk Man Looks at the Thistle':

> And O! to think that there are members o'
> St Andrew's Societies sleepin' soon,
> Wha tae the papers wrote afore they bedded
> On regimental buttons or buckled shoon,
> Or use o' England where the UK's meent.

The Conservatives want to go on believing that political Union is essential
at once to the economy of the archipelago, to Britain's influence in Europe,
and – in more mystical vein – to maintaining the civilised norms of British
administration and culture. But what is the real historical nature of the
Union thus defended? Two books, *A Union for Empire: Political Thought and
the Union of 1707*, edited by John Robertson, and *The Autonomy of Modern
Scotland* by Lindsay Paterson, represent very different new approaches to
the question.[2] They assume, surely correctly, that it is a genuine puzzle.
There is nothing either self-explanatory or standard about the survival of a
united kingdom based on England, from early-modern times until practically the end of the second millennium.

John Robertson's collection of academic studies examines the origins of
its most important axis, the parliamentary unification of Scotland and
England in 1707. Lindsay Paterson's long polemical essay looks at the
consequences of that for the Scots – a near-unique form of 'autonomy' as
unusual as the state of which it is a part. Scotland's silent way, he contends,
allowed far more effective self-rule than most commentators have recognised. Nationalists have treated institutional autonomy as second-rate or
instrumental. With their emphasis on all-British virtues, Unionists have also
until very recently regarded it as relatively unimportant, or even as a mere
relic. Paterson's view is that though unusual it was, and remains, a more
respectable form of evolution than general theories of progress have allowed
for. These have been based on the nation-state, and hence have overlooked
the case of a stateless yet quite successful nation.

Both books bear on the current debates about devolution, constitutional
reform and Europe. Robertson's academic volume naturally disclaims
partisanship. Yet he cannot help hoping that better historical understanding
may 'help to clear the way for the formation of a viable modern alternative
to the Union'. For his part, Lindsay Paterson argues that a better grasp of

the real story of autonomy may sanction moves to recover political authority in Edinburgh. But paradoxically, it may also render independence less significant. A new Scottish democracy demands more distinct political representation; according to the author this need not entail the restoration of statehood or a literal dissolution of the Union. Rather than being simply a forlorn pre-modern accident, in fact, the silent way may presage the post-modern development of other countries inside a European Union.

Battle of the Cases

This places Paterson firmly among the nationalists rather than among the Nationalists. Politics in Scotland has turned into an orthographic battle between the Upper and the lower cases. Almost everyone is some sort of nationalist, including even Michael Forsyth, the new Tory Secretary of State for Scotland. In retreat, the Conservatives have discovered that true Union-ism awarded Scotland just as much nationalism as was good for it, via Scots law, institutional autonomy and new devices like the national health trusts. Much of their speeches these days are devoted to extolling the modest merits of enough-as-is-good-for-you national self-reliance. One might almost think that the aim of Union and Empire had all along been to foster this better class of Scottish and Welsh nationalism. Some in their audience are of course bound to think, if it has been so marvellous then might not more be better still? 'Ah, but it would bring disaster!' is the official reply – the agonising abyss of separatism, etc. But just why would healthy self-management lapse so swiftly into chaos?

Because the serpent will have bitten the apple, say Forsyth and his Scottish Office servants. He means the serpent of politics. This is also the problem for a growing intermediate stance in Scotland – those who find themselves somewhere in between the upper and lower cases (a position corresponding perhaps to 'small caps' in font design). These are people who, while not exactly yearning for a return to nationhood, perceive no likely stopping-place on the nationalist track short of whatever the European Union currently recognises as statehood or 'independence', and who have become increasingly matter-of-fact about the prospect. This is not surprising. No manifest disaster is equatable in today's Europe with 'being like Denmark', or the Netherlands or Finland. Scots of this persuasion tend to be more definitely pro-European than similar strata in England, and for that reason also inclined to scepticism about the dread abyss of separate statehood.

And then there is full upper-case Nationalism, which does indeed yearn for the 1707 Parliament to be recalled, for the Scots to abandon their silent way and recover voice and presence within the arena of nation-states. Many but not all Nationalists are in the Scottish National Party, or sometimes vote for it. However, there seem to be plenty of both upper-case and small-cap Nationalists in the Scottish Labour Party, and also among the Liberal Democrats, while an unknown number of small- or tiny-'n' nationalists support the SNP less for its ideology than because it registers the most effective protest against Them. In existing circumstances 'They' are of course bound to be mainly English, or at least perceived as held in the southern thrall.

Already confusing, the scene has become more so since the recent by-election at which Roseanna Cunningham won the rural and small-town constituency of Perth and Kinross for the SNP. Ethnicity-gaugers found the whole thing disorienting. Ms Cunningham is a vociferous Republican, Socialist and Feminist who refused to scale down any of her capital letters for electoral motives. This made no difference to the result. She thus succeeded one of Europe's outstanding politiclowns, the late Sir Nicholas Fairbairn.

Normally garbed in tartanic garments designed by his own hand and inhabiting a nearby castle, Sir Nicholas had been famously critical of the SNP's open-door citizenship policy which would, for example, allow the illegitimate offspring of black American GIs stationed in Scotland to be as Scottish as, well, Sir Nicholas himself. Vote Tory to preserve the Scot-Brit race. This eccentric addendum to the Unionist creed was not openly endorsed by Fairbairn's successor as candidate, a generally pitied young lad called John Godfrey. However, he did open up by routinely denouncing the Nationalists as Nazis, and the Tory campaign as a whole did little to redeem governmental fortunes. In fact all it did was mimic governmental fortunes, in the sense of staggering from one gaffe to another for three weeks like a Perthshire heifer struck down by 'mad cow' disease.

Before Nationalism

The road to this plight from 1707 has been a long one. Neither Union nor Empire then meant what they came to signify for the nineteenth and twentieth centuries. Robertson argues that the terms figured in a long and complex European debate within which the Edinburgh–London negotiations were only a minor episode. 'Empire' meant at that time not colonies and subject populations but something closer to today's notion of 'sovereignty'. 'Union' enjoyed a double-barrelled usage, as incorporation or confederation. The mounting absolutism of European monarchies encouraged the former but at the same time 'there had also emerged a second, rival concept of union understood as a confederation of more or less equal states' like the Dutch United Provinces. The rival sides in the 1706–7 argument looked back over these seventeeth-century disputes and struggled to adapt them to the new situation.

The 1707 deal was justified as an 'incorporating Union'. Yet the main agency of incorporation, all-powerful monarchy, had been destroyed by the mid-century revolutions in both England and Scotland. A landowners' parliament had risen to dominate one country, and a militant Protestant church had become crucial in the other. Patriotic lairds like Andrew Fletcher opposed incorporation not with independence in today's meaning but with a version of equal-state confederation. Yet that position too was weakened at its heart by memories of the revolutionary era. Everyone knew about, and in 1707 a few individuals could actually recall, the dire events of the 1650s when (in Robertson's words):

> The armies of the Commonwealth succeeded where so many kings had failed, and summarily conquered both Ireland and Scotland. The experience of defeat, followed by enforced union, changed for ever the relationship of each country to England ... never again could the Scots deceive themselves that the English lacked the will or the means to conquer them.

No really equal confederation of states was possible. Recent subjection had only emphasised a fundamental and inescapable imbalance. Today England represents about 85 per cent of the United Kingdom, Scotland about 9 per cent. Historically the latter's population was relatively bigger (before the great emigrations of the nineteenth century) but its resources were relatively less. There never was a time when it (or even all the fringe nationalities together) was anything like Hungary inside the Habsburg Empire, or even Slovakia within pre-1992 Czechoslovakia. Like German dominance in Central Europe, English domination of the British Isles was a mixture of commanding geography, overwhelming demography and economic power. This did not mean that political mastery was equally preordained or natural; but English leaders could easily pretend or assume that it was.

The pretence was important above all for the English self-image. Most of the time, for most social purposes, nine-tenths of any group can ignore the remainder. They will do so all the more easily when the statistical effect is amplified by advantage in other domains, like ownership, social class, cultural or military achievement. The resultant hegemony appears more natural to those exerting it than to whoever is in its train, or under its wheels. 'Use o' England where the UK's meant' has always been an irritant to the fringe but inevitable for the majority. The latter rarely mean to rub in their authority. They just don't think about it, nor, in most times and places, is there really much reason why they should. What is natural in the situation is that when they should, they usually have to be reminded.

This English absence of self-definition (or glib over-identification with Britain) flows from an ethnic dominance established well before the time when ethnic traits assumed the central historical and political significance they came later to possess. The last episode in that establishment was the abolition of the Irish Parliament in 1801. But the 1707 Treaty of Union was arguably its most important moment. Through it the biggest rival *ethnos* of the archipelago was subordinated well before nationalism turned into a general motor of political discontent and mobilisation in Europe. The beginning of the nineteenth century – after the American Revolution, after 1789 and the Irish risings of the 1790s – proved too late for another lasting 'incorporating Union'. Instead what became a quite standard form of European ethno-religious nationalism was to be pioneered there. Looked at in terms of the later mainstream of nationalist development Ireland turned into a typical part of Eastern Europe, disconcertingly located on the Western seaboard.

At the beginning of the eighteenth century, however, neither democracy, nor Enlightenment, nor Romanticism had accomplished enough of their fertilising work. Since confederation was impracticable the Scottish governing classes fell for incorporation. Because absolute monarchy had been defeated, however, they were able to qualify and limit their subordination in remarkable ways, through what they (but not the English government) regarded as in effect a written constitution: the Treaty of Union. Popular wishes had nothing to do with the 1707 deal. But that fact too was only part of the seventeenth century or early-modern package. Scott, firm Tory Unionist though he was, encouraged no illusions among his readers on this score. In *Tales of a Grandfather* he admitted that 'the Union was regarded with an almost universal feeling of discontent and dishonour':

> The Scots felt generally the degradation, as they conceived it, of their country being rendered the subservient ally of the state, of which, though infinitely more powerful, they had resisted the efforts for the space of two thousand years. There was, therefore, nothing save discontent and lamentation to be heard throughout Scotland, and men of every class vented their complaints against the Union the more loudly, because their sense of personal grievance might be concealed and yet indulged under popular declamations concerning the dishonour done to the country.

He exaggerates the point revealingly. The two thousand years were fantasy, and it was not even true that the Scots and English had been mostly in conflict over the centuries between the Wars of Independence (thirteenth–fourteenth centuries) and the time he was writing. Yet psychologically he was right: that seems to have been the way most people felt. Dishonour was taken in a recklessly personal way which, under any form of democracy, would certainly have doomed the Treaty. He points out perceptively how the poor reacted more strongly than the wealthy, 'because they had no dignity or consideration due to them personally or individually, beyond that which belonged to them as natives of Scotland'.

A Union for Empire does not waste time going over the old story of sleaze. Scott's *Tales* covered that angle as well as anyone has ever done. The cash was sent up from London in wagons for the upper-class begging-bowl. When he has finished stressing how providential this whole event was, Scott concedes that – 'The distribution of the money constituted the charm by which refractory Scottish members were reconciled to the Union [and] it may be doubted whether the descendants of the noble lords and honourable gentlemen who accepted this gratification, would be more shocked at the general fact of their ancestors being corrupted, or scandalised at the paltry amount of the bribe.'

But still, these were 'the people' who counted, not the mere dishonoured

mob in the Edinburgh streets. What anyone today would recognise as a
proto-nationalist fury might be inflaming the latter, but in early-modern
terms the former were the effective 'citizens'. The contemporary Scottish
jurist Gersholm Carmichael pointed out how

> the composition of the citizens, properly so called, is to be gathered from the
> laws and customs of each state. When I use the word people I mean the
> citizens who are so called in a more eminent sense, those who by direct
> consent and agreement entered into with the sovereign himself originally
> instituted the state [and] not all heads of households qualify.

That was the real point of course, not the bribery. The eminent people
had been rendered (so to speak) structurally corrupt already, by the
previous century during which Royal authority had moved south to London
and taken the great machinery of patronage with it. They had got used to
dependence, then had it confirmed by defeat – defeat from below by
religious enthusiasm, and afterwards from outside, by Cromwell's army. As
for the less than eminent, those who failed to qualify, their secular national
passion was as yet ineffectual. It still took the form of riot, not a national
movement.

The Time of Nations

A Union for Empire has essays devoted to Scotland's independent attempt at
colonial empire, the Darien Scheme, and to religion, law and theology. Two
separate chapters are concerned with the operations of that wily English
rogue Daniel Defoe, and the dean of early-modern studies, John Pocock,
delivers a thoughtful contribution on the relationship of the Union to the
American Revolution. But the book's two key items are Robertson's own
articles, and particularly the second, 'An Elusive Sovereignty'.

Here he traces the course of the arguments about Union from 1698 up
to 1707. In spite of the previous history and the disaster of the Darien
Scheme, there were still many who sought to avoid incorporation. Andrew
Fletcher was not alone in his patriotic and idealist opposition. But such
opponents faced a fundamental intellectual problem. 'Radical and imaginative as their thinking was', observes Robertson, 'those who would uphold
Scotland's sovereignty, and preserve the kingdom from incorporating
union, were faced with the frustration of their efforts to identify an
institutional framework equal to the challenge'.

The debate was in any case rigged by Queen Anne's ministers and agents,
determined to get their way this time. But that they did so quite easily only
underlined another weakness: the Scottish Parliament lacked the prestige
and wider popularity of its English counterpart. Hence there was no
indisputable focus of political mobilisation and resistance against London's
manoeuvrings. No single redoubt commanded either the traditional or the
popular forms of national feeling. Allegiances were profoundly fractured.

The Glorious Revolution of twenty years before had united England, but divided Scotland and Ireland.

The exiled Stuart monarchy was still influential, and its supporters knew very well that one essential purpose of Union was to keep it in exile. A non-state institution, the Presbyterian Kirk, enjoyed something of the morale and prestige normally given to parliaments. But, although self-consciously national and hostile to incorporation, it did not really think statehood was essential to its other-worldly goals. The mental world of Scottish theocracy stopped well short of political nationalism, and (as later times would show) was tendentially rather opposed to it. The most democratic Scottish institution was therefore persuaded that, given enough guarantees, it could cut its own deal with a unified British realm. The Church of Scotland is unmentioned in the Treaty of Union itself. But this is only because it was shrewdly promised its own separate legislation – a second treaty, in effect, establishing its autonomous rights for 'all time coming'.

Nationalists have always denounced the Treaty as sell-out for a mess of pottage. What Robertson's book shows is how strong were the structural constraints which forced decisions into this mould. In that particular historical plight the absence of a valid 'institutional framework' inevitably made short-term considerations predominate. Scotland's old institutions had partially collapsed, and yet it was too soon historically for others to be improvised by nationalism. Thus an elusive sovereignty came fatally to be weighed against 'the prospect of material improvement and the apparent benefits of participation in a British Empire', as well as against fears of Catholic re-expansion in Europe and the French 'universal monarchy'. Within this balance the individuals who counted could all too easily perceive their own advantage as identified with the national interest. Saving one's estate from creditors coincided happily with the good of Scotland.

In parliamentary circles, though not in the street, this blessed coincidence had by 1707 already made the alternative – continuing the old unequal struggle for national honour – appear a dream. In the 1706 Parliament Lord Belhaven made his famous over-the-top lament for 'Mother Caledonia', piling one bit of myth-history upon another in a surfeit of sentimental metaphors. Englishmen present already failed to understand what he was going on about. In fact he was trying to express a sense of incalculable loss, of a fate implicit in their proceedings which lay far beyond short-range profit and party tactics. There was nothing absurd about that. It echoed the fury in the High Street and has been transmitted in one form or another, dimly yet hurtfully, as nostalgia or its opposite – hard-nosed realism – to each successive generation in Scotland. On the day, however, it provoked hilarity, and Patrick Hume of Marchmont's equally famous one-liner put-down: 'Behold he dreamed, but lo! when he awoke, he found it was a dream.'

In truth the short range advantages turned out to be themselves disconcertingly far off. As Scott put it sourly, after Union was obtained one delay and obstacle after another then 'interposed a longer interval of years betwixt the date of the treaty and the national advantages arising out of it, than the term spent by the Jews in the wilderness ere they attained the Promised Land'. Nearly forty years later anti-Union resentment was strong enough to carry Charles Edward Stuart close to an overthrow not just of the treaty but of the Hanoverian state. And only after the 1745 rebellion did conditions improve enough to resemble the improvements promised an earlier generation.

This time-lapse is another feature defining the early-modern nature of the British Union. At no later period in history could any government have hoped to postpone benefits for so long and get away with it. With the revolutions of the later eighteenth century, in technology and agriculture as well as in America and France, time itself came to assume a different and more urgent meaning. Measurable change entered more decidedly into mass awareness; expectations intensified and focused more clearly on futures realisable, if and when social conditions are altered to allow them. The psychic world of nascent nationalism is one where all lands become 'promised', and not by divine intervention alone. An accelerated sense of the transitory and the possible makes any wilderness that much less tolerable; and hence, mobilisation for exit becomes that much more appealing and necessary. Such a consciousness would become general in the nineteenth century, then universal in the twentieth. But in the 1707–45 era it remained embryonic, at least in Scotland. This is why the mechanics and arguments surrounding the Union Treaty appear so archaic. They did indeed occur 'in another time', or more precisely within another temporality where vital things are missing which we take for granted today.

The Early Modern in Aspic

A *Union for Empire* helps us understand better what these things are. So does Paterson's *Autonomy of Modern Scotland*, though from a strikingly different and contemporary viewpoint. His book follows two other recent general reassessments of Scottish post-Union society, Jacques Leruez's *L'Écosse: une nation sans état* (1983) and David McCrone's *Understanding Scotland: The Sociology of a Stateless Nation* (1992). He gives a more political twist to these important analyses, attempting indeed what amounts to a general ideological reassessment of post-1707 history:

> In effect, if not in constitutional theory or political rhetoric, Scotland had been autonomous for most of the three centuries since the Union – not a fully independent state, of course, but far more than a mere province. It has been at least as autonomous as other small European nations [and] closer to the partial independence of Norway, Finland or Hungary than to the dependent condition of the Czech lands or Poland.

Most of the time, over most areas of social existence, a kind of self-management has prevailed. Until the twentieth century London intervened very little. Rule was so indirect that the state seemed a remote entity impinging hardly at all upon the native institutions left in place by the Treaty – the Kirk, the law, the educational system and (later on) a distinctive apparatus of local government. Scots liked to think of these bodies as 'civil society': it is no accident that this deeply mysterious term originated in Edinburgh. Originated, that is, in the conditions of a lean-to social formation which, very unusually, had a powerful Treaty-guaranteed interest in the illusion of being self-standing. Idealist philosophers like Hegel would later develop the idea further. It evolved into the general concept of a stateless or market-governed society, magically shorn of abstract or merely political authority.

Paterson reminds us that such generalisation had a concrete source, in the Scottish managerial belief that

> The whole point of the Union was to remove the oppressions of politics on the Scottish character. Government, it was felt, should have nothing to do with moulding the character of a people; on the contrary the nature of a government should be derived from the pre-existing culture that it was supposed to serve.

Much of the author's effort goes into defending the resultant managerialism. He insists repeatedly that Adam Ferguson's conception of an oppression-free civil society was justified, and proven by the Scottish example. Caledonia's institutional bourgeoisie has often been scathingly denounced as servile, cringing, routine-minded and unadventurous. In Paterson's reverse image it shows up quite differently: rational, sensible, shrewd, 'showing a wise appreciation that there are multiple sources of social authority', and knowing where its true interests lay within the old British imperium. Thus 'canny' is transformed from accusation into general plaudit. Keeping one's head down was an inevitable part of the silent way; and rightly so, argues this book, since it preserved autonomy and the integrity of a system where 'the daily lives of people in Scotland remained thoroughly Scottish because emphatically local. By European standards Scottish autonomy was at worst normal, at best actually quite privileged.'

One can see an interesting mechanism of psychic reversal at work in *The Autonomy of Modern Scotland*. In only a few pages (pp. 27–45) Paterson tells the reader that Scotland's elite is 'not abject', does not consist of 'dupes', does not deserve its 'reputation for cravenness', and is by no means always 'timid' and 'dependent'. He significantly labours the point. And the obverse of this is over-emphasis upon its supposed contrary, a practically infallible rationality. Our ancestors weren't just not abject, they were positively brilliant: they astutely converted weakness into strength and displayed 'sensible *Realpolitik*', a people that 'chose quietness, because it genuinely believed in the common destinies of all the British peoples', preserving the moderate demeanour of a 'dual identity' which balanced Britain and Scotland – 'British for formal and public matters, Scottish for the family and home and community'. Essentially, what today's all-or-nothing Nationalism denies is this complex if unromantic inheritance. It has 'forgotten about the partial, negotiated, but nevertheless real autonomy of domestic sovereignty'.

A series of comparisons with other nineteenth-century European countries is then used to underline the non-romantic virtues. Judged by progress towards independent statehood Scotland may have been backward; but in terms of broad liberal criteria it did rather well. Liberty, economic development and middle-class culture all flourished within the Union, encouraging Scottish intellectuals to go on cultivating their backyard autonomy rather than attempt organised political dissent. In Scotland 'civil society' was after all a virtual *chasse gardée* of the intellectual trades: there were almost no English Kirk ministers, lawyers or teachers in this job reservation, and hence no threat to its national integrity. Those who felt stifled by the backyard could emigrate. They did so in great numbers, bearing to London, Canada or Australasia what Paterson identifies as the virtues of apolitical Scotland – more or less the opposite of the Irish emigrant culture, with its inclination towards machine-politics, conspiracy and grand rhetoric.

One result was the absence of a key social factor connected in most other countries with nationalism. A famously educated culture produced no intelligentsia. The circumstances of 'autonomy' bred intellectuals who were either over-employed managing 'domestic sovereignty' or in a curious sense lost to normal nationhood through outward osmosis. Paterson would probably not admit the dilemma implicit in his own analysis, but I think it can be seen in the social history of many Scots intellectuals. 'I kent his faither' – the choice inherent in the structure he describes was indeed like that from John Buchan's father to Buchan himself: small-town stuffed-shirt to high-administrative panjandrum. Both very successful, of course: one cannily beneath nationality in the troublesome sense, and the other philosophically far above it, in the Tory clubland pantheon of those who have risen. The same point can be made in other terms (which the author also avoids). 'Nationality' in that sense came to mean politics. But politics is of course the one thing that modern Scots are most conspicuously bad at. Their best-known gift to twentieth-century UK politics, Ramsay Mac-Donald, was also its worst calamity. Yes, Scotland had opted out of the 'oppressions of politics'; and out of its opportunities and collective rewards as well.

Identity Displays

Now it is trying to opt back in. Autonomy has at last begun to yield to democracy, even in Scotland. Paterson describes how in the first half of the present century 'the UK welfare state took a distinctive form in Scotland, to such an extent that Scotland can be described as having had a welfare state of its own'. Autonomy begat the Scottish Office – 'a uniquely bureaucratic form of national government' deploying vast powers of co-option and patronage, supervised only in dim and sporadic fashion by Westminster committees and late-night sittings. Though rooted in the older, simpler entities protected by the 1707 Treaty, like Kirk Presbyteries, the Court of Session or the eighteenth-century sheriffdom, Scottish institutional identity attained its fullest flowering only in quite recent times.

What is 'institutional identity'? What kind of national character does it represent? Paterson wishes above all to dispel the familiar notion of Scotland's being deformed or deeply defective in some way – a cripple or half-wit among the nations, demeaningly glad to be allowed to run its own backyard without the usual accompaniment of a parliament, an army and so on. Speaking as one guilty of disseminating this libel in times past, I feel obliged to utter a few words in its defence.

Institutional identity seems to me broadly the same as managerial identity or, less flatteringly but more familiar to theorists, 'bureaucratic identity'. The self-management of civil society historically found in Scotland implied a corresponding managerial or bureaucratic ethos, the customs of a stratum or class which administers and regulates rather than 'rules' in the more ordinary sense of political government or direction. Max Weber described its origins and character as one of the pivotal features of modernity. In *Economy and Society* he showed how superior such management is to all its predecessors, and how

> Experience tends universally to show that this bureaucratic type of organis-ation is from a purely technical point of view, capable of attaining the highest degree of efficiency and is in this sense formally the most rational known means of exercising authority over human beings.

No one would in this sense deny the rationality so strongly endorsed in *The Autonomy of Modern Scotland*. However, Weber also pointed out the drawbacks of instrumental or short-range reason. The very strength of such bodies and the kind of self-sustaining momentum they acquire poses a threat, the danger

> that the world might be filled with nothing but these little cogs, with nothing but men clinging to a little job and striving after a slightly bigger one, men who need 'order' and nothing but order, who become nervous and cowardly if this order wavers for a moment.[3]

Bureaucracy had an egalitarian side to it and within limits was a social leveller, especially in contrast to aristocracy or older, class-bound societies. But that should not be confused with democracy. It also lends itself rather to petty or low-level authoritarianism – sticking to the rules or (in the Scottish phrase I always thought of as timeless, until I read Paterson's book) 'doing as one's telt'. Weber also remarked on how this sort of thing tended to 'parcel out the soul', before concluding that an over-dominance of the 'bureaucratic ideal of life' was something to be fought and averted at all costs. Simplifying for the sake of polemic, I would suggest that this dominance is indeed a fundamental trait of post-1707 Scotland. *The Autonomy of Modern Scotland* puts a spotlight on it much more effectively and passionately than any previous analysis, seeking to redeem and justify institutional identity as the bedrock of Scottishness – the explanation of Scotland's place within the British Union and of the relative satisfaction and quiescence which attended that place until quite recently.

But for many observers the spotlight will only deepen the surrounding darkness. After all, the most common identity stereotypes of Scottishness are wildly different. Nervousness and cowardliness are not ideas which suggest themselves to anyone who has witnessed the crowd at a Scotland–England international, nor do they feature in the Scottish Tourist Board's promotion of a castellated and kindly-peasant wilderness. Eagles, lairds, bagpipes and scones are the grist of Scotland's Heritage mills – not little cogs, canny Cooncil-men or the quangocracy manipulated from St Andrew's House in such prodigious and democratically unaccountable numbers. At the literary level a similar puzzlement seems in order. What about the weird country depicted in James Kelman's stories, for example, where demotic-proletarian saints find themselves forever knackered by sadist-authoritarian bullies or preached at in Malcolm-Rifkind English by *bien-pensant* hypocrites and child-molesters?

One easy answer, itself now a form of cant, might be the post-modern alibi: there are multiple or equivalently valid identities coexisting in no special order of significance. Another and, I believe, more convincing reply is the other one from which Paterson firmly averts his gaze. Since Walter Scott's time, the Scots have indulged in chest-beating display identities *because* the one he singles out as 'real' has been in certain important respects both deeply unpalatable and functionally useless. In some ways institutional identity may indeed have been the blessing depicted in *The Autonomy of Modern Scotland*. In others it has been more like an unavowable curse.

Whatever else is involved, 'identity' is the answer to a question. In a large and growing number of characteristically modern situations, 'Who are you?' is inevitably a collective rather than an individual query. Its real sense is 'What do you mean?' as a sample or representative of some broader entity. While one may of course be 'a Catholic', 'a stamp-collector' or a Friend of the Earth, the most useful, all-purpose handle here remains one's nation. There is, literally, no getting away from it. Nationality is not in the genes; but it is in the structure of the modern world, much more prominently and inescapably than it was in ancient times, or than in the early-modern world to which the Treaty of Union has for so long pinned down the Scots.

Now, no one ever responded to this interpellation with a short lecture on the beauties of the sheriff system, the merits of Scottish generalist education or the advantages of not having one's own politics. Or if anybody ever did, it would only have been to see the interlocutor's eyes glaze over in bored disbelief. As Robert Louis Stevenson remarked in one of his letters home from Germany, in that situation you just find yourself gabbling on about clanship, tartans, Jacobites and whatever else will make the necessary effect.

Silence would imply oblivion – dismissal as an ignoble province, a mere part of England. Yet the long story is incomprehensible in normal conversation. It takes articulate theoretical animals like McCrone and Paterson around 250 pages to account for their oddity in the zoo. Shorthand is as inescapable as nationalism: the culture requires it. It must therefore be faked, with whatever materials come to hand. It is this sense that the fakelore of Gaelicism and assumed Highland identity is by no means accidental, or simply the consequence of bad faith and culpable romantic escapism. Phoniness is its unavoidable accompaniment, of course, as is the kind of uneasy half-belief which most Scottish Lowlanders have half-indulged in about it since Victorian times. However, all that really means is that since Paterson's 'real' identity cannot be deployed for certain important purposes, a display identity is needed to fill the gap. Intellectuals are often terribly sanctimonious about the results, but should waste less breath on it. I speak as one who has in the past expended all too much of the precious stuff on the follies of tartanry. A cure will be found in politics, not in aesthetic disdain or a stand-off intellectualism.

Paterson's analysis consistently counterposes these real interests and motives of domestic sovereignty to the external realm of Britishness. He argues that backyard autonomy is where most people are at, most of the time, and so the Scots should congratulate themselves on preserving so much sage, short-range control over 'their own affairs'. Carried away by a commendable and intensely Scottish argumentative passion he ends by over-endorsing institutional identity, and ignoring its awful shortcomings. It is quite possible – and in fact the common Scottish plight – to be attached to domestic sovereignty and yet unwilling to be bored to death by it. He fails to perceive how 'autonomy' itself has generated the more celebrated Kitschland which now stands in for Scotland in the world's consciousness. Rob Roy is not all down to Hollywood, Michael Caton-Jones or Alan Sharp, nor even to Walter Scott's original tale of honour misplaced and traduced. Its nerve lies in a sense of intolerable loss which has always been as 'real' as the short-term gains linked to silent-way managerialism. The same sense animates Kelman's violent repudiation of a fallen middle-class universe whose increasingly nervous and cowardly cogs revenge themselves on underlings – the Hell of a dead-end autonomy, as it were, from which an unseen God will permit neither advance nor exit.

From a Shallow Grave

A few years ago there was a Court of Session meeting concerned with the poll tax. The Edinburgh lawyer Randolph Murray had complained that it was illegal in Scotland since it contravened the Treaty of Union. As part of the proceedings photocopies of the original Treaty document were ordered up, and I recall vividly the eerie sensation of seeing the ushers solemnly bear in the large sheets and place them before Lord President Hope and his two colleagues. The judges then studied the relevant clauses for some minutes, only a few yards from the Parliament Hall where Belhaven and Patrick Hume had argued over it two hundred and eighty-four years previously. Unrequited ghosts hovered over the proceedings, their dispute still unresolved. Afterwards Lord Hope observed that this was a matter of such fundamental importance that the High Court would need a little time to reach its decision.

A fortnight later he published a verdict of exquisite moderation denying that the Treaty had been betrayed. Hume was still in charge (though other recent decisions suggest Fletcher and Belhaven may at last be staging a comeback). I think that few of those involved in the poll-tax action ever paid the damned thing, but that was not because Autonomy shielded us. We simply joined the mutiny against it, along with millions of others in both Scotland and England. Everyone there – small-'p' and large-'P' patriots alike – knew perfectly well that no Scottish legislature would ever conceivably have imposed such a tax to begin with, and that any Scottish representative body, were it no more than the equivalent of an old French *conseil régional*, would have denounced it. The only reason for our futile day in court was the complete absence of a political alternative.

One of Paterson's shrewdest points is his depiction of how often the Scots themselves have been responsible for Anglicisation. In true colonial situations the metropolis imposes its equalising will. But under self-colonisation it may very well be those indirectly ruled who seek assimilation as the way to equal treatment. Where the dependent or autonomous structure offers no alternative formula, then – paradoxically – a kind of self-preserving nationalism can move them towards integration. Nationalism's aim is equality with one's own first-class compartment. When the latter is ruled out, however, then it may be felt better to move into the majority's indisputably first-class accommodation than lapse visibly into the second-rate. This is most likely to be true where assimilation in one particular sphere is not apprehended as too threatening. What does it matter being 'just like them' here or there, while, as Paterson shows, the main bulwarks of civil identity remain unassailable?

Recognition of this reveals another uncomfortable aspect of his position. If nationalism accounts even for assimilation, then it must really be endemic at some deeper level. *The Autonomy of Modern Scotland* counterposes a sage domestic-sovereignty outlook to 'romantic' nationalism. But of course this is also a contrast between two sorts of nationalism: the canny calculations of self-colonisation versus the heedless and emotive assertion of equal status. Furthermore, the second must underlie the first. A sense of loss, limitation and separateness can help to explain the deviousness and the main-chance opportunism of the Scots, but not vice versa. In any case, 'romantic' is only a dismissive label in this context. The Patrick Humes have always employed it to keep politics out of court, as if it were an ailment or weakness to which the post-Enlightenment world had unfortunately succumbed. This is historical nonsense. Like nationalism, romanticism is more an integral element of modernity than a reaction against it.

Thus the road not taken haunts the one actually followed by a self-managing (and self-limiting) civil society. Nationalism is like a *deus ex machina* to Paterson's whole argument. It motivates the whole complex machinery he describes: institutional identity, self-preservation and, where needed, self-suppression. In that sense the Treaty of Union came just in time to bury a nascent Scottish nationalism, but could only put it into a shallow grave. Consent was the key to its remaining there. Yet to give such continuing consent it could never be really buried and forgotten. Robertson and Paterson show how the deal was meant to work out among the living, but neither accounts sufficiently for the illustrious cadaver of the seven-century-old Kingdom. In 1707 it was decreed undead, not dispatched to genuine oblivion. Embalmed by Union far more efficiently than Lenin or Clement Gottwald were, it has not ceased to exert the profoundest influence upon each new generation. Has 'autonomy' conserved it, as Paterson maintains? Or is it more accurate to say that that profound influence has kept autonomy working and in effective adaptation for so long? All recent experience suggests how persistent and apparently indelible nationhood can be. Once nationality reaches or crosses the threshold of modern development it is rare indeed for it not to attain political realisation, or at least go on struggling towards it. The autonomy of modern Scotland was intended to be a stable, self-reproducing system of dependency. But however artfully designed and maintained, dependency depends: it assumes the permanence of a wider system. If the latter collapses or shrinks, then it may only have been an odd way of cold-storing nationhood. The corpse may simply step out from temporary interment to resume his rights. He was never really sleeping anyway.

15

Sovereignty After the Election

Sovereigntyscapes[1]

I desire a perfect Union of Lawes and persons, and such a Naturalizing as may make one body of both Kingdomes under mee your King. That I and my posteritie (if it so please God) may rule over you to the world's ende; Such an Union as was of the Scots and Pictes in Scotland, and of the Heptarchie here in England. And for Scotland I avow such an Union, as if you had got it by Conquest, but such a Conquest as may be cemented by love, the only sure bond of subjection or friendship.

King James VI and I, speech to Both Houses of Parliament at Whitehall,
31 March 1607[2]

The week before the 1 May General Election, Robert Harris wrote in his *Sunday Times* column that the interminable electoral campaign had probably been a waste of time for the outgoing government. It had made no difference to voting intentions because 'the tectonic plates had shifted' already to determine the outcome. I think this was more than just a striking phrase. Deeper pressures had indeed asserted themselves, and are continuing to do so. The fault-lines are still widening, and we are still trying to work out just what they are.

Theorists of nationality politics have invented the term 'ethnoscape' to describe certain aspects of traditional national identity.[3] By analogy, what we are dealing with here might be called the 'sovereigntyscape' of the United Kingdom – the deeper configuration of central authority inherited and taken for granted, and in practice grafted on to most ideas (including popular ideas) of the nation, of 'what it means' to be British or English. I think it is in this zone that the tectonic shifts are occurring. The two outstanding manifestations so far have been the precipitous decline of the monarchy since around 1990, and 1997's electoral earthquake, 'the Labour landslide' as most comment called it – appropriately enough in the context of Harris's metaphor. But there is another old-fashioned metaphor which might be applied too. It could equally be said that 'a crisis of the state' is going on. Marxists used to be fond of this idea, which implied that social forces, notably economic ones, were outpacing and undermining the existing power structures, and hence bringing about an inevitable 'collapse' (with any luck, a 'revolution') from which Progress would emerge victorious, guided by Marxists. A crisis of the state is by definition a crisis of sovereignty.[4]

Sovereignty is the ultimate or last-resort power of decision over a given population and territory.[5] The question is a fundamental one, but I do not propose to tackle its philosophical side directly here. Everyone knows that in Great Britain a peculiar mysticism attaches to the notion, reflecting the metempsychosis of the late-feudal Crown into a representative Parliament, after the revolutions between 1640 and 1688. Given the aristocratic or patrician nature of the resultant English representation, an extraordinarily centralised and elitist apparatus of power and administration was created. It was voiced literally by James VI and I in the above quotation, at the moment of birth of the British Union. Then the Crown-in-Parliament became the sovereignty mode of what Liah Greenfeld has called 'God's first-born' – the early-modern or primitive template of the nation-state.[6] This lasted three centuries, plenty of time to acquire delusions of immemoriality. Round about its three-hundredth birthday in 1988, however, in the thirty-sixth year of the reign of Elizabeth II and I – and the ninth of counter-sovereign Margaret – it began to exhibit serious symptoms. As if stricken by a premonitory curse, the Crown abruptly de-metempsychosed into a tacky Heritage sideshow, leaving Parliament as sole manager of the national team identity. Westminster was poorly equipped for the role: *hauteur*, immemoriality and Empire had long ago immured it into a traditionalism immune from 'that sort of thing'. So the deposition of Margaret in 1990 consigned Britain to a sort of Hades, John Major's grey nether kingdom of dinge, sleaze, *rigor mortis* constitutionalism, tread-water triumphalism and anti-European xenophobia.

It is tempting but erroneous here to speak of the old regime as having 'scraped the bottom of the barrel'. That would imply that there had been something else in the barrel, previous stratagems or reforming devices attempted and found wanting until, *in extremis,* the political class just had to go for the bilge water. Of course this was not so. Mother-of-Parliament-land had no requirement for such stratagems and devices: historic-exemplary status implies that nationalistic status anxiety is for wimp lands alone. Where first-born nationhood is threatened, therefore, there is only the barrel bottom: it can't be our fault, so *they* must be to blame. Hence identity may legitimately be redefined by the crudest means to hand: in this case a spluttering concoction of warm beer, bicycling clerics, filthy abattoirs, plotting foreigners and Sir James Goldsmith.

Beneath the rotting barrel lies the sand, fortunately: a 'sovereignty' which will outlast the fall of Britain. But the banks of sovereignty are now themselves shifting rapidly in new tides. The locus of debate has at last shifted decisively from the economy to the state. It always used to be said by conscious and unconscious apologists of Old Corruption that the people 'had no interest in constitutional questions'. Well, they seem to be acquiring one fast. That was in any case always a piece of Westminster dullardry. Ah for the days of such pseudo-shrewdness and unflinching self-admiration! *Naturally* there was little popular concern with reforming a Constitution which everyone had been taught to revere alongside the State Opening and Vera Lynn. But all this meant is that people used to behave themselves. In the 1980s they stopped behaving themselves. Then the Royal Family and the Tory Party stopped behaving themselves too. And finally Britain's last hope of rectitude, the Labour Party, embarked upon a noisy and compromising – though possibly brief – *affaire* with democracy. About the same time as the National Lottery, identity angst crept at last into the British soul and led it to query 'the way we're governed' – which means sovereignty.

Occluded Multi-nationalism

Thus did 1989's End of History (etc.) reach Ukanian shores, only eight years late. One effect of the original event had been a great expansion of the view, as historians realised that the fateful eternity of the Cold War had been but one dismal chapter in a longer and more interesting story. Similarly, in archipelagic terms we ought to try and perceive archaic-British sovereignty as an episode now approaching its end. It started with the late-feudal assimilation of Wales and ended – morally speaking, at least – amid the strident hysteria of Tory no-surrender Unionism between 1992 and 1997.

The United Kingdom state was neither a standard-issue nation-state nor an *ancien régime* comparable to the Habsburg and other empires. It escaped from the latter by stopping James's posteritie well short of the world's ende, but never made it as the former. However, the important thing is to recall that it never *had* to make it in that way. This was because of its *sui generis* location within modernity. The prime mover would not itself be directly configured by the developmental process to which it gave rise. Here is the reason why down to the present the dominant British Isles *ethnos* remains so studiedly vague and indefinite about being English. On that fundamental level – the plane of sovereignty – today's 'Englishness' is a long-term locational effect rather than, as often said, a natural or ethno-genetic one.

Remaining an early-modern state-nation within what became the nation-state world presented certain problems. One of these was dealing with the other archipelago *ethnies*. A crucial part of the evolution of Britain and Britons lay within the formative interim of 1688 to 1789 – in post-feudal but pre-nationalist times.[7] Wales had been absorbed by crass pre-modern techniques before this moment, but after 1688 these were no longer usable. From 1650 to 1660 Cromwell's proto-Jacobin experiments with terror and assimilation had also proved futile. To align them with the new dominant-state project of overseas mercantile conquest and colonisation, different techniques of subordination or co-option were required for the larger nationalities of Ireland and Scotland. Such methods failed with the Irish, but succeeded for a long time with the Scots. It is the breakdown of that longer-lasting success which provides the context of the Blair government's 'devolution', and our subject today.

Today's crisis of the state returns us logically to another, that accompanying the establishment of the Williamite regime (1688–1702). Before the Prince of Orange's great *coup d'état* of 1688, the Stuarts had done their best with perfect Union. James launched it with great enthusiasm and determination. I mentioned him to begin with because he deserves greater recognition: the wisest fool in Christendom who not only invented 'Great Britain' but tried extraordinarily hard to make it work. It was an eerie experience rereading his addresses to the English parliament earlier this year, at the same time as John Major was perched on his campaign soapbox squawking about saving the Union. In the good old pre-1989 days – when a decade felt a long time everywhere, and an eternity in Britain – 1603 had appeared coeval with the Ark. Abruptly the truth dawned: it was yesterday afternoon. The primal posteritie may have mostly departed, but much of its vessel was left behind. In fact we are still aboard the damned thing, and it's sinking. Abrupt psychic reversal can occur at such moments. Suddenly it became clear how 'too long ago to matter' was itself mere ideology – the aura of a wilfully timeless statehood, in which the same prime minister could blather about Britain's 'thousand years of history' without someone dialling 999 for help. The problem was up-ended, too. No longer, 'how can such an immemorial polity ever end?' – and more like, 'how on earth has it kept going at all? Under *this* management?'

One vital element in that survival has been what one could call an occluded multi-national state. This is how the formative crisis of the contemporary British polity was resolved in 1707, by the Treaty of Union with Scotland.[8] That crisis itself derived from the failure of absolute monarchy. Had Jacobean Mark-I sovereignty lasted longer, then the English unitary state would presumably have expanded more straightforwardly, like the French one. Whether as royal despotism or as a successor republic, it would have sought to repeat the Welsh experience in Scotland and Ireland. We can be reasonably sure that such a state would not have 'solved' the national questions of the British Isles; but it might have installed a somewhat more ordinary pattern of nationality politics.

Instead, absolutism was struck down by a mixture of decapitation, socio-religious revolt and military invasion, and gave way to the formidable elite authority mentioned before, that of an English-style *parlement* which incorporated itself as collective sovereign. This Leviathan then retained the actual (personal) monarch as a dependent or (ultimately) as a national-popular mascot. The shift in the centre of gravity was confirmed by the 1689 Declaration of Rights that greeted and allowed William's accession to the throne. Perfect Union by royal sovereignty had failed in practice but (more important) had now become impossible in principle. This was the heart of the formative crisis. Any new approach had to be parliament-centred, and involve complex negotiations and a written treaty – which would also be the written bit of William's Great British constitution – with the parliament of Scotland.

But these were mainly uncharted waters in 1700 Europe. Such a non-regal union of states – but not of nations – implied an original configuration of sovereign power: an elite-civic supranational identity, as it were, which either disregarded nationality and religious faith or treated them as quite separate (and subordinate) issues. Both parliamentary elites had interests in striking such a deal, summarised by Brian Levack as follows:

> The two parliaments were reduced to one, and Scots and Englishmen were given complete freedom of trade in either kingdom, but the administration of the two countries was never fully unified, and their laws and churches were kept separate. This arrangement, which lacks any parallel in Europe, has been described as quasi-federalism. Whatever one may call it, it has been responsible for maintaining Scotland as a 'satellite' of England.[9]

The 'occluded' bit of the bargain is indicated by the last sentence. For the resultant multi-national character would remain of great importance to the 'satellite' (or weaker partner), and yet – in the longer term – be largely hidden from the dominant one. The 'quasi' part of 'quasi-federalism' has the same meaning. Federation in a more modern sense rests upon constitutional agreement among at least notionally equal governments, who retain some separate representation and voice – a guaranteed if reduced sovereignty. Whereas here the whole point was to remove such representation and voice – without the trouble of transforming or removing the nation behind them. The Jameses, the Charleses and Oliver Cromwell had all tried that and failed. The formula now to be employed was an 'incorporation' of states which left nationhood – notably institutional nationhood – alone. 'The Treaty established a British state', concludes Levack, '. . . nothing more and nothing less.'

Unreformable Unitarism?

The underlying demography and economics of the archipelago – with England representing more than three-quarters of the whole – meant that such a state could then behave pretty well 'as if' it was a unitary polity. Approaching the year 2000 we still inhabit 'as if' land. Although the most significant of the national minorities, the Scots were (and maybe still are) too few, far off, ill-organised and (in European terms) 'unconnected' to interfere with such a de facto interpretation of Britishness. In practice the English parliament simply turned into the United Kingdom parliament and got its own way with a name change. Later such unitarism was buttressed by a nineteenth-century reconstruction of the monarchy. Transformed into a popular ideology code, this worked as a state-ordained nationalism-substitute until the collapse of the 1990s.[10]

The old interpretation still prevails, of course. But it is ceasing to do so, because of the new crisis of sovereignty created by a combination of British decline, the European Union, and the advance of non-elite (or anti-elite) democracy. As a result the crisis of dis-formation of Crown-in-Parliament absolutism is now seriously upon us. 1997's electoral lurch was another symptom of this – whether or not it indicates any deeper will to escape. And one of its victims now seems certain to be the style of multi-national sovereignty whose origins we have been looking at.

Occluded multi-nationalism depended completely upon the absence of political voice in its 'satellites'. That was the single most important meaning of 'incorporation'. More exactly, it was that meaning *from the majority or main-body standpoint*. But the point has never been taken in the same way by the satellites themselves. As Harris pointed out in the article quoted before, not much was said of any importance during the longest election campaign in history. Among the important statements, however, were some made at its outset by Conrad Russell on the Constitution.[11] Rereading the Treaty of Union, he underlined how it was in fact 'an international treaty between two equal sovereign states ... [which] may be thought by some to be capable of renegotiation', and also recognised 'a residual Scottish sovereignty'. This may be a museum piece in England, but lives on in the satellite: 'What the Scots have wanted ever since 1603 is recognition as equal partners in a union with England. This the English, because of their unitary theory of sovereignty, have consistently denied them.' In other words, when Scots have talked about 'being British', staying in the Union and so forth most of them have never meant what the English – and especially English political leaders – thought they meant by these apparently harmless phrases. Such misunderstandings are vital to an unwritten constitution. Though less blatantly obvious than in the case of Northern Ireland, Scottish and Welsh *mésententes* are just as profound, and just as reflective of the present crisis. Hence, Russell continues, 'For Scots the point of devolution is to destroy this unconscious English supremacism ... Something like two-thirds of Scots want to preserve the Union with England, but they do not want, and have never wanted, to preserve it on exclusively English terms.'

Some other conclusions seem to me to follow from his acute observations. 'Devolution' is for London precisely that: 'power retained', or a way of preserving the old terms, while affecting the more democratic or liberal approach made obligatory by the post-1989 climate. Lady Thatcher's version lay in pretending to devolve power to 'the individual' – entrepreneurs, families and so forth. Blair, on the other hand, in the phrase which the election campaign made sadly famous – though naturally more in Scotland than in England – would rather give nothing away to a northerly 'parish council'. Since his Scottish Party is fixated on this aim, he has no option. But like nearly everyone in England he interprets the Scots Assembly as simply a more democratic form of administration, a benign modernisation move in no way affecting the existing structure of sovereignty. The Scots by contrast (including many in the Labour Party, and many Conservatives) will welcome the reconstituted parliament as a reappearance, albeit one-legged, of sovereignty among them – something more like equality, 'their due' in the sense of what the Treaty should have meant, and so on. Could misunderstanding be deeper, or more total?

In sovereignty questions, voice is all.[12] This did not *seem* to be true for long enough, granted. But that was because a kind of compensated anaesthesis was kept in place as long as the collective Scottish voice was (so to speak) being rerouted via the Westminster modem and translated into unitarist-speak. In that sense, 1707's 'incorporation' was a devious form of strangulation, for long justified in the name of British progress. Notoriously, Scots of all classes had for long a strong interest in British and imperial progress: hence their silence was compensated, and half-bearable during the decades of empire and a centrally administered welfare state. But even then it never really signified *to them* submergence in a perfect Union or – as James fantasised it later on in the same speech – 'Golden conquest cymented with Love'.[13]

The Leopard's Spots

The main body has two ways of tackling its satellite problem. One was the perfect rigidity of the stick insect (Thatcher and Major); the other is a display of Lampedusan zeal for as much of the New as can be counted on not to disturb the Old too much (Blair). I realise anyone making such a glum suggestion during the euphoria of the moment is liable to be dismissed as a curmudgeon. After twenty years of constitutional catatonia someone appears to actually *change* something, and all you do is sneer.

So let me defend a more sober stance on New Everything as follows. In general terms, there is likely to be less ground for the negotiation of novelty into the system than appears at first sight – particularly in a period of euphoric expectation. A state in steepening long-term decline will tend to consolidate or fall back upon its essence, even while it searches – avidly, as at present – for new survival formulae. The Labour government inherits easily the most dense, refractory and metropole-centred power system in Europe. That historical unitarism was borne to a new level altogether by the reforming passion of Baroness Thatcher, who in some respects remains Blair's heroine and model. He wants to move in a different direction, but 'as she did' in the sense of rapidly, popularly and decisively – even ruthlessly. Furthermore, he has something she didn't: a new party. The new premier's authority enjoys the crucial vehicle of a 'modernised' party where greater individual democracy has been counter-balanced by intensified central domination. To regain office, in other words, Kinnock, Smith and he were forced to transform Labourism along parameters which were, immediately, those of 'Thatcherism' but, more profoundly, could not help also being those of an ultra-centralist polity near the end of its tether. They made Labour a party of power rather than protest; but 'power' is not an abstraction. A party reconfigured in these circumstances unwittingly became the prime bearer of actual 'sovereignty'. For all Britannic subjects power has the defined form of Crown-in-Parliament, the airless courtroom-chamber by the Thames, the wondrously flexible Constitution (and so on – all the rest of it). Also, we know how New Labour has attained its object:

through the kind of absurd tip-over inherent in the ancient electoral system
– too great a victory, in other words, and one owed to the mechanism of
elite representation rather than democracy. It would seem to follow that the
'presidentialism' so many commentators have depicted is not a passing or
merely personal phenomenon. It is most probably – in the terms I
recommended earlier – a further phase in the crisis of the state: from
monarch-substitute to pretend-president.[14]

Yes, it could be all be different *if . . .* but I think I should refrain from
speculation about the subjectivity and 'real intentions' of the new regime.
There are others who know them far better than I ever will. My point is that
the sovereignty problem is structural, not personal. And also that most of it
seems inscribed in the original historic solution found for the (temporary)
transformation or extension of England into 'Britain'. That solution was a
by-product of early Enlightenment civism: by definition it avoided the perils
and tumults of the nationalism which subsequently informed such alterations of the map. However, it took place well before democracy, too; and
hence was never sanctioned by popular will or what Ernest Renan called the
'daily plebiscite' of wider representation. The absence of further revolutions
of the state – so lauded by system-worshippers – meant that this primitive
civic nationalism was also preserved in the aspic of its time. The price of
non-revolution was a palimpsest nature, in other words, later coded by
Burke as 'evolutionary', 'gradual' and superior to the rest of the post-1789
world.

One aspect of the palimpsest was 1707's treaty preservation of an
institutional national society and a strong national consciousness, albeit
exiled to 'satellite' limbo. National*ism* – in what would become the standard
ethno-linguistic sense of the nineteenth and twentieth centuries – was slow
to evolve there for a perfectly obvious reason: in Scotland, there was no
'nation' to be built, redeemed, 'imagined' and so on by means of the usual
formulae. The nation was there already. It had been around as long as
England, and – whatever the long-run faults of the Union – was neither
dismantled, nor suppressed, nor seriously under-developed.[15] 'Incorporation' was not colonisation, even if it meant a good deal of (so to speak)
self-colonisation. It follows that national liberation is not much like decolonisation either. 'Disincorporation' would be a more accurate phrase – so far,
a relatively low-key process marked by successive attempts at reconstituting
a broadly based civic-political (rather than an ethnic) identity. The reacquis-
ition of voice has been as odd as the way it was lost three centuries ago.

West-Lothianitis

'It is no accident that . . .', another fine old Marxist phrase. It gives me great
pleasure to revive it as well, by pointing out that by no accident is Conrad
Russell an authority on the seventeenth-century foundations of sovereignty,
and hence sees the contemporary dilemma so clearly. Accident would be an
equally poor explanation for the fact that the most persistent and celebrated

critic of devolved government in Britain over the last twenty years is a living
relic from the same century. I refer of course to Tam Dalyell, MP of The
Binns, in West Lothian. Since 1 May we have seen him remount on the
umpteenth leg of his crusade to save the Union. Where his ancestor General
(or 'Bloody') Tam used musket and sabre on the underlings, today's Laird
wields the West Lothian Question. He has laid about him with it for over
twenty years now, smiting liberal smartasses and heeding no man lest the
(nationalist) Devil steal his tongue. 'One day...' he recently told *Sunday
Times* readers,

> a government will come which will not tolerate a situation where my successor
> and the other West Lothian member, Robin Cook, will still be able to vote
> on housing, education and health in West Bromwich but not in West Lothian.
> A Prime Minister and a government which set such store by doing what is
> right in the long term cannot shrug off this problem by intoning: 'Sufficient
> unto the day is the evil thereof'. Just how will the White Paper address the
> problem of setting up a subordinate parliament in part – though only part –
> of a Kingdom which above all one wishes to keep united?[16]

Did 'one' not know the context and the man, another 999 call might
seem appropriate. This is at first glance the language of sandwich-board
salvationism. *What* 'evil thereof', intoned upon which wrathful 'day'? As for
'subordinate parliaments', isn't today's Europe carpeted with them from
the River Oder to the Atlantic? What Biblical doom can possibly be hastened
by a few more in the British Isles?

But of course the man is a familiar, like that darker sense in which he
does know what he is talking about. Being from the seventeenth century he
bears sovereignty in the blood, and understands that 'subordinate' would
actually mean 'insubordinate'. Beneath the studied phraseology of the West
Lothian Question lies an invocation of terror and the Last Days. *There is no
way* in which some sense of sovereignty regained can be prevented from
informing a new Scottish parliament. And hence, no way in which a counter-
sense can be prevented from arising in the old British-English parliament.
No way (consequently) of avoiding some kind of struggle over where the
last word lies – on what, eventually, might be any number of subjects.

For Dalyell and his numerous class (the artificers and loyal servitors of
Union) such a struggle must be prevented at all costs. The only sure way of
doing so is by abortion. Unfortunately, this particular abortion lobby has
got used to phrasing its message in the deliberately quaint litany imposed
by its author: legislating on sewage, road signs, toilet paper, class sizes and
e-coli outbreaks 'in West Bromwich but not in West Lothian', or an English
resentment of too many Scots at Westminster – that bothered King James
also. Such matters have of course been straightforwardly resolved by other
regional or subordinate national constitutions round the world, and there
would be nothing to prevent that here – *if we had a new, general, written
constitutional settlement to replace 1688 sovereignty.*[17] A redrafted, democratic

Union could then build in some new quasi-federative, confederal or other partnership scheme for the *ethnies*. But this is Tam's real point, one to which he has never wanted to draw overmuch attention. Heavy concentration on hypnotically engulfing detail dispels the uneasy radicalism attaching to such notions. The truth is not only that we do not have such a settlement. In itself that might just be a remediable accident. The more effective truth – best not dwelt on for the sake of democratic sanity – is that in this Kingdom which 'one' (Dalyell, the Queen, Tony Blair and so on) wishes to keep united to the world's ende, we *never will*.

Make Up or Break Up

At the end of his 1607 speech to the English Houses of Parliament, James lapsed into an appeal to them all to trust his own person:

> Studie therefore hereafter to make a good Conclusion. Avoid all delays, cut off all vain questions, that your King may have his lawfull desire, and be not disgraced in his just endes. And for your securitie in such reasonable points of restrictions, whereunto I am to agree, ye need never doubt of my inclination. For I will not say any thing which I will not promise, nor promise anything which I will not swear; What I swear I will signe, and what I signe, I shall with God's grace ever perform.

In the beginning lay the end. Tony Blair's fustian resembles King James's so closely because the deeper problematic of sovereignty is the same. There is actually only one solution to West-Lothianitis and the quandaries of devolution: recognition of the sovereign character of the new – or more precisely, the restored – Scottish parliament. If that is not given, it will end by imposing itself. The 'New Britain' everyone has heard so much about for the last six months requires a new Treaty of Union. This has to be renegotiated: in 1998–99, it can no longer be imposed. But renegotiation needs at least two parties, in order to guarantee consent, wholehearted democratic agreement – and all the other watchwords. If a substitute for equal partnership is imposed by one side alone – as appears likely – it can only end up as provisional, incessantly contested and probably bad-tempered.

If there is anything in the longer-term perspective I have argued for here, then 'devolution' will be like the application of a Band-Aid to a broken leg. Thus far it remains founded – like Labour's previous 1978 Bills – upon solemn listings of discrete 'powers'. These may be either given to the new assembly, or – in the formula reputedly more favoured by Blair – 'withheld' from it as the imperial responsibilities of Westminster. That may make a difference to legislative progress through the House of Commons but in no way affects the principle. In the light of sovereignty, both formulae are absurd. They disregard and offend the 'residual Scottish sovereignty' which Russell has rightly diagnosed in the post-1707 legacy. The only way this can be avoided is by treating the resurrected assembly as a constituent or 'convention parliament', one of whose tasks – probably the most important – will be to strike a new deal with Westminster and replace the old Treaty, on behalf of the Scottish nation.[18] In 1689 convention parliaments redefined sovereignty after the Stuarts, and established the new system of representative, corporate rights. Further conventions are needed to establish democracy, along the lines argued for by Charter 88 in England and the Constitutional Convention in Scotland.

Apropos the latter – and in case people feel uneasy with the abstraction of 'the nation' – let me remind them of recent concrete history. The Scottish Constitutional Convention was a broadly based body which included the Labour Party, the trade unions, the churches, and representative of the most important institutions. Not without reason was it parodied as a constellation of the Scottish great and good, convened in definitely Godly style by a cleric of the Episcopalian Church, Kenyon Wright. The Convention met patiently for years in the 1980s and produced the over-modest home-rule scheme on which any new legislation will largely be founded.[19] But in 1988 – the 300th anniversary of William's accession – it also published a *Scottish Claim of Right* signed by most Labour and Liberal Democrat MPs, which attributed all sovereign rights in Scotland to the Scottish people, rather than to the Crown in Westminster. Did they mean it? Well, presumably the signatories did mean it, at least while their pens were scratching the declaration paper. Some of them may now be telling themselves it is irrelevant, or has been superseded by the newly Glorious & Bloodless Accession of 1997. If so, they are mistaken.

Such recusants have probably been stricken by the curse of the New. Living inside a cadaver has certain risks, including a belief in miracles. Since spontaneous regeneration is difficult – implying a revolution, a new constitution and so on – the temptation is to hope that marvellous short cuts, ingenious tricks and wheezes, might do instead. Thatcherism was a hothouse for this sort of thing, and a Left modelled by its influence has partly succumbed to it too. Mrs Thatcher felt the need for change, and the hunger for it. But her government also rested upon a Tsarist resolve to maintain the old Union regime unchanged. Hence non-state or socio-economic transformations had to be feverishly stimulated or at least – where they turned out to be hard, or impossible – fantasised about: crowned entrepreneurialism, America minus the democracy and egalitarianism – everyone here will recall only too well these and other half-wit formulae of the 1980s. An instant intelligentsia and formulae industry arose to supply them. The authentic philosophy of the Anglo-British domain had been empiricism, but in the 1980s this was abruptly – and maybe fatally – deposed. John Locke, Michael Oakeshott and nearly everyone in between were consigned to the bin. Where superior somnolence had reigned, think-tanks mushroomed and prophets power-breakfasted with ministers.

I mention all this now not out of hostility to the post-modern, but to try and locate it better.[20] It may not be so easy to distinguish death throes from the stirrings of the New. Any suggestion of this kind – that nation-states are the likely inheritors of the British Union – is bound to encounter the accusation of archaism. All think-tanks seem to have it in for nationalism and nation-states: outmoded, narrow, obstructive, reactionary, inward-looking and immune to alternative intellectual medicine. As a modernising addict, I sympathise with much of this. None the less, if the question of sovereignty is taken seriously, then the emphasis has to be put the other way. A degree of anachronism remains inseparable from solutions to that question in the United Kingdom, because the context itself remains so deeply anachronistic. There can be no magic leap out of it. Democracy won a remarkable victory on 1 May; but so (unavoidably) did archaism. We don't yet know which aspect will be the more important; but of course the argument advanced here implies the second. Power may or may not corrupt 'absolutely'; it will as sure as hell tend in that direction. In such an old-fashioned framework, old-fashioned solutions remain not only inevitable but at least provisionally desirable. If the President continues his successful appropriation of the former charisma of royalty, and the framework gets even more old-fashioned beneath all the trappings of the New, then they will become that much more desirable. This is why the Convention and its *Claim* remain justified – and much more justified in principle than in the over-praised detail of the self-rule schemes which it and other bodies have so laboriously considered.

Trapped in the Interim

The present British sovereignty system arose in the interim era between absolutism and (with 1776 and 1789) the advent of democracy. Its terminal crisis is occurring in another interim: that between the national-identity states of 1789–1989 and the formation of a democratic European polity. Historical and developmental location explains most of what matters about nationalism. The point can be put more crassly, too: things happen when they have to, usually at the 'wrong time'. There is a deeply – and in its own way essentially – accidental side to progress, which has consistently mocked blueprint-makers from the Enlightenment onwards. This has nothing to do with irrationalism or 'human nature' in the fatidic sense, though it helps to explain the formation of mythologies of that kind. The wrong time which we happen to be in is the one between the endlessly analysed 'decline of the nation-state' and a European successor in which ethno-linguistic and political differentiation can assume renewed and stable forms.[21]

It would of course be awfully convenient if Scotland, Wales and Ulster could fast-forward into that regional/national condition of the future. There is no lack of voices urging them to do so, and thus avoid the perils of nation-statehood and atavism as well as the delusions of sovereignty in a globalised world. These same admonitory voices have discovered how the abandonment of old-style sovereignty can be awfully good for you – how societies may actually gain in effective authority (as well as in economic terms) through a pooling or merging of statehood, and this without sacrificing 'identity' in the psychic or communitarian sense.[22] Well, that may be so, and be absolutely splendid, *for those with the stuff to give away*. For those without it, who possess nothing resembling sovereign power to 'pool', 'merge' or gallantly sacrifice, the prospect is necessarily a bit different. Sovereignty-rich metropolitans may enjoy such snakes-and-ladders; sovereignty-deprived satellites wouldn't mind just getting into the game. For the latter the UK and French Leviathans appear quite differently: not only did they appropriate smaller-nation sovereignty, they think they can give it away on our behalf as well.

Scotland has plenty of its own fast-forwarders, some of them in the Scottish National Party – which has been brandishing 'Independence in Europe' for many years. As usual, I suspect they actually mean something different by it, not necessarily appreciated from a distance. As a formulaic long-term solution, the thought may appeal of being an autonomous region, or region-nation inside European Union – whatever 'independence' turns out to mean there. In the shorter term, however, as a way of avoiding trouble, strife and secession, there is always another implication present, but possibly less evident in the London/home county conurbation. It is that England – or maybe even regions of England – must move *at the same time* towards some similar or equivalent status. Indeed – since that happens to be where sovereignty is unjustly concentrated – it would plainly be easiest for the metropolis at least temporarily to lead the way in such sacrifice.[23]

So on with the pooling and merging, Britons. Until merger is achieved and 'sovereignty' decently buried, however – that is, until the interim becomes a bit less interim, just to be going on with – could the peripherals please have some ordinary, boring, narrow, dangerous, egotistical, potentially atavistic (etc.) sovereignty? In an epoch of the provisional, the sole solution remains the actually attainable one: that which looks back as well as forward – sovereign statehood, also known as independence, and prescribed by the general rules still prevalent in Europe and the UN world.[24] Though some of its members-to-be may not yet grasp the implication, the new Scottish parliament does have a sovereignty ambit defined for it in advance by the history I have tried to over-view here: from the 1689 *Claim of Right* down to the new 1988 one squeezed out by the pressures of Thatcherism. That is where it will really start from. In the new parliament there may also be plenty of 'good boys' – including I hope 50 per cent of women – who wish above all to conduct themselves with devolved propriety inside the pseudo-immemorial rules of Ukanian hegemony, antique and New. This is already known as 'making the parliament work'. I suspect they will be wasting their time. Seen in the sovereignty terms we have been looking at – the rise and fall of Britishism – ordinary nation-statehood and responsibility (also known as freedom) may turn out to be a lot less trouble.

Readers may have noted something odd about this manner of argument. It amounts to saying that a frankly sovereign parliament and its eventual accompaniment, a Scottish state, are both the most likely and the best solutions to the emerging dilemma, and yet employs no standard-issue nationalist rhetoric to do so. This is because the case does not depend – and actually never has depended – upon such familiar motifs and incantations. It may also be why the latter sound a bit odd in the UK context, as if an important message was somehow getting mistranslated into the wrong tongue. The general, hence unavoidable, speech mode of nationalism never accords with the particular problematic of the England–Scotland relationship. It *does* fit Ireland, and half-fits Northern Ireland/Ulster. But that is because Irish nineteenth-century and early-twentieth-century development was so much closer to European and global norms: in comparative terms, it was more 'modern' than main-island politics – not more backward, atavistic and so forth. The political die for that development was cast by the incorporation of the Irish parliament in 1800 – across the threshold of nationality politics, as it were, two and a half centuries after Welsh assimilation and one after the Treaty of Union.

This can be put in another way, by asking what the Scottish electorate now votes for. In one sense, of course, it votes via the Westminster *table d'hôte* menu of different parties inherited from the long epoch of political incorporation. However, it can also be seen as voting in a fairly unanimous (70 to 80 per cent) manner for a decided if ill-defined direction of affairs, described in innumerable surveys and polls as 'more say in our own affairs', 'home rule' and so on. With a degree of relief, some commentators regularly point out that only one part of this registers on the Thames-side Richter scale as overt 'separatism' – the 20 to 25 per cent supporting the SNP. This is true, but the relief is misplaced. The point can be put more Irishly: in Scotland, home rule is far too serious a matter to be distracted by independence.

What most voters may really be supporting is (so to speak) the Sovereignty Party, a movement now addressing itself to the people in many different party and non-party guises – and with increasingly open support from within the ranks of Scottish Conservatism. It could also be called the right-to-decide party. The most important thing for a recalled parliament to decide, I need hardly point out, is not raising or lowering income tax by a few per cent. It will be whether to try to alter the conditions of UK affiliation. Like many, possibly most, adherents of 'right-to-decide', I think that once it comes into existence only a Scottish parliament will have the right to decide such questions. Of course this body might meet only once and decide to follow 1707 precedent, by requesting reincorporation at Westminster with a few modernising touches. I would be disappointed by the verdict but would certainly accept it on democratic grounds; just as I assume opponents would accept any eventual verdict on disincorporation or seeking 'independence in Europe'.

The right-to-decide party is about democracy, not ethno-cultural nationalism. At the same time, it recognises that democracy retains a predominantly national configuration capable of transformation but not (or not yet) of supersession or transcendence. British Unionism was a short-lived pseudo-transcendence whose day is over. The 1997 election result opens the door to (at least) begin an escape from it, I hope we can get some way through that door before it closes again.

Notes

Introduction: On Studying Nationalism

1. A talk originally given to students at Edinburgh in early 1997.

2. The last time I heard him say it was on a car trip through the Prague suburbs in 1993. The theme is adumbrated in trenchant, almost aphoristic style in his posthumous volume *Nationalism*, London, 1997. But see also *Nations and Nationalism*, London, 1983, pp. 19–38, 'Industrial Society'. His most entertaining reflections on the subject may be an essay on Hegel called 'The Absolute in Braces', in the collection *Spectacles and Predicaments: Essays in Social Theory*, Cambridge, 1979.

3. *Nationalism*, London, 1960: 'National self-determination is, in the final analysis, a determination of the will; and nationalism is, in the first place, a method of teaching the right determination of the will.'

4. See *Illuminations*, trans. Harry Zohn, London, 1973.

5. Douglas Dunn, *Northlight*, London, 1988, p. 13. Nine years after the publication of 'Going to Aberlemno' the referendum of September 1997 brought a second vote for self-government and opened the way to the election of another Scottish Parliament.

6. I am using these terms as redefined in Régis Debray's new and unsettling study *Transmettre*, Paris, 1997, which proposes more systematic examination of the processes of both transmission and communication.

7. See Sidney Pollard's *Peaceful Conquest: The Industrialization of Europe, 1760–1970*, Oxford, 1981, especially the section 'The Leading Industrial Regions', pp. 87–106.

8. See for instance John A. Armstrong's *Nations Before Nationalism*, Chapel Hill, 1982, and Anthony D. Smith's *The Ethnic Origin of Nations*, Oxford, 1986.

9. *Saints of the Atlas*, London, 1969.

10. The most succinct version of this widely felt critique is that given by Perry Anderson in his essay on 'Weber and Gellner' in *A Zone of Engagement*, London, 1992: 'The most arresting feature of Gellner's theory is its single-minded economic functionalism. Whereas Weber was so bewitched by the spell of nationalism that he was never able to theorize it, Gellner has theorized nationalism without detecting the spell' (p. 205). Anderson concludes also that the ambiguities of nationalism really demand 'an account that is temporally and spatially more differentiated'.

11. *Selected Poetry*, ed. Timothy Webb, London, 1991, p. 124. The editor notes that although Yeats may have had in mind 'the turbulence of contemporary Ireland', the famous poem's final version is 'entirely void of all historical specificity'.

12. See Barth's introduction to *Ethnic Groups and Boundaries*, Boston, 1969, and Eriksen's *Ethnicity and Nationalism*, London, 1993.

13. A condemnation most eloquently conveyed in Conor Cruise O'Brien's despairing tract for the times, *On the Eve of the Millennium*, London, 1996. A previous study, *Ancestral Voices: Religion and Nationalism in Ireland,* Dublin, 1994, provides the context for such

despair. It was criticised at the time by Gellner in one of the essays in his *Encounters with Nationalism*, Oxford, 1995.

14. Reproduced in *Nations and Nationalism*, vol. 2, Part 3 (Cambridge, 1996), as 'The Nation: Real or Imagined?' Gellner's intervention was called 'Do Nations have Navels?', and his answer was on this occasion 'not necessarily'.

15. Liah Greenfeld's *Nationalism: Five Roads to Modernity*, Cambridge, Mass., and London,1992, is the most important recent contribution to the general theory of nationalism, which also inclines noticeably to explanation in terms of collective psychological terms: 'ressentiment' is her chosen category, applied to the five main roads to modernity. She has since developed these views for work as yet unpublished, and I am very grateful to her for sending me indications of this work in progress (as well as to her general example).

16. *In the Blood*, London, 1996, pp. viii–ix, based upon a 1996 BBC2 television series of the same title. The Human Genome project based at the Centre des études des Polymorphismes Humaines in Paris is briefly described in chapter 1, 'The Paradox of Armageddon'. A longer account of both this programme and the intellectual background of contemporary racism can be found in Marek Kohn's *The Race Gallery*, London, 1995.

17. On archaeology, see for example *Nationalism and Archaeology*, Glasgow, 1996, and *Nationalism, Politics and the Practice of Archaeology*, ed. P. Kohl and C. Fawcett, Cambridge, 1995.

18. George Steiner's *After Babel: Aspects of Language and Translation*, new edn, Oxford, 1993. The Introduction to this second edition is addressed to 'those who experience language as formative of their humanity [and] know that the affair at Babel was both a disaster and – this being the etymology of the word "disaster" – a rain of stars upon man' (p. xviii).

19. Roger Lewin, *Bones of Contention: Controversies in the Search for Human Origins*, Chicago and London, 2nd edn, 1997, p. 319. A 2nd-edn 'Afterword' describes the impact of genetics upon the search for origins, and the prolonged controversy between 'Regionalists' and 'Africa-firsters'.

20. One of the most interesting and contentious attempts to establish an intelligible link between the biological and the social is found in Pierre Van Den Berghe's studies, *Human Family Systems: An Evolutionary View* (1979) and *The Ethnic Phenomenon*, 2nd edn, London, 1987. Van Den Berghe's view is that inherent 'nepotism' (in a redefined sense) is carried forward and incessantly reconfigured as the basis (real and metaphorical) of all modern social formations.

21. As quoted in Chapter 1 of D.H. Akenson's biography of O'Brien, *Conor: A Biography of Conor Cruise O'Brien*, Ithaca, 1994, p. 5; the original source was 'The Parnellism of Sean O'Faolain', *Irish Writings*, no. 5 (Dublin, July 1984).

22. The contrast indicated here is vividly brought out in the collection *Questions of Consciousness*, ed. Anthony P. Cohen and Nigel Rapport, London, 1995. The theoretical approach of the editors is conveyed in their Introduction, on 'Consciousness in Anthropology': 'An anthropology of consciousness should contribute to the "decolonization" of the human subject: to a liberation from what we have for so long presented as overdetermining cultural conditions and social institutions' (p. 11). Cohen's *Self Consciousness: An Alternative Anthropology of Identity*, London,1996, takes the same argument much further.

23. I have attempted to tackle aspects of this in chapter 5 below, pp. 90–112.

24. In *Words and Things: A Critical Account of Linguistic Philosophy and a Study in Ideology*, London, 1959, an attack which blighted the author's relationship with the UK philosophical tradition, rather as just previously *Pourquoi des philosophes?*, Paris, 1957, put Jean-François Revel into permanent bad odour with French-language academic philosophy.

Part I: *The Internationale*

1. 'Le danger des nationalismes', *Le Regain démocratique*, Paris, 1992, pp. 499–500 (author's trans.).

2. *Le Point* (Paris), No. 1098, 2 octobre 1993, p. 33 (author's trans.).

1 Internationalism: A Critique

1. I am especially grateful to Niels Kadritzke of *Kursbuch* (Berlin), where this article originally appeared, for editorial and critical help. It also appeared in the first number of a short-lived review, *The Bulletin of Scottish Politics*, published from Edinburgh by Michael Spens of the SNP and myself in the period 1979–81. Both the article and the publication itself were essentially acts of defiance against the failure of the Scottish Home Rule referendum in 1979, aimed at counteracting the long wave of defeatism and hopelessness which followed.

In very adverse circumstances, a small majority had actually voted in favour of the Labour government's devolution Act, and yet been frustrated by a mixture of old imperialism and the 'internationalism' analysed here. Puzzlingly, the key vehicle of defeat (Labour MP George Cunningham's '40% rule') had been furnished by the Left itself, from inside a British government nominally favourable to the restoration of a Scottish parliament. Eighteen years later, when Donald Dewar announced the success of another referendum on the morning of 12 September 1997, he took care to underline how its 75% majority had also easily satisfied the requirement that 40% of registered electors support the change. Many listeners must have had little idea what he was talking about.

Few in 1979 England understood the elements of profound ideological conviction which figured in this drama. The operative idea (transmitted from the seventeenth or even the sixteenth century) was of the Scots as an elect or chosen people – i.e. chosen *not* to be a political nation but, rather, to guide other peoples away from that trap on to a Godly plane of inter- or post-national reality. After the Scottish Labour Party's abandonment of home rule in the 1950s, this weird conception had evolved into a justifying and often passionate orthodoxy. Hence in 1974–75 the Scottish Party had needed – equally puzzlingly – to be bullied by its London colleagues into re-embracing home rule, as the sole plausible riposte to the rise of nationalism. This was because by that time many Labourites perceived the Scottish National Party as a work of the Devil, to be foiled (at least in the first instance) by fanatical defence of the United Kingdom. Impassioned 'internationalism' was one part of that strategy. At bottom it was signalling a superior destiny, that of a Saint among nations.

By contrast, the Nationalists of that era merely wanted a nation among nations. Yet they also could not help feeling in terms of the elect and the damned, and so denounced Labour's Unionism as a 'treachery' of the latter. Such awesome roots ennobled the resultant struggle in the instincts of the actors, but made it fairly incomprehensible to outsiders. Two battles were being fought concurrently, as it were, one in 1679 and the other in 1979. Though nominally devoted to questions of 'class', economics, social policy, the fate of the new North Sea oil industry, etc., Scottish politics were in that profounder sense about the National Question – with a distinctive resonance unavoidably conditioned by the country's past national (i.e. religious) revolutions. The drama was later publicised to the Southern audience through the archaic figure of Tam Dalyell MP and his 'West Lothian question'. This was never a question at all. It is essentially a 1679 Lairdly castigation of re-emergent Sin – unleashed, in its author's view, from irresponsible dissolution of the Union Treaty's Protestant polity.

Written under conditions of personal adversity as well as national disorientation, 'Internationalism' was an attempt to unravel something of that conflict from the angle of the professed ideology of the Left. The article appeared initially in Germany (as recorded), where the old West German Left had been forced to wrestle in a different way with the contradictions of internationalist ideology. As far as I know it made no impact upon opinion on either side of the quarrel. The archives of the *Bulletin* were long ago lost, and its circulation was tiny.

2. V.I. Lenin, 'Critical Remarks on the National Question', Oct.–Dec. 1913, in *Collected Works*, vol. 20.

3. As quoted in R.J. Barnet and R.E. Müller, *Global Reach: The Power of the Multinational Corporation*, New York, 1974, pp. 14–15.

4. T.J. Schlereth, *The Cosmopolitan Ideal in Enlightenment Thought*, London, 1977, p. 2.

5. Eugène Ionesco, *Théâtre*, vol. 1, Paris, 1954, pp. 96 ff. (author's trans.).

6. Jules Humbert-Droz, *L'Origine de l'International Communiste: de Zimmerwald à Moscou*, Neuchâtel, 1968, p. 7 (author's trans.).

7. *International*, vol. 4, No. 2 (London, Winter 1977). The accidental death of Neil Williamson in October 1978 was a tragic loss for the Scottish national and communist movements. One of his last reproaches to me was that (much as he disagreed with many of my views) he thought I was not a consistent enough iconoclast. I have tried to honour him in retrospect.

8. See especially Walter Kendall, *The Revolutionary Movement in Britain, 1900–1921*, London, 1968, Chapter 7, 'Clydeside in Wartime'; and John Maclean, *In the Rapids of Revolution: Essays, Articles and Letters, 1902–23*, ed. and intr. Nan Milton, London, 1978.

9. I am very grateful to Fred Halliday for making this point, and for discussing his forthcoming work on internationalism with me on several occasions.

10. H. Gorter, *Der Imperialismus*, 1915, translated into English in *Pannekoek and Gorter's Marxism*, ed. D.A. Smart, London, 1978, quotation from this edn.

11. *Marxismus und Nationalismus*, Hamburg, 1978.

12. *Memoirs of a Jewish Revolutionary*, London, 1989.

13. Fernando Claudin, *The Communist Movement: From Comintern to Cominform*, English trans., London, 1975, p. 91.

14. Georges Haupt, 'Les marxistes face à la question nationale: l'histoire du problème', in *Les Marxistes et la question nationale, 1848–1914*, Paris, 1974, with Michael Löwy and Claude Weill, p. 12.

15. *The Right of Nations to Self-determination*, 1914, from *Collected Works*, vol.20.

16. E.J. Hobsbawm, 'Some Reflections on The Break-up of Britain', *New Left Review*, No. 105, Sept.–Oct. 1977.

17. This was written in the winter of 1979–80.

18. Marx and Engels, *Collected Works*, vol. 3, from the 'Introduction' to the *Critique of Hegel's Philosophy of Right*, pp. 177–87.

19. P.N. Fedoseyev and others, *Leninism and the National Question*, Moscow, 1974, English trans. 1977, p. 212.

20. See, e.g., W.B. Maass, *The Netherlands at War, 1940–45*, London, 1970, ch 6.

2   The Owl of Minerva

1. First appeared as 'Beyond Big Brother' in the *New Statesman*, 15 June 1990.

2. Eric Hobsbawm, *Nations and Nationalism Since 1780: Programme, Myth, Reality*, Cambridge, 1993.

3. *Nations and Nationalism* (1983), p. 119.

4. Arvydas Sliogeris, in *Radical Scotland*, May 1990.

5. See 'Nationalism', in *Thought and Change*, Chicago, 1975.

6. Later he explained the same point to a largely East European audience in Budapest, giving a guest lecture at the Central European University in 1992. See *New York Review of Books*, 16 Dec. 1992, pp. 62–5, and the collection *On History* (1997), ch. 1.

7. Hélène Carrère d'Encausse, *L'Empire éclaté*, Paris, 1978, reissued 1990, trans. as *End of the Soviet Empire: The Triumph of the Nations*, New York, 1994.

3   Demonising Nationality

1. First appeared in *London Review of Books*, vol. 9, no. 4 (1993).

2. The infamous phrase was first coined by an unfortunate UN representative, José-Maria Mendiluce, as recounted in Laura Silber and Allan Little, *The Death of Yugoslavia*, London, 1995, ch. 16, pp. 245–8.

3. Ken Jowitt, *New World Disorder: The Leninist Extinction*, Berkeley, 1991.

4. *New Left Review*, May–June 1992.

5. Signatories include Timothy Garton Ash, Norberto Bobbio, Pierre Bourdieu, Anthony Giddens, Simon Schama, Arthur Miller, and Jonathan Fanton, Director of the New School for Social Research in New York (where the Appeal was launched).

6. *New Left Review*, March–April 1991.

7. Some of Gellner's recent contributions include: 'Nationalism and Politics in Eastern Europe', *Le Débat*, Jan–Feb, 1991, and *New Left Review*, Sept.–Oct. 1991; Introduction to *The Soviet Empire: Its Nations Speak Out: The First Congress of People's Deputies, Moscow, 25 May to 10 June 1989*, ed. O. Glebov and J. Crowfoot, Yverdon, 1989. Other interesting essays include Branka Magas, 'Response to Ernest Gellner', *New Left Review*, Nov.–Dec. 1991; and Slavoj Zizek, 'Republics of Gilead', *New Left Review*, Sept.–Oct. 1990.

4   From Civil Society to Civic Nationalism: Evolutions of a Myth

1. I am grateful to Bob Lumley of the Italian Department at University College, London, for an invitation in April 1997 to give the talk on which this paper is based.

2. Ernest Gellner, *The Conditions of Liberty: Civil Society and Its Rivals*, New York, 1994.

3. Ibid., p. 1.

4. Ibid., p. 5.

5. See Krishan Kumar's short account of 'civil society' in *The Blackwell Dictionary of Twentieth-Century Social Thought*, ed. William Outhwaite and Tom Bottomore, Oxford, 1994, pp. 75–7, for example. The same account is greatly amplified in the same author's important article 'Civil Society: An Inquiry into the Usefulness of an Historical Term', *British Journal of Sociology*, vol. 44, no. 3, Sept. 1993, pp. 375–92.

6. Much more ambitious and long-range etymologies have also been invented, reaching back to the Renaissance and Aristotle, but I doubt if these have other than rhetorical significance. I have assumed here that, like 'nationalism', 'civil society' belongs to modern times – i.e. to the Enlightenment and after. Just as ethnicity and nationality politics preceded the abstract concept of modern nationhood, so of course urban, commercial or 'middle-class' society preceded its conceptual reification; but the abstractions are what count in the present context.

7. Adam Ferguson, *An Essay on the History of Civil Society*, ed. Duncan Forbes (1966).

8. It has been in the news recently, after the succession of the 11th Duke, a South African engineer called John Murray. The commander of today's 'army', Andrew Gordon, was relieved to learn of 'the new Duke's determination to maintain tradition and keep things as they are'. The original Atholl Brigade (1689) took the Jacobite side and was destroyed at Culloden. The later 'Atholl Highlanders' (from which today's stage army descends) was raised only in 1775, and then transformed into a ceremonial bodyguard by Queen Victoria in the nineteenth century. So the tradition actually represented by its pageantry is that of the British Constitution's revived monarchism (of which Adam Ferguson would certainly have approved).

9. David Kettler, *The Social and Political Thought of Adam Ferguson*, Ohio, 1965, p. 46, citing Colonel Yorke's 1746 letter in *Life and Correspondence of the Earl of Hardwicke*, Cambridge, 1913, vol. 1, p. 500.

10. John Small, 'Biographical Sketch of Adam Ferguson', *Edinburgh Review*, vol. CXXV, no. 255 (1867). In the *Essay* Ferguson observes how the feudal nobility may have 'formed a strong and insurmountable barrier against a general despotism in the state [but] they were themselves, by means of their warlike retainers, the tyrants of every little district, and prevented the establishment of order, or any regular applications of laws' (Section II, 'History of Subordination', in Forbes's edn, op. cit., p. 131).

11. The best short biography of Ferguson is Jane Bush Fagg's Introduction to *The Correspondence of Adam Ferguson*, ed. by Vincenzo Merolle, 2 vols, Aldershot, 1995.

12. This later became Hegel's definition: the collection of extra-familial entities through which individuals are socialised. See Charles Taylor's exposition of the point in his *Hegel*, Cambridge, 1975, pp. 431–8: 'The family is inadequate alone as *Sittlichkeit* (second or

ethical nature) for within it man is not really an individual and the allegiance to the common life is not founded on reason but on feeling only. Hence beyond the family, man is in another community in which he operates purely as an individual. This is what Hegel calls civil society.' As Taylor observes, economic or market relations are prominent in this 'community', and were destined to grow much more so with the development of capitalism. The best recent account of how this functioned in post-Ferguson Scotland is given in Lindsay Paterson's admirable *The Autonomy of Modern Scotland*, Edinburgh, 1994, which contains a general developmental comparison with other and more politically normal small European societies in the nineteenth century (see chapter 14 below).

13. Forbes, op. cit., p. xxxix.

14. Writing sixty years later, Sir Walter Scott called Scotland's 'the silent way' – the non-political or stateless way – to progress: 'No longer the object of terror to the British government, Scotland was left from the year 1750 under the guardianship of her own institutions, to win her silent way to national wealth and consequence. Contempt procured for her the freedom from interference, which had formerly been granted out of fear' (*Thoughts on the proposed Change in Currency*, 1826). The silent way was in effect the non-nationalist way, representing the persistence of an early-modern pattern into the environment of modernity. This environment (as Gellner explained more convincingly than anyone else) normally required political nationalism as a developmental lever. See the seminal essay on 'Nationalism' in his *Thought and Change*, Chicago, 1975. The only serious attempt to construct a model based on Scottish-style 'dependent development' remains that of the historian T.C. Smout. His debate with Immanuel Wallerstein on this appeared first in *The Review*, vol. III, No. 4, 1980 and is reproduced in *Bulletin of Scottish Politics*, Edinburgh, no. 1, 1980.

15. Most comprehensively tracked in Louis Schneider's 1967 anthology *The Scottish Moralists: On Human Nature and Society*, Chicago, 'Heritage of Sociology' series. Another celebrated description is Gladys Bryson's *Man and Society: The Scottish Inquiry of the Eighteenth Century*, Princeton, 1945. The most detailed recent account of the period's general intellectual ambience can be found in Ian Simpson Ross's *The Life of Adam Smith*, Oxford, 1995. In his introduction to the 1966 edition of *Civil Society* Forbes acutely observes how close these analyses were to Emile Durkheim's later 'current of energy' flowing from society through the individual, in *Elementary Forms of the Religious Life* (1912).

16. Kumar, op. cit., p. 381. The reference is to the vivid depiction of American social association and its political importance in *De la démocratie en Amérique*, vol. II, Part II, chapters V–VII, *Oeuvres*, II, Paris, 1992, pp. 620–34.

17. *Selections from Prison Notebooks*, London, 1971, trans. and ed. by Quintin Hoare and Geoffrey Nowell Smith, pp. 208–9. For the famous justifying passage on the contrast between East and West, see ibid., pp. 235–9.

18. 'Intellectuals, Socialism and Proletariat', in *Intellectuals and Politics: From the Dreyfus Affair to Salman Rushdie*, ed. J. Jennings and A. Kemp-Welch, London, 1997, p. 211.

19. In an earlier essay (*Bulletin of Scottish Politics*, 1980, reproduced here as Chapter 1, 'Internationalism') I looked critically at the origins of 'internationalism', at its complex function as an alternative moral agenda and its utility in the spiritual transformation of defeat. Gramsci's *Quaderni* and the accompanying *Prison Letters* can also be seen as the most complete exemplification of these themes, and the greatest expression of the element of nobility inherent in them. Alas, such virtues are all too compatible with the elitist vices described by Neil Harding in the new assessment quoted above.

20. In 1987 I was associated with a film documentary commemorating the fiftieth anniversary of Gramsci's death, *Gramsci: All that Concerns People* (Pelicula Productions, Glasgow, for Channel 4). The writer and Italianist David Forgacs inquired at that time why Gramsci's thought and personality had had such a strong impact in Scotland. On the spot neither the producer Douglas Eadie nor I had a ready answer to his question; but in retrospect one suggests itself. It was a case of one illusion feeding off another. Gramsci's enforced preoccupation with 'civil society' found a natural echo within a country still condemned to the depoliticised history mentioned above. Sardinia was read as being like Scotland and (in effect) Mussolini as a forerunner of Mrs Thatcher.

NOTES TO PAGES 85–102 231

21. *Civil Society: History, Theory, Comparison*, ed. John A. Hall, Cambridge, 1995.

22. 'Civil Society and Its Future', ibid., pp. 323–4.

23. This view of things was also in conformity with deeply rooted Western notions of general superiority and advancement, as Adam Burgess underlines in his *Culturally Dividing Europe*, London, 1997. He observes ironically that although East Europeans had themselves rediscovered and practised 'civil society' (notably in Poland), they were then told this was by no means good enough. No, greater attention to Western models of civism and associational spirit were required in order to retrain ethnic demons (etc.), and overcome inherited backwardness.

24. See Charles Turner's essay 'Civil Society or Constitutional Patriotism?', *Democratization*, special issue ed. by Robert Fine and Shirin Rai, vol. 4, no. 1, Spring 1997.

25. For an argument to just this effect, see Robert Fine's 'The "New Nationalism" and Democracy: a Critique of Pro Patria', also in *Democratization*, vol. 1, no. 3, Autumn 1994. Fine's intention is 'to sound a warning note lest nationalism be dressed up in democratic cloth', as thinkers like Michael Ignatieff, Jürgen Habermas, Julie Kristeva and Dominique Schnapper have been attempting to do. But if they are all mistaken, then this is Giner's 'bleak universe' indeed. In fact the rate of successful dressage has greatly increased since around 1980, and shows no sign of slowing down. It has been estimated that over 60% of UN members are now democracies, at least in a formal sense; in the 1970s less than 40% of them were.

26. David McCrone, *Understanding Scotland: The Sociology of a Stateless Nation*, London, 1992.

27. It is worth noting that Finlay's life in the Lanarkshire of that time (the 1980s) had long been made miserable by incessant, vengeful and philistine persecution over property rates from officials of the local government area in which he lived, Strathclyde Region. They always appeared anxious to cut the great Scottish modernist down to size, as it were: in the terms outlined here, to the size of a castrate or low-political society in which 'civil' had come finally to mean 'none of that damned nonsense!'

5   The Curse of Rurality: Limits of Modernisation Theory

1. Based on an article in *London Review of Books*, vol. 18, no. 19 (1996), then developed further for a commemorative volume on Ernest Gellner, *The State of the Nation*, ed. John A. Hall, Cambridge, forthcoming (1998).

2. Ben Kiernan, *The Pol Pot Regime: Race, Power and Genocide in Cambodia under the Khmer Rouge, 1975–79*, New Haven, 1996.

3. London, 1977.

4. As quoted in Karl D. Jackson, 'The Ideology of Total Revolution', in *Cambodia 1975–1978: Rendezvous with Death*, Princeton, 1989, p. 73.

5. Kiernan, op.cit., p. 460, 'The End of the Pol Pot Regime'.

6. Jackson, op. cit., pp. 74–5.

7. Autarchy (or 'autarky') was the doctrine of absolute economic self-reliance, prominent between the world wars in both fascist states and the USSR. 'In the 1930s the drive to self-sufficiency or autarky was founded on the desire to achieve power to control one's own destiny, generally by states which were despotic in their internal politics and felt victimised internationally' (Robert Skidelsky, *The World After Communism*, London, 1995, pp. 62–3). It represented only an ideal type extrapolated from Friedrich List's theory of economic nationalism or protectionism: there are no examples of effectively autarchic states in modern times – with the dubious and transient exception of Pol Pot's Cambodia.

8. Jackson, op. cit., p. 242.

9. Eric Robert Wolf, *Peasants*, Englewood Cliffs, 1966.

10. As quoted ibid., pp. 106–19, 'Peasant Movements'.

11. Kiernan, op. cit., p. 22–3 (including following quotation).

12. Michael Vickery, *Kampuchea: Politics, Economics and Society*, London, 1986.

13. Ph.D. Thesis, Monash University, Australia, 1991.

14. By far the most persuasive analysis of this dimension is that given by Anthony

Barnett in '"Cambodia Will Never Disappear"', *New Left Review*, No. 180, March–April 1990. He argues that what Pol Pot and the leadership clique absorbed from France was its chauvinism rather than its variant of Stalinism. Prince Sihanouk 'was and remains the incarnation of the French myth of Cambodia', while the radical nationalism of his Khmer Rouge opponents was also 'expressed within the parameters of the French ideal'. The cult of Angkor Wat and the delusions about the ancient Khmer hydraulic system also find their place in Barnett's brilliant profile of Cambodian nationalism.

15. François Ponchaud, *Cambodia: Year Zero*, London, 1978.

16. British TV viewers with recollections of the 1960s and 1970s would recognise him instantly as something like 'Alf Garnett': comic, tear-jerking, randy, foreigner-despising, royalty-loving and irreversibly Tory. However, Garnett was a Chaplinesque and urban figure of fun, a pre-war Londoner risen (or half-risen) above proletarian origins.

17. *Chauvin, le soldat–laboureur: Contribution à l'étude des nationalismes*, Paris, 1993.

18. On the theme of the relationship between nationalism and the intellectuals, see for the French case *Naissance des 'intellectuels'*, by Christophe Charle, Paris, 1990. The same author has more recently carried his analysis on to a much wider canvas with *Les Intellectuels en Europe au XIXe siècle: essai d'histoire comparée*, Paris, 1996.

19. One striking example of this is the nexus of myths and observances attaching to French cuisine and gastronomy. This represents an 'earthy' (peasant) tradition which is now both perfectly urbanised and strongly identified – indeed over-identified – with national distinctiveness. The peculiar salience of *la bouffe* in contemporary France may arise partly from its function as an uncontroversial cementing factor between two nations of the mind: the land of Chauvin (Pétain, Le Pen, etc.) on one hand and that of the neo-Jacobins and Radicals (Zola, Mendès-France, 1968, etc.) on the other.

20. 'Max Weber and Ernest Gellner', in *A Zone of Engagement*, London, 1992, pp. 204–6. It is not irrelevant to the point here to recall a reminiscence of Gellner passed on to me by John Hall (and cited elsewhere in this book). For all his irony about ethnic passion and misrepresentation, Gellner (who was an adept with the mouth-organ) loved playing Czech folk-tunes and would sometimes burst into tears after doing so. In a postcard to me he once wrote: 'I was brought up among Ruritanians and Megalomanians and to this day can remember and play many folk-ditties (both real and invented) on the mouth organ. For some reason which escapes me, these seem never to give pleasure to the listeners.'

21. In a 1934 speech to unemployed workers, Heidegger suggested this was what urbanisation had brought them. The solution was a return 'to soil and land' which could renew German community. In a radio address of the same period, he even compared philosophical reflection to peasant labour: 'This philosophical work belongs right here in the midst of the peasants' work. My work is intimately rooted in and related to the life of the peasants [and] comes from a centuries-long and irreplaceable rootedness in the Alemannian-Swabic soil.' See Michael E. Zimmerman, *Heidegger's Confrontation with Modernity*, Bloomington, 1990, pp. 69–71. Another important discussion of the issue is Robert Minder's article 'Martin Heidegger et le conservatisme agraire', in *Allemagnes d'Aujourd'hui*, no. 6, Jan.–Feb. 1967. Pierre Bourdieu's *L'Ontologie politique de Martin Heidegger*, Paris, 1988, gives the complete low-down on his 'louche' philosophical rendition of folkish nationalism.

22. In 'Nationalism and the Politics of Resentment' (*The American Scholar*, vol. 63, no. 3, Summer 1994), Eugen Weber tries to estimate the limits of right-wing nationalism in contemporary France. But perhaps the most significant limit lies in the post-war transformation described in Henri Mendras's *La Fin des paysans: suivi d'une réflexion sur la fin des paysans vingt ans après*, Arles, 1984.

23. In *European Modernity and Beyond*, London, 1995, Göran Therborn shows that on the eve of World War II Europe was 'still a predominantly agrarian society', and only in the 1950s to the 1970s was 'the compressed end of immemorial agrarian society' witnessed – one generation ago, in fact (pp. 65–73). Except in the British Isles and one 'corridor from Switzerland to Sweden', industrialisation was rapid, one-way – and remarkably short-lived. By the 1980s, de-industrialisation was already under way. In this context of ultra-rapid transitions, perhaps what Therborn calls in his general conclusion 'the cunning

survival capacity of historical traditions' (ibid., p. 359) deserves greater emphasis than it has usually received.

24. 'National Revivals and Violence', in *Archives européennes de sociologie*, vol. XXXVI, no. 1 (1995).

25. Ibid., p. 35, where the author is quoting from Orest Subtelny's *Ukraine, a History*, Toronto, 1988.

26. 'Nationalism and the "idiocy" of the countryside: the case of Serbia', *Ethnic & Racial Studies*, vol. 19, no. 1, January 1996, pp. 70–71. See also her book *Balkan Babel: The Disintegration of Yugoslavia from the Death of Tito to Ethnic War*, Boulder, 1995.

27. On this topic the reader must turn first of all to Gérard Prunier's brilliant and corrosive study, *The Rwanda Crisis 1959–1994: History of a Genocide*, London, 1995. The parallels to be drawn with Barnett's profile of Cambodian nationalism – see ' "Cambodia Will Never Disappear" ', note 14 above – are especially striking as regards both the ideological origins of the conflicts and the potentially lethal authority of one-party rule within peasant societies.

28. It failed to yield much before the author's earlier effort, *The Break-up of Britain*, London, 1977, which entirely failed to register the socio-historical dimension emphasised here. Gellner wrote a typically amusing and acerbic notice of this work in *Political Quarterly*, vol. 49, no. 1, 1978, which was republished later in his collection *Spectacles and Predicaments: Essays in Social Theory*, as 'Nationalism, or the new confessions of a justified Edinburgh sinner'.

29. See 'God's Firstborn: England', in *Nationalism: Five Roads to Modernity*, Cambridge, Mass., 1992.

30. Gellner was an enthusiastic pro-European, but always had difficulty fitting the British Isles into his grand schema of modernisation through nationalism. It seems to me his most acute critique of his adopted nation's culture is contained in an early and famously abrasive study of its indwelling philosophical mystique, 'British empiricism': *Words and Things: An Examination of and an Attack on Linguistic Philosophy*, London, 1979. Only an outsider could have dealt such a memorable blow to the native identity. On the other hand, he did become more of an insider, and later always gave the impression that there was much – indeed more and more – to be said in defence of God's First-born. It may also be worth observing here that the First-born is not really unique. Actually, His Second- and Third-born are in similar sorts of trouble today, as the USA and France also labour towards long-overdue reform of their own almost equivalently gerontocratic versions of 'the Western model'. It looks as if the general fate of revolutionary models is to become outdated, and then discover what an impossible nuisance further political revolution is.

31. Ernest Gellner, *Nations and Nationalism*, Oxford, 1983.

32. New York and London, 1981, p. 329.

33. Some readers may detect an odd echo effect between the lines here. In the 1960s Perry Anderson and I evolved a theory of Britishness which proclaimed that everything in the United Kingdom was, in effect, far sooner than most opinion believed. First published in the *New Left Review*, the so-called 'Nairn–Anderson theses' asserted, not without passion, that the great vanguard State of European Modernity was in truth a pitiable and quasi-feudal reliquary fit only for history's museum, or perhaps just its dustbin. We too were victims of the foregone conclusion, alas. It occurred to neither of us that the reliquary would rattle on into the third millennium, or that forty years later a New Labour government might be in power devoted to pathologically cautious rearrangement of the bones – for example, phasing out the hereditary principle in the House of Lords (while conserving lordship and monarchy themselves).

6 Race and Nationalism

1. First appeared in *London Review of Books*, vol. 18, no. 6 (1996).

2. Marek Kohn, *The Race Gallery: The Return of Racial Science*, London, 1995.

3. New York, 1982.

7 Cities and Nationalism

1. First appeared as 'At the Fairground', *London Review of Books*, vol. 19, no. 6 (1997).
2. London, 1996.
3. Martin Thom, *Republics, Nations and Tribes*, London, 1995.

8 Andorra

1. First appeared in *The Scotsman* (Edinburgh) in Sept. 1993.

9 Micro-states

1. Based on seminar talks given at a Freudenstadt Symposium in 1994 and another at the 'Boundaries and Identities' conference at Edinburgh University, 1996.
2. The 'pyramid' of a modern educational system (he notes in *Nations and Nationalism*) – 'provides the criterion for the minimum size for a viable political unit. No unit too small to accommodate the pyramid can function properly. Units cannot be smaller than this. Constraints also operate which prevent them being too large, in various circumstances; but that is another issue.'
3. London, 1996.
4. The term 'offshore' entered the general vocabulary of most languages around this time. It can be found (e.g.) in the *Petit Larousse* dictionary, listed as reluctant French ('anglicisme déconseillé') rather than in the pink pages at the middle of the book as a locution *étrangère*. It meant the practice – originally marginal and apparently of minor importance – of registering the legal seat of businesses in some tiny and fiscally generous territory which allowed firms to avoid taxes and other constraints imposed by their own countries.
5. Michael Chabot, 'Les 22 plus petits états du monde', *L'événement du jeudi*, 28 juillet–3 août 1994. A more academic attempt at defining the terrain has been made by Laurent Adam in 'Le concept de micro-Etat: Etat lilliputien ou parodies d'Etats?' in *Revue Internationale de Politique Comparée*, vol. 2, no. 3, 1995. Adam's definition is more ample than Chabot's: 'Le nombre d'habitants inférieur ou égal à 1 million; la superficie inférieure à 6000 km^2' (ibid., p. 587). This gives a total of 34 microstates in the UN list.
6. Those who suggested at the time the sole way out might be artificial statehood for the islanders were derided. Was it not obvious that independence for just 2,000 people on a few barren rocks would always be wholly unviable?
7. The former British colony of Bahamas recently held a referendum on statehood which returned a majority for retaining the links with Great Britain.
8. London, 1994.
9. Ibid., pp. 15–19.
10. *The Empire of Civil Society: A Critique of the Realist Theory of International Relations*, London, 1994, especially Chapter 5, section 6, 'Karl Marx's Theory of Anarchy'.
11. Six have accomplished this since 1990: Liechtenstein (1990), the Marshall Islands and Micronesia (1991), San Marino (1992), Monaco and Andorra (1993). It is especially noticeable that they may now beat larger competitors to the mark. No Andorran (e.g.) will miss an opportunity to emphasise, especially in the presence of someone from Barcelona, that Catalan language and culture first resounded in the international arena through their admission, and not that of Catalonia itself.
12. Paris, 1993.

10 A Civic–Nationalist Divorce: Czechs and Slovaks

1. Remarks made at a conference in Edinburgh in early 1994, attended by representatives from the Czech Republic and Slovakia, including Ernest Gellner, and former prime ministers Peter Pithart and Jan Carnogursky. Reprinted in *Scottish Affairs* (Edinburgh).
2. A summary of the 1944 report can be found in Eugen Steiner's *The Slovak Dilemma*, 1973, chapter 6, 'The Struggle in Exile' (from which the quotes here are taken).
3. New York, 1979.
4. *National Conflict in Czechoslovakia: The Making and Remaking of a State, 1918–1987*, Princeton, 1988, Part V, 'Federalization and the Czech-Slovak Relationship'.
5. Published as 'Beyond Reason: The Nature of the Ethnonational Bond', in *Ethnic & Racial Studies*, vol. 16, no. 1 (1992).
6. Peter Rutland, 'Thatcherism, Czech-style: Transition to Capitalism in the Czech Republic', *Telos* (1993).
7. See Jiri Musil's analysis of 'Czech and Slovak Society', *Government and Opposition*, vol. 28, no. 4 (Autumn 1993).

11 Ulster

1. First appeared in *London Review of Books*, vol. 17, no. 6 (1995).
2. *Ancestral Voices: Religion and Nationalism in Ireland*, Poolbeg, 1994. An acute and astringent critique of O'Brien's position can be found in Ernest Gellner's latest collection of essays: *The Sacred and the National, Encounters with Nationalism*, Oxford, 1994.
3. 'As part of the agreement the Irish Government will introduce and support proposals for change in the Irish Constitution reflecting the principle of consent in Northern Ireland and demonstrably be such that no territorial claim of right to jurisdiction over Northern Ireland contrary to the will of a majority of its inhabitants is asserted ('Northern Ireland Framework Document', 22 Feb. 1995).
4. 'When we get the healing done', from *Too Long in Exile* (1993).
5. 'Nationalism and the International Order', in op. cit., p. 31.
6. *The Edge of the Union: The Ulster Loyalist Political Vision*, Oxford, 1994, pp. 142–6.
7. New York, 1994.
8. 'The Ends of History', in *A Zone of Engagement*, London, 1992, p. 280.
9. See Boyle and Hadden, op.cit., 'Attitudes and aspirations', pp. 59–62, where they conclude that in spite of cantonal apartheid 'On some matters the two communities overlap to such an extent that it becomes questionable whether it is not better to say that there is a large community of opinion in the centre and two much smaller communities with sharply polarised views on the extremes'.

12 Palestine

1. First appeared in *London Review of Books*, vol. 16, no. 17 (1994).
2. Edward W. Said, *The Politics of Dispossession: The Struggle for Palestinian Self-Determination, 1969–1994*, London, 1994; *Representations of the Intellectual*, London, 1994.
3. 19 Feb. 1993.

13 Identities in Scotland

1. Based on a talk given at the International Congress of Scottish Studies held in Grenoble in March 1991. This appeared in another version in the Congress Proceedings, *Etudes écossaises*, no. 1 (Grenoble, 1992) as 'Scottish Identity: A Cause Unwon'.
2. New York, 1978.
3. London, 1984.

14   Empire and Union

1. First appeared in *London Review of Books*, vol. 17, no. 16 (1995).
2. *A Union for Empire: Political Thought and the Union of 1707*, ed. John Robertson, Cambridge, 1995. Lindsay Paterson, *The Autonomy of Modern Scotland*, Edinburgh, 1994.
3. The argument is summarised in *From Max Weber*, ed. H. H. Garth and C. Wright Mills (1970), ch. VIII, 'Bureaucracy'.

15   Sovereignty After the Election

1. This essay is based on a lecture given to the Sovereignty Seminar, Birkbeck College, London, June 1997, at the invitation of Anthony Barnett.
2. This and other references to King James are from Johann Sommerville's *King James VI and I: Political Writings*, Cambridge, 1994.
3. I owe the term to Anthony Smith, who employed it in a recent address on 'Sacred Territory and National Identity' at the University of Edinburgh, 1 May 1997.
4. An earlier argument along similar lines was made by David Marquand in his pamphlet *Faltering Leviathan: National Sovereignty, the Regions and Europe*, London, n.d. The basis of his position was: 'The fact remains that Britain's political culture remains unusually – perhaps uniquely – unfavourable both to the devolution of power from the national to the sub-national level, and to the kind of power-sharing implied by membership of the European Community . . .' (pp. 14–15). On 1 May the observation was still true.
5. All reflections on sovereignty are of course situated in a longer perspective stretching from Jean Bodin down to Dicey's *Law of the Constitution*. However, the thoughts expressed here owe most to recent work on the early-modern period, like J.G.A. Pocock's many studies, and Martin Thom's *Republics, Nations and Tribes* (London, 1995; discussed in chapter 7 above); or to very recent views on the democratic reconfiguration of sovereignty, like Bernard Manin's *Principes du gouvernement représentatif*, Paris, 1995, Philip Pettit's *Republicanism. A Theory of Freedom and Government*, Oxford, 1997, and Dominique Schnapper's *La Communauté des citoyens: l'idée moderne de nation*, Paris, 1996.
6. Liah Greenfeld, *Nationalism: Five Roads to Modernity*, Cambridge, Mass., and London, 1992, chapter 1.
7. Linda Colley's fundamental exploration of this theme, *Britons*, New Haven, 1993, concentrates on its development in the eighteenth century, from 1707 up to Queen Victoria's accession in 1837 – most of it in this early-modern or transitional era before the contemporary one of national-identity politics.
8. As described in Brian Levack's invaluable and thorough survey, *The Formation of the British State: England, Scotland, and the Union, 1603–1707*, Oxford, 1987, especially the Introduction and chapter 6. On the immediate circumstances of the 1707 Union, the standard account remains that of George Pryde, in *The Treaty of Union of Scotland and England, 1707*, London, 1950, which contains the text of the Treaty in an appendix. But the Treaty text has been reproduced in Paul Henderson Scott's useful anthology *Scotland: An Unwon Cause*, Edinburgh, 1997, alongside other related material.
9. Levack, op. cit., p. 222.
10. I argued this case in a book called *The Enchanted Glass. Britain and Its Monarchy*, London, 1988, which had the misfortune to appear just before things got serious and sovereignty lost its royal alibi. How complete the loss now is was shown in the famous Carlton TV programme in January 1997, where a telephone poll produced – for the first time – an anti-monarchical majority in Scotland.
11. 'In Search of the Constitution', *Times Literary Supplement*, no. 4901, 7 March 1997.
12. Voice was allowed in the Stormont Parliament at Belfast from 1922 until 1974, certainly, on condition it maintained the complete traditional alignment of Protestant Loyalism with the sovereign-imperial perspective. As soon as that ceased, it was dissolved.
13. In this context, it is interesting to note how in Scotland political science has been

in practice a branch of pathology – one might say perhaps: from speech defect to autism, via inarticulacy, abject mimesis and the endless taxonomy of body-language nationalism. The spread of participative democracy since the 1960s weakened that anaesthesis, while 1989 signalled its imminent end, even in Britain. But the ending has now coincided with the disappearance of all the other ambient conditions which for so long underwrote voiceless incorporation: a non-party hegemonic elite ('the Establishment'), the Crown, the Empire and relative economic success. Hence the crisis.

14. The less noticed aspect of the 1997 election result was that it deprived the British countries of genuine democracy, quite possibly – as far as the 'British' bit is concerned – for the last time. The government which the multi-national electorate voted for was, in proportional terms, a Labour–Liberal Democrat alliance under which a longer-lasting Left–centre regime was quite conceivable, and constitutional change might have stood a far better chance of realisation. Instead, the Labour Party's winner-take-all majority could very well end by returning everyone to Hades: that is, to a revanchiste Conservatism swept back on the turning tide, and perhaps even more devoted to Union-mania and liberation from Europe. Unless proportional representation is established, one presidentialism will sooner or later lurch over into another.

15. In his *The Political Development of the British Isles 1100–1400*, Oxford, 1990, Robin Frame argues that two centuries before James's accession to the English throne – and three before the Union Treaty – the determining fact of British Isles life was its permanent-seeming partition between two monarchic states, the northern one remarkable for its 'stability and recuperative qualities' and much better organised than a later romantic and Unionist historiography would concede.

16. 'Devolution: Now It's the West Bromwich Question', *Sunday Times News Review*, 18 May 1997.

17. The point most regularly made by defenders of devolution is that a supposedly analogous system has worked in Spain for peripheral countries with national pretensions. Unfortunately, more rigorous examination shows the crucial weakness of the model, when casually transferred to the UK. Post-Franco Spain created the all-embracing constitutional order of *l'estado de las nacionalidades* precisely in order to accommodate subordinate sovereignties – without which nothing would have worked. British Unionism, by contrast, is a belief either that nothing like that is needed at all or – if some changes tiresomely force themselves – that they will always be marginal, on the cheap, and unhampered by dire foreign constitutionalism. In the system's subconscious, Edmund Burke remains firmly in charge of the sovereigntyscape.

18. Debate about the likely meaning of devolution is dominated in Scotland itself by Lindsay Paterson's remarkable book *The Autonomy of Modern Scotland* (Edinburgh, 1994), an account of the 'self-management' history of Scottish institutions from 1707 down to the present (see chapter 14 above). 'Low politics' – as he puts it – have always remained mainly in native hands: why therefore should setting up a new national assembly change things much? This perspective seems to me to ignore the fundamental nature of sovereignty: a parliament is not in fact just another institution of civil society, devoted to the extension or completion of 'low politics'. Quite apart from its significance for 'identity' – under-rated in Paterson's optic – it implies a qualitative shift to the 'high politics' of last-resort responsibility and extra-local status. The commanding general text on Scottish politics remains Michael Fry's *Patronage and Principle: A Political History of Modern Scotland*, Aberdeen, 1987, an acid account – in the author's words – of 'just how bad the Scots have been at politics'.

19. By the way, during these manoeuvrings it was plainly indicated to the Scots great-and-good class how post-1998 sovereignty is likely to function. Irritated by Tory badgering over a possible 'tartan tax', Blair abruptly announced that not just a referendum, but a referendum *on being taxed* would be required to set up the Edinburgh Assembly. This device, unique in referendal history, is now on the way to being implemented. It is certain to produce an unprecedented tidal wave of jokes about the contents of Scottish pockets/sporrans. More seriously, a petty campaigning nuisance was elevated by fiat into what felt like a matter of state in the satellite. The Constitution Convention was not even consulted

about the switch. After so many years of quiet democratic effort that body thought it had earned a voice which might be heard – especially since it was dominated by Blair's own party. Indeed it had come to fancy itself as a kind of shadow-parliament. All in all, a valuable lesson in sovereignty, unlikely to be forgotten when the actual parliament meets.

20. Scotland has certainly not lagged behind in cultivation of the New. In fact the Enlightenment strain in its culture has allowed it to make contributions which no one would align with think-tankery, like Bernard Crick and David Millar's admirable pamphlet *To Make the Parliament of Scotland a Model for Democracy*, Edinburgh, 1995. But in the sovereigntyscape argued for here, it remains unlikely that such a model could ever be created without a national state.

21. Just how far we may be from that condition is illustrated by two commanding recent discussions of European Union, Alan Milward's *The European Rescue of the Nation-State*, London, 1992, and Perry Anderson's recent essays on Europe, published originally in the *London Review of Books* (Jan. 1996) and republished in Peter Gowan and Perry Anderson, eds, *The Question of Europe*, London, 1997. The same author's incisive essay, 'The Invention of the Region', was published by the European University College's 'Working Papers' series, Florence, 1995.

22. Geoffrey Mulgan's recent study *Connexity. How We Should Live in the 21st Century*, London, 1997, is a comprehensive overview of this perspective on matters of culture and sovereignty.

23. The new government's proposals for an elected London council and mayor may mark a significant turning point for regionalism in England. However, that may depend in turn upon areas where greater restiveness has been shown in the past, like the north-east and Cornwall.

24. These rules are changing, naturally, but have always tended to trail far behind actual or coal-face alterations. Today they are still anchored to the era well described by Professor Gerry Simpson in 'The Diffusion of Sovereignty in the Post-Colonial Age', *Stanford Journal of International Law*, vol. 32, no. 2, 1996. Simpson contends that there is a new post-1989 tendency to 'rethink self-determination', which could entail that 'Even secession, long the pariah of international law, is making something of a comeback'.

Index